THE ROUGH POETS

McGill-Queen's Rural, Wildland, and Resource Studies Series
Series editors: Colin A.M. Duncan, James Murton, and R.W. Sandwell

The Rural, Wildland, and Resource Studies Series includes monographs, thematically unified edited collections, and rare out-of-print classics. It is inspired by Canadian Papers in Rural History, Donald H. Akenson's influential occasional papers series, and seeks to catalyze reconsideration of communities and places lying beyond city limits, outside centres of urban political and cultural power, and located at past and present sites of resource procurement and environmental change. Scholarly and popular interest in the environment, climate change, food, and a seemingly deepening divide between city and country is drawing non-urban places back into the mainstream. The series seeks to present the best environmentally contextualized research on topics such as agriculture, cottage living, fishing, the gathering of wild foods, mining, power generation, and rural commerce, within and beyond Canada's borders.

5 Time and a Place
An Environmental History of Prince Edward Island
Edited by Edward MacDonald, Joshua MacFadyen, and Irené Novaczek

6 Powering Up Canada
A History of Power, Fuel, and Energy from 1600
Edited by R.W. Sandwell

7 Permanent Weekend
Nature, Leisure, and Rural Gentrification
John Michels

8 Nature, Place, and Story
Rethinking Historic Sites in Canada
Claire Elizabeth Campbell

9 The Subjugation of Canadian Wildlife
Failures of Principle and Policy
Max Foran

10 Flax Americana
A History of the Fibre and Oil That Covered a Continent
Joshua MacFadyen

11 At the Wilderness Edge
The Rise of the Antidevelopment Movement on Canada's West Coast
J.I. Little

12 The Greater Gulf
Essays on the Environmental History of the Gulf of St Lawrence
Edited by Claire E. Campbell, Edward MacDonald, and Brian Payne

13 The Miramichi Fire
A History
Alan MacEachern

14 Reading the Diaries of Henry Trent
The Everyday Life of a Canadian Englishman, 1842–1898
J.I. Little

15 Cultivating Community
Women and Agricultural Fairs in Ontario
Jodey Nurse

16 Being Neighbours
Cooperative Work and Rural Culture, 1830–1960
Catharine Anne Wilson

17 The Lives of Lake Ontario
An Environmental History
Daniel Macfarlane

18 The Rough Poets
Reading Oil-Worker Poetry
Melanie Dennis Unrau

THE ROUGH POETS

READING OIL-WORKER POETRY

MELANIE DENNIS UNRAU

With poems by
Ross Belot, S.C. Ells, Peter Christensen, Dymphny Dronyk, Mathew Henderson, Naden Parkin, Lesley Battler, Lindsay Bird, and Kelly Shepherd

McGill-Queen's University Press
Montreal & Kingston • London • Chicago

ISBN 978-0-2280-2293-0 (cloth)
ISBN 978-0-2280-2294-7 (paper)
ISBN 978-0-2280-2338-8 (ePDF)
ISBN 978-0-2280-2339-5 (ePUB)

Legal deposit fourth quarter 2024
Bibliothèque nationale du Québec

Printed in Canada on acid-free paper that is 100% ancient forest free (100% post-consumer recycled), processed chlorine free

This book has been published with the help of a grant from the Canadian Federation for the Humanities and Social Sciences, through the Awards to Scholarly Publications Program, using funds provided by the Social Sciences and Humanities Research Council of Canada.

Funded by the Government of Canada | Financé par le gouvernement du Canada | Canada | Canada Council for the Arts | Conseil des arts du Canada

We acknowledge the support of the Canada Council for the Arts.
Nous remercions le Conseil des arts du Canada de son soutien.

McGill-Queen's University Press in Montreal is on land which long served as a site of meeting and exchange amongst Indigenous Peoples, including the Haudenosaunee and Anishinabeg nations. In Kingston it is situated on the territory of the Haudenosaunee and Anishinaabek. We acknowledge and thank the diverse Indigenous Peoples whose footsteps have marked these territories on which peoples of the world now gather.

Library and Archives Canada Cataloguing in Publication

Title: The rough poets : reading oil-worker poetry / Melanie Dennis Unrau ; with poems by Ross Belot, S.C. Ells, Peter Christensen, Dymphny Dronyk, Mathew Henderson, Naden Parkin, Lesley Battler, Lindsay Bird, and Kelly Shepherd.
Names: Unrau, Melanie Dennis, author.
Series: McGill-Queen's rural, wildland, and resource studies series ; 18.
Description: Series statement: McGill-Queen's rural, wildland, and resource studies series ; 18 | Includes bibliographical references and index.
Identifiers: Canadiana (print) 2024037519X | Canadiana (ebook) 20240375289 | ISBN 9780228022930 (cloth) | ISBN 9780228022947 (paper) | ISBN 9780228023388 (ePDF) | ISBN 9780228023395 (ePUB)
Subjects: LCSH: Canadian poetry—20th century—History and criticism. | LCSH: Canadian poetry—21st century—History and criticism. | LCSH: Petroleum industry and trade in literature. | CSH: Canadian poetry (English)—20th century—History and criticism. | CSH: Canadian poetry (English)—21st century—History and criticism. | LCGFT: Literary criticism.
Classification: LCC PS8147.P48 U57 2024 | DDC C811/.54093553—dc23

This book was designed and typeset by studio oneonone in Minion 11/14

Contents

Figures

Acknowledgments

This book was written on the traditional territory of Anishinaabeg, Cree, Oji-Cree, Dakota, and Dene peoples and the homeland of the Red River Métis – Treaty 1 territory/Winnipeg. I want to thank the caretakers of this land on which I live as an uninvited guest, and I also want to thank the land itself, which has held and sustained me my whole life and despite everything. May the future of our relationships and land relations in this place be de(anti)colonial and more just.

Thanks to the oil-worker poets who wrote the powerful works I discuss in this book and who, along with their publishers, granted permission to reproduce their poems. I am honoured and delighted to highlight their work in this way. Thanks to David Brydges, Peter Christensen, Dymphny Dronyk, Kathy Fisher, Naden Parkin, Kelly Shepherd, and Tom Wayman for conversations about oil work and work poetry.

This book began as a dissertation, and I am so grateful for the insightful, practical, and challenging feedback and support of my committee members at the University of Manitoba (U of M), Warren Cariou, Diana Brydon, and Dawne McCance, and of my external examiner, Catriona Sandilands (York University). Thanks to Warren for bringing me in on his petrocultures and petrography research and for the research trips to Fort McMurray (along with Teddy Zegeye-Gebrehiwot), Virden, and the S.C. Ells fonds at Library and Archives Canada; thanks, also, for continuing to mentor me after the

PhD. Other vital PhD support came from Alison Calder, Glenn Clark, Anita King, Vanessa Warne, and David Watt at the U of M, and Jeff Derksen at Simon Fraser University. I'm grateful to my postdoctoral supervisors Jennifer Wenzel at Columbia University and Emily Eaton and Michael Trussler at the University of Regina (U of R). Thanks to Emily and the U of R for the research trip along the Athabasca River and for the related collaborations to come.

At McGill-Queen's University Press, thanks to Ruth Sandwell for reading my dissertation and seeing the potential to publish it in the Rural, Wildland, and Resource Studies series. My deep appreciation to the two anonymous peer reviewers who enthusiastically supported the book while also pushing it to be better. Thanks to my acquiring editor Kyla Madden, to managing editor Kathleen Fraser, to copy editor Susan Glickman, to the series editors, and to the other members of the publishing team.

I reworked the project into a book during the COVID pandemic, workshopping my writing with Siobhan Angus, Sarah Bezan, and Kevin Coleman, and working remotely alongside Sarah Bezan, Rina Garcia Chua, Sarah Deckert, Jennifer Hedges, Hee-Jung Serenity Joo, Ekene Emeka Maduka, and other participants in the University of Manitoba Institute for the Humanities (UMIH) online writing sessions. Even thinking about what it would have been like without you makes me want to doom-ugly cry, so thank you!

An earlier version of chapters 2 and 4 was published as "Rig Talk and Disidentification in Peter Christensen's *Rig Talk* and Mathew Henderson's *The Lease*" in *Canadian Literature*, no. 243 (2020): 15–38. Parts of chapters 1 and 7 were previously published in "Founding Fathers (in a Tailings Pond)," as part of a special issue, "Critical and Creative Engagements with Petro-Media," edited by Rachel Webb Jekanowski and Emily Roehl for *Imaginations: Journal of Cross-Cultural Image Studies* 13, no. 1 (2022). Thanks to the editors and the anonymous peer reviewers at both journals who made the work stronger. This book has also been influenced by the "Poetics and Extraction" issue of *Canadian Literature* I co-edited with Max Karpinski, and the forums on the same theme I co-hosted with Max and Warren Cariou at the UMIH in 2022 and 2023. Thanks to Max, Warren, Christine Kim and the editorial team at *Canadian Literature*, and the contributors, including oil-worker poets Lesley Battler, Ross Belot, Lindsay Bird, and Kelly Shepherd.

I presented on and workshopped parts of this project in *Mosaic* journal's "Relative Time/Little Time" lecture series; at the British Academy/CIFAR

(Canadian Institute for Advanced Research) Symposium "What Is a Good City?"; at the Environment, Justice, and the Politics of Emotion Symposium at UC Riverside; as lectures in the Departments of English at the University of Regina and the University of Calgary; at conferences of the Association for Literature, Environment, and Culture in Canada (ALECC), the Association for the Study of Literature and Environment, the Association of Canadian College and University Teachers of English, the Canadian Association for Work and Labour Studies, and Petrocultures; and at the University of Manitoba with the Critical Environment Research Group, the St John's College Fellows, and the Globalization and Cultural Studies reading group. Thanks to everyone who discussed this work with me, especially my students in English and cultural studies at the University of Winnipeg, and my grad-student and postdoc colleagues at the University of Manitoba, including Ifeoluwa Adeniyi, Ademola Adesola, Chigbo Arthur Anyaduba, Melanie Belmore, Warren Bernauer, Melanie Braith, Kirsty Cameron, Karla Ferreira da Costa, Karalyn Dokurno, Katelyn Dykstra, Mandy Elliott, Kate Grisim, Mike Hayden, Isabella Huberman, Micheline Hughes, Ishrat Ismail, Jessica Jacobson-Konefall, Golnaz Jamshidi, Michelle Keller, Michelle Lietz, Amal Majumder, Sabrina Mark, Andrea Mattos, Erin Millions, Michael Minor, Gustavo Moura, Vanessa Nunes, David Shaw, Jeremy Strong, Joanne Struch, Mya Wheeler, and Libe García Zarranz.

Thanks to my colleagues and communities at St John's College, the English and Rhetoric departments at the University of Winnipeg, *The Goose* journal, ALECC, the Decolonial Cities Collective, the artist-mothers' group at Mentoring Artists for Women's Art, *Geez* magazine, and the Manitoba Energy Justice Coalition. I am deeply grateful for my scholarly, creative, and organizing communities and interlocutors (including any I have neglected to mention here), and I'm sorry I can't name everyone, but you know who you are. Thank you! And, of course, any errors in *The Rough Poets* are my own.

Thanks for doctoral and postdoctoral fellowships, research funds, and publication funding are due to the Social Sciences and Humanities Research Council; the Arts Publication Fund, President's Publication Fund, Research Office, and Faculty of Arts at the University of Regina; and the Faculty of Graduate Studies, the UMIH, and St John's College at the University of Manitoba.

To my family, chosen family, community, and faith community, thank you for your care and support. To my little family – Jason, Courtney, Sheldon, and Ollie – thanks for loving and caring for me, giving me space and time to do this big thing, and keeping me grounded and making me smile. You mean the world to me, and you help me remember who I am and what matters.

Timeline of Oil-Worker Poetry in Canada

Including some relevant historical events, with oil-worker poetry titles (and other related titles) in bold.

1858 First oil well in North America in Oil Springs, Ontario (one year before the Drake well in Pennsylvania); discoveries of oil and gas in Ontario, Alberta, and the Northwest Territories follow.

1869 ***Poems Satirical & Sentimental, On Many Subjects Connected with Canada, Including a Complete Exposure of Our County Court, and Division Court System, in Several Theatrical Acts & Dialogues, Showing How the People Have Been, and Are Now Victimized. All Tending to Prove on the Part of Those Indicated, A Complete Conspiracy Set Up by Them for the Purpose of Enslaving the People of this Country. Also a Dissertation on the Doings of the Canada Company's Land, Jobbing, and Other Matters*** **by Robert McBride (Dawson & Brother, Book & Job Printers).** McBride was an Irish-Canadian merchant, poet, and businessman who lived in Oil Springs beginning in 1862. He pursued a number of business ventures in Oil Springs, including oil extraction.[1] The book includes six poems about oil: "To Oilsprings Birds of Passage" (111–12), "Answer to H.J. Nelson" (138–40), "The Theology of Mr. S. on Sunday Labor, Paraphrased with a Moral" (160–2), "Lines, On the Duty Lately Put on Petroleum Oil, 29th

April 1868" (213–15), "The Queerest Man in Sarnia" (216–18), "On Internal Taxation Such as Is on Petroleum Oil, &c." (269).

1913 S.C. Ells first investigates the tar sands on behalf of the federal government and ships bitumen south by scow along the Athabasca River.

1930 Mineral rights in western provinces are transferred from the federal government to the provinces.

1938 ***Northland Trails*** **by S.C. Ells, 1st ed. (Garden City Press).** Discussed in chapter 1.

1947 Imperial Oil drills Leduc #1 in Leduc, Alberta, known as the birthplace of the modern oil industry in Canada.

1956 ***Northland Trails*** **by S.C. Ells, New and Enlarged Edition (Burns & MacEachern).** Discussed in chapter 1.

1960 Organization of Petroleum Exporting Countries (OPEC) founded.

1967 Opening of the Great Canadian Oil Sands near Fort McMurray, Alberta.

1973 OPEC oil embargo and oil shock.

1977 Exxon climate scientists first link climate change to fossil fuel consumption.[2]

1980 Pierre Trudeau's Liberal government introduces the National Energy Program (NEP).

1981 ***Rig Talk*** **by Peter Christensen (Thistledown).** Discussed in chapter 2.

1981 ***Going for Coffee: Poetry on the Job,*** **edited by Tom Wayman (Harbour).** Includes works by three oil-worker poets: four early versions of *Rig Talk* poems by Christensen (54–6; 58), "Tripping" by Deena Hunter (56–7), and "Blind Rivers of No Sun" by R.A. Kawalilak (59). Kawalilak's bio indicates that he was working on a poetry collection about "sweat spent in the oil and gas fields around Rainbow Lake in northwestern Alberta" (203), but I have found no indication that the book was ever published.

1982 Oil glut causes prices to fall.

1982 Ocean Ranger drilling rig sinks off the coast of Newfoundland, killing eighty-four people.

1984 Brian Mulroney's Progressive Conservatives defeat the Liberals and scrap the NEP.

1986 Oil bust: prices collapse.

1988 Intergovernmental Panel on Climate Change established.

1990–91 Gulf War.

1991 ***Paperwork: Contemporary Poems from the Job*, edited by Tom Wayman (Harbour).** Includes "They Said Women Always Quit" by former refinery worker Donna Langston (81–2).

1992 Rio Earth Summit.

1990s Escalating ecoterrorist sabotage of sour gas wells in the Peace Country, attributed to Wiebo Ludwig and the Trickle Creek community.

1998 Canada signs the Kyoto Protocol, committing to reduce greenhouse gas emissions.

2003–11 Second Gulf War.

2006 Stephen Harper's Progressive Conservatives win a minority government on a platform that includes scrapping Canada's Kyoto targets.

2006 Oil prices reach record high.

2007 ***Contrary Infatuations* by Dymphny Dronyk (Thistledown).** Discussed in chapter 3.

2008–09 Global financial crisis and oil bust.

2009 ***Alberta Holed 'Em: Playin' for Girls, Gold and Oil* by Ada Sharpe and Sarah-Jean Krahn (self-published).** Poetry zine modelled after a deck of cards, made while taking a course on "Gendering the Boom." Ecofeminist gender analysis of life as women in Alberta. Links extraction to violence against women.

2009 ***So You Want to Be a Roughneck: Tales from the Alberta Oil Rigs in the 1960s* by Howard Brown (self-published).** Chapbook/memoir. Insider work poems – narrative, lyric, vernacular. Brown includes a glossary of oil-rigging terminology.

2010 ***Deepwater Vee* by Melanie Siebert (McClelland & Stewart).** Siebert's poetry is based on her experience working as a wilderness guide on northern rivers, including the Athabasca and the North Saskatchewan. Includes poems written to/about Sir Alexander Mackenzie, the eighteenth-century Scottish explorer after whom the Mackenzie River is named, who noted the presence of bitumen in the Athabasca region.

2011 Canada withdraws from the Kyoto Protocol.

2012 ***The Lease* by Mathew Henderson (Coach House).** Discussed in chapter 4.

2013 ***Crude Truths* by David C. Brydges (Brydge Builder Press).** Chapbook. Insider poetry about Brydges's work as a construction worker and migrant labourer who travels to Fort McMurray for the shutdown seasons (spring and fall) at the Suncor refinery powerhouse.

2013 An oil-by-rail explosion kills forty-seven people in Lac-Mégantic, Quebec.

2014 ***Fort McMurray Tricksters* by Kelly Shepherd (Alfred Gustav).** Chapbook. Insider work poetry about Shepherd's time working in Fort McMurray. The poems from this chapbook are collected in Shepherd's book *Shift* (Thistledown, 2016).

2014 ***Prologue for the Age of Consequence* by Garth Martens (Anansi).** Insider work poetry about residential construction work in the tar sands and the Alberta oil patch.

2014 ***Prairie Wheel: A Vision of Turnaround* by Kathy Fisher (self-published).** Chapbook. Oil refinery/oil work poetry written by an outsider/visitor to the refinery. Fisher, an Edmonton poet and artist, was one of ten artists commissioned to visit the Shell Scotford refinery during turnaround in 2013 and produce artworks.

2014 ***A Relationship with Truth: Poem and Verse Born in the Canadian Oil Patch* by Naden Parkin (self-published).** Discussed in chapter 5.

2014 After prices averaging US$110 per barrel since 2011, oil prices collapse, falling to less than half that value, triggering layoffs, automation, and other cost-reduction strategies in the industry.

2015 ***Endangered Hydrocarbons* by Lesley Battler (BookThug).** Discussed in chapter 6.

2015 Justin Trudeau's Liberals win a majority government on a platform that includes a commitment to climate action.

2015 Canada signs the Paris Agreement to limit global warming to two degrees above pre-industrial levels.

2016 ***Digsite* by Owain Nicholson (Nightwood).** Insider poetry about doing archaeology work for the mining and oil industries.

2016 ***Shift* by Kelly Shepherd (Thistledown).** Work, nature, philosophical poetry. Insider work poetry about a variety of jobs, including pipeline construction in Fort McMurray.

2016 Oil prices reach a low point of US$29 per barrel and begin a slow recovery.

2016 The wildfire known as "the Beast" rages through Fort McMurray.

2016 The Trudeau government announces a federal benchmark for carbon taxes and invites the provinces and territories to develop their own carbon tax plans by September 2018.

2017 ***The Oil Patch (Cowboy Poems Four)*** **by Ron Gale (self-published).** A chapbook-length collection of insider "cowboy" poetry about oil work, written, according to the dedication, between the 1940s and the 2000s. Gale lives in Alberta, but he has also worked in offshore oil (Ellesmere Island).

2018 ***Tar Swan*** **by David Martin (NeWest).** Poetry about the work of early oil-sands developer Robert C. Fitzsimmons, written by an outsider/researcher.

2018 ***Insomnia Bird*** **by Kelly Shepherd (Thistledown).** Poems mostly about living and working in Edmonton. Most of the poems are collages of found text, lyric lines, and Alberta vernacular, so the references to the oil industry, oil work, and work in Fort McMurray are dispersed throughout.

2018 The Trudeau government purchases the Trans Mountain pipeline from Kinder Morgan to guarantee that a proposed expansion will be built.

2019 Implementation of carbon tax in all Canadian provinces and territories.

2019 ***Boom Time*** **by Lindsay Bird (Gaspereau).** Discussed in chapter 7.

2019 Alberta premier Jason Kenney (United Conservative Party) establishes the Canadian Energy Centre, also known as the "war room," with a mandate to combat "misinformation and lies" about the Canadian oil and gas industry;[3] he launches an inquiry into foreign funding of environmental groups that will find no evidence of wrongdoing.[4]

2020 Following "Shut Down Canada" blockades in solidarity with Wet'suwet'en camps protesting the Coastal GasLink pipeline in British Columbia, Alberta introduces "critical infrastructure" legislation to criminalize blockades.

2020 ***Work of Words*** **by Max Vandersteen (self-published).** Insider poetry about work as a pipefitter in oil and gas and the oil sands, also about the role of Canadian corporations in global extractive industries.

2020 The economic slowdown due to the COVID-19 pandemic causes oil prices to plummet below US$20 per barrel in April; Canadian producers respond with layoffs and predict a slow, partial recovery.

2022 ***Ducks: Two Years in the Oil Sands*** **by Kate Beaton (Drawn & Quarterly).** Graphic memoir (not poetry) about living and working in tar-sands work camps near Fort McMurray between 2005 and 2008.

THE ROUGH POETS

First Day

Ross Belot

Gulf Oil refinery Clarkson, Ontario, 1979

Two men blinded by hydrofluoric acid
yesterday. The skin of one
absorbed acid
                    and it ate his bones.
He died this morning.
The gate's safety sign says
12 hours worked
since the last lost time.

The safety trainer lectures.
Hydrogen sulphide.
At high concentrations it causes olfactory paralysis,
you can't smell it. Then you fall down
unconscious and next you die. If you see a body
on the ground
you must:
        check wind direction,
        move upwind,
        call for help.
Imagine your best friend Bill
on the ground,
how it would feel to leave him.

This is your first day,
wear workboots, learn work rules,
get the paycheque, go home to Shelley
pregnant with Neil, looking after little Heather –
do the right thing, be a good boy,
come home safe
ten thousand more times.

"First Day" by Ross Belot, reprinted with permission of the press and author from *Moving to Climate Change Hours* (Hamilton, ON: Wolsak & Wynn, 2020), 11.

Introduction

Ross Belot is an engineer who worked for Imperial Oil for more than thirty years before he retired in 2014. Since then, he has devoted his time to poetry, filmmaking, photography, and writing opinion pieces on energy and climate change. Belot's poem "First Day" – an apt poem to begin both his poetry collection *Moving to Climate Change Hours* (2020) and this volume – portrays a worker's first day at the Clarkson Refinery in Mississauga, Ontario.[1] Narrated in a second-person present-tense voice that makes "your first day" also a first day for the reader, the worker starts a new job the day after an accident that killed one worker and blinded another. In a common industry practice, the safety sign at the entrance gate frames accidents as *lost time incidents*. It is meant to demonstrate the efficiency and safety of the refinery, and to inspire pride and care among workers, but today, its paltry count of "12 hours worked / since the last lost time" emphasizes, more than usual, that the refinery is a site of dangerous and sometimes deadly work. Despite this, the first line of Belot's second stanza gives the impression – through its dull phrasing ("The safety trainer lectures") and its abrupt end to a sentence after only one line – that the mandatory safety training is tedious yet also alarming. The trainer describes fatal exposure to hydrogen sulphide and the steps workers must take if they see another worker collapsed on the ground – steps that amount to saving oneself and letting the other worker die.

Belot uses indented lines to itemize the steps, ending the list with a period, but I can't help also reading the next, un-indented but still imperative lines as part of the instructions:

> check wind direction,
> move upwind,
> call for help.
> Imagine your best friend Bill
> on the ground,
> how it would feel to leave him.

While the indented lines might seem to keep this hypothetical experience at arm's length, the lines that follow collapse the difference between imagination and reality, as well as between the worker and the reader. The end-stopped but also enjambed line break between "call for help." and "Imagine your best friend" draws readers into a moment of reflexivity about the realities of working in the oil and gas industry. It materializes endangerment, risk, and the expendability of workers in extractive industry by asking readers to imagine it is "you" and your friend risking life and limb for a paycheque.

The final stanza, which opens with the line "This is your first day," levels the experiences of oil workers and readers. On his first day, the naïve new worker knows as much about working in a refinery as non-oil-worker readers. This stanza focuses on how the refinery worker must learn to perform as a "good boy" – a heteropatriarchal worker, father, husband, and citizen who goes through the paces ("wear workboots, learn work rules / get the paycheque, go home to Shelley" and so on) to support his family. Whereas many Canadians might find it easy to stereotype and judge workers for doing physically, ecologically, and ethically dirty work, this simple free-verse poem suggests both that it could be "you" doing this work and that such work is essential to the smooth operation of Canadian culture, from the level of the household to the industry and the nation-state. Belot pulls readers close, drawing us into proximity with workers and offering a sense of what it's like to be an oil worker inhabiting the era of climate change and the early stages of an energy transition away from fossil fuels.

The setting of the poem in 1979 is significant in framing climate change as a process – a poetics – that was already in motion four decades ago. Recent exposés have shown that in the 1970s and 1980s, oil companies Exxon and

Shell were funding research on climate change (then known as the greenhouse effect) and already knew it was caused by the combustion of fossil fuels. Once their own scientists had proven that the oil industry was responsible for climate change and that the process of "moving to climate change hours" referred to in Belot's title (perhaps a shift in the way we think about both work and time) was already underway, the companies shifted tactics to denial and misinformation.[2] If the early research served a purpose like the safety sign at the Clarkson Refinery, demonstrating a minimal commitment to monitoring and preventing harm, Big Oil's response to the research was like removing the sign. Despite this, as anthropologist Elizabeth Povinelli writes about the oil shocks of the 1970s, it was around this time that "the thought that their mode of existence was not merely fueled by carbon but also fueling the conflagration of the earth itself" entered the consciousness of "the affluent West."[3] Today, in an uncanny meeting of the refinery safety sign and the Doomsday Clock, "climate change hours" count down, not up, as all of humanity faces the cataclysmic effects of decades and centuries of bad decisions, often made by the most powerful and least likely to suffer.

The setting of "First Day" is also significant to me personally. Born in 1979, I can interpret the poem as if I am the unborn child Neil, or Neil's sibling "little Heather," born into and raised by the "good" subjects, the profits, and the harmful land, gender, class, and race relations of an extractive settler-colonial state that was already "moving to climate change hours" when I took my first breath. I begin *The Rough Poets* with "First Day" because it positions the book as being about class, about care and harm, about feelings, about extractivism and how it operates, about Canadian culture and the vital role that extraction workers play in it, and about dynamic processes of moving toward and away from fossil fuels and climate change that I call *petropoetics*.[4]

■ ■ ■

The Rough Poets: Reading Oil-Worker Poetry identifies oil-worker poetry as a little-known tradition that already exists in Canadian literature, stretching back to the very beginning of the oil industry in Canada (as the timeline that precedes this introduction shows), yet that has received little critical attention to date. This book reads twentieth and twenty-first-century oil-worker poetry collections as foundational Canadian petropoetry. Laying groundwork for a thorough investigation of the poetry and poetics of oil in Canada,[5] it treats the poetry collections both as representative of the genre of petropoetry and as astute, embedded working-class theorizations of the power dynamics and structures of feeling of a broader petropoetic process of world-making with fossil fuels. The seven chronological chapters focus on full poetry collections about oil work by writers who have done the work themselves. Like this introduction, each chapter is preceded by an individual poem written by an oil worker that is interpreted in the chapter.

With Canadian culture modelled more than we might realize after the boom-and-bust cycles and the fraught aesthetics of resource extraction, this book uses a cultural-studies methodology that rejects distinctions between "high" and "low" cultural forms, that trusts worker poets to theorize petropoetics and just transition for themselves, and that focuses its analysis on social change. Facing the problem of climate change as not only scientific or technical but also social and cultural, this book asks what oil-worker poetry contributes to the fields of Canadian literature and the energy humanities (also known as petrocultures),[6] and also to ongoing conversations about, movements for, and shifts toward energy justice.

This interdisciplinary study is grounded in literary and cultural studies, but it also draws on history, politics, environmental studies, labour studies, settler-colonial studies, and gender and sexuality studies. This book is also grounded in, and limited by, my embodied perspective as a white settler of mixed European ancestry, a cisgender woman, and a first-generation university student and scholar who grew up in a working-class home kitty-corner to a hydroelectric station, with a parent working in the electricity industry. I have benefited throughout my life as a privileged resident of a petrostate[7] where oil lubricates the workings of government and my access to social services, where energy companies employ my family members, and where my consumption of abundant cheap energy links me to global warming, dispossession, and harm. I am not an oil worker, and I knew very little about oil work before beginning this project. Despite my attempts to learn,[8] I remain an outsider to oil work. I approach the study of oil-worker poetry and of petropoetics as a literary scholar and poet, as an anticolonial feminist, and as a working Canadian deeply concerned about the environmental and social impacts of the ongoing extraction, refining, and combustion of fossil fuels.

The Rough Poets hypothesizes that we are currently living in a moment of overlap between two poetic processes – one dominant but waning, the other emergent and still taking shape. The first is *petropoetics*, the production and combustion of fossil fuels, an extractive capitalist and colonial process which not only fuels but also shapes modern cultures, economies, and ways of life.[9] The second poetic process is an energy transition away from fossil fuels, which is already underway, despite the well-known delay tactics of the ruling class (also known as "the One Percent") and the corporations, lobby groups, and nation-states they steer. This process can be seen in the broad consensus that climate change is scientifically proven and caused by humans;[10] in the uneven and as-yet inadequate adoption of climate-change mitigation and adaptation measures by governments, corporations, communities, and individuals;[11] and in the corporate and populist backlash against these changes.[12] Energy-justice activists consider the current planetary crisis as an opportunity to make our energy systems just. Although the movement is a grassroots phenomenon with diverse expressions, energy-justice groups generally advocate for a just transition that replaces extractive economies with regenerative, living economies. This includes calls for equitable access to energy for Indigenous, racialized, and working-class communities; putting control of the means of energy production in the hands of frontline, marginalized, and vulnerable communities; equitable distribution of not only the benefits but also the environmental and health impacts of energy systems; and reparations for historical injustices including colonization, slavery, and environmental racism.[13] Meanwhile, just transition legislation (such as Canada's long-awaited Sustainable Jobs Act) is slow in coming and less transformative than what energy-justice advocates are demanding.[14] It remains to be seen whether energy transition will be a just transition or one that entrenches and exacerbates existing injustice. *The Rough Poets* reads oil workers' poetry to ask what it contributes to conversations about energy justice and the poetics of just transition.

Petropoetics

In this book, I use the term *petropoetics* expansively to refer to material, cultural, and relational processes that range from the extraction of oil to the writing of poetry and the making and unmaking of petro-cultures and worlds. This is rooted in the meaning of *poesis* as not only the making of poetry or art but also "[t]he process of making; production, creation; creativity, culture."[15] Beginning from a narrow definition of *petropoetics* as poetry about oil or oil work, the scope of *The Rough Poets* extends outward toward a broader petropoetics – a way of living and understanding the world that is centred on the extraction and combustion of fossil fuels. With the energy humanities already theorizing such world-making processes as *living oil*, *carbon democracy*, oil as neoliberal *lifeblood*, *fossil capital*, *dead labour* as racial capital and fossil capital, the *carbon nation*, *petro-masculinity*, and *geologic life*,[16] a focus on *petropoetics* can sharpen our analysis of how we got into our present predicaments and how we might get out.

Petropoetics is a colonial, extractive way to relate to and live on land. Following Métis discard studies scholar and artist Max Liboiron's argument in *Pollution Is Colonialism*, I see petropoetics as a colonial resource logic premised on the theft of Indigenous territory and made up of ecocidal and genocidal practices that pollute the land and cause environmental effects, including global warming.[17] Petropoetics contradicts Indigenous knowledges and practices of good land relations. Métis/settler literary scholar Warren Cariou has summarized traditional Indigenous teachings about energy as being about "*energy intimacy*" – "the relationship between the people and their land," through which "every community member necessarily has direct and personal relationships with the sources of their energy."[18] Rather than an Indigenous perspective that sees non-humans as kin (what Métis/settler anthropologist Zoe Todd terms "*relatives* not *possessions*"),[19] petropoetics is premised upon what anthropologist Elizabeth Povinelli refers to as a *geontological* division "between Life and Nonlife,"[20] which treats fossil fuels and other so-called natural resources as dead and extractible while portraying Indigenous lifeways based in other ways of seeing the world as backward and nonsensical. Petropoetics denies the significance of energy intimacy; it treats energy as an object or property that is easily extracted, transported, and consumed to enrich multinational corporations and their shareholders. Such treatment is rooted in racial-capitalist logics that also treat Indigenous and racialized peoples and their homelands as objects that can be exploited, depleted, destroyed, and turned into surplus value within what Macarena Gómez-Barris has termed the *extractive zones* of global capital.[21] It is not a coincidence that while petropoetics has had devastating consequences for planetary life, it has disproportionately affected racialized and marginalized people both in Canada and globally. Like the systematic exploitation and endangerment of workers to generate profit, the dispossession especially of Indigenous, Black, and racialized people through land theft, pollution, and altered physical and cultural landscapes is a feature, not a bug, of petropoetics.[22]

Colonial land theft and bad land relations are continually justified and obscured in Canadian culture, including Canadian literature. Oil-worker poet Lesley Battler references this by calling Canada "the gentle colony / of bitumen worshippers."[23] Canada's reputation as a gentle country is belied by its existence as a settler-colonial state whose past and present treatment of Indigenous peoples and their territories has been documented as genocidal,[24] as the home of global mining companies known for their human-rights abuses,[25] and as a state that persists in extracting and exporting fossil fuels in a climate crisis.[26] Similarly, Canadian literature has recently been described as "in ruins," plagued by controversy and injustice, including its exclusion or extractive inclusion of Indigenous, Black, and diasporic, migrant, queer, trans, crip, and femme/women's perspectives and texts.[27] In *Literary Land Claims*, Margery Fee problematizes the "settler-nationalist" project of using literature to build a nation and a home on stolen land.[28] Canadian nature poetry and ecopoetics are particularly complicit in such land claims, as is the related subgenre of petropoetry, a diverse assemblage of poetic texts that at turns document, reflect, critique, problematize, and attempt to transform petropoetics. For instance, oil rigger Peter Christensen's poem "We Are New Here" replaces Northrop Frye's framing of settler identity as the perplexing and disingenuous riddle "Where is here?"[29] with a worker's critique of an extractive colonial gaze that frames land as resources to be dug up "until the mountains / are empty."[30] As a medium tuned to extraction, petropoetry is poised to contribute to and reflect on the fraught state of Canadian literature and settler-colonial land relations that leave workers, as Mathew Henderson writes, "with no sense of what is yours, and what is not."[31]

If petropoetics is an exploitative and harmful relationship with fossil relatives as well as other human and non-human relations, there remains open a transformative possibility for a [petro]poetics of relating differently with land, fossils, and one another. A poetics of care that overthrows colonial geontologies suggests itself as an alternative to extraction, and one that might become a different petropoetics. Yet, Indigenous scholars including Cariou and Liboiron are clear that Indigenous land relations, as well as the work of decolonization, cannot be appropriated to fix settler-colonial land relations. If Canadians' very understandings of life and the worlds we inhabit have been shaped by flawed colonial ways of being and seeing, a call for the overthrow or transformation of petropoetics is a call to welcome the decolonial horizon of "the end of this world" as the basis for more just futures.[32] As Liboiron explains, we all have responsibilities to enact good relations in the places and communities we inhabit; for non-Indigenous folks, critiquing extraction while striving to enact ethical relations, in solidarity with and accountable to Indigenous communities, is properly described as anticolonial (not decolonial) work.[33] I situate my work on petropoetics and its transformation as anticolonial energy-justice work.

Oil-Worker Poet

According to Energy Safety Canada compilations of Statistics Canada data, the oil and gas industry (including oil sands) employed 177,380 workers in November 2023, with 128,368 in Alberta, 17,588 in British Columbia, 13,068 in central Canada, 10,144 in Saskatchewan, and 6,848 in Atlantic Canada. These figures include workers in the sub-sectors of exploration and production, oil and gas services, and pipeline transmission; they reflect a reduction of employment in the industry from its ten-year high point of 228,996 in 2014 before a sharp decline with an oil bust beginning that year, followed by further declines attributed to COVID-19 as well as some modest recoveries. Indigenous workers made up 8 per cent of the oil and gas workforce in 2021, with women at 22.2 per cent,[34] immigrants and non-permanent residents at 27.2 per cent, and youth between the ages of fifteen and twenty-four at 13.3 per cent.[35] To account for and emphasize the importance of the oil and gas industry in Canada, the oil lobby adds a broader definition of what might count as oil work to these statistics. The Canadian Association of Petroleum Producers (CAPP) includes "direct" and "indirect" jobs in its estimate that "[i]n 2019, Canada's oil and natural gas industry supported more than 500,000 jobs either directly or through its supply chain."[36]

While the list of oil-worker poetry collections in the timeline in the first pages of *The Rough Poets* includes what may be considered direct and indirect oil work (for example, former construction worker Garth Martens and archaeologist Owain Nicholson write about indirect oil work), my analysis in the remainder of this book focuses on poetry written by workers directly employed inside the oil industry. I also make a distinction between poetry about oil work written by an outsider (for instance, David Martin's *Tar Swan*, which is about the work of tar-sands industry founder Robert Fitzsimmons) and the kind of poetry that work-poetry anthologist and advocate Tom Wayman has called "the new, insider's, work writing";[37] the poets I identify as oil-worker poets write about oil work from an insider's perspective, having done the work themselves. Following the editors of *Working for Oil: Comparative Social Histories of Labor in the Global Oil Industry*, I do not limit my analysis to either "manual or blue-collar labor" or "the sphere of production."[38] In addition to the poetry of oil rigger Peter Christensen, production tester Mathew Henderson, and drilling fluid specialist Naden Parkin, I consider poetry written by three women, Dymphny Dronyk, Lesley Battler, and Lindsay Bird, whose work – writing emergency response plans and negotiating surface rights, managing projects and communication on behalf of an oil company, and working in the tool crib and the office in a work camp at an oil sands mine, respectively – is farther removed from the materiality of oil but still situated directly within the industry. I also include the poetry of S.C. Ells, a civil servant who not only managed but also participated in the intensely physical labour of tar-sands surveying, extraction, separation, and transport in the early twentieth century. Although I have found and included in my timeline some poetry written by workers in refineries (Belot, Donna Langston, and David Brydges), and one poet who has written about pipeline construction work (Kelly Shepherd), I have not yet found full poetry collections about these jobs. Perhaps because of my location in western Canada, I also have not found much poetry about work in offshore oil, although I expect that this poetry exists. The study of oil worker poetry should expand from here to include poetry by indirect oil workers, including gas jockeys, factory workers, sex workers, truckers, hospitality workers, temporary foreign workers, and more.

I regret that this study focuses on a white or white-passing archive and does not include a more diverse group of authors. My primary texts are reflective of power dynamics and demographics inside the oil and gas industry that privilege men over women or non-binary workers, and white workers over Indigenous workers and other workers of colour. Dronyk's, Battler's, Bird's, and Langston's poetry describe the struggles of being the only woman, or one of only a few women, in a workforce mostly made up of men,[39] but I have not yet found poetry collections that convey the experiences of Indigenous, Black, and other racialized workers.

In their study *Indigenous Gendered Experiences of Work in an Oil-Dependent, Rural Alberta Community*, Angele Alook, Ian Hussey, and Nicole Hill use an intersectional analysis to demonstrate that Indigenous people, women, and people of colour face discrimination in the oil industry. They describe the power dynamics of the Alberta oil patch: "Albertans are living in a corporate-dominated province overly focused on the oil and gas sector, in a settler-colonial country that is built on an intersectional hierarchy of value that sees white, male workers benefit because of the super-exploitation of gendered and racialized people (as well as other intersections of marginalization not focused on here). That is, in a corporate-capitalist economy like present-day Alberta, even high-wage workers are in some respects exploited, but gendered and racialized people tend to be confined to precarious, marginal positions in which their low wages contribute to especially high profits."[40] Indigenous workers report that they are often hired last and laid off first, are placed in unskilled jobs, and struggle to advance in their careers. This is in keeping with Yellowknives Dene political scientist Glen Sean Coulthard's argument that when it comes to Indigenous people, Canada is more intent on appropriating their land than their labour: "the history and experience of *dispossession*, not proletarianization, has been the dominant background structure shaping the character of the historical relationship between Indigenous peoples and the Canadian state."[41] Alook and her collaborators note that Indigenous workers can mitigate the negative effects of discrimination by operating their own businesses and employing other Indigenous workers, but Indigenous workers also face a conflict between extractive work and Indigenous identity.

In the absence of poetry written by Indigenous oil workers (which I still hope to find), it is helpful to read oil worker poetry alongside Indigenous poetry. See, for example, Cree poet Marvin Francis's work poetry in *Bush Camp,* where Francis offers an Indigenous railroad worker's take on extractivism:

he didn't
"get in   get rich   get out"

he was already there
he was poor
and
he loves the muskeg[.][42]

Responding to the "get in, get rich, get out" mantra of extractive workers doing difficult jobs, Francis critiques the colonial and alienating position that extraction puts workers in and highlights a tension for Indigenous extractive workers. The work contradicts, for example, the Cree poetics of "*miyo-pimatisiwin* (the good life)":[43] since "he loves the muskeg," not the money, and since he sees the land not as inert resources but as kin, the worker must negotiate conflicting understandings of wealth and what makes for a good life. I believe that many extractive workers feel this tension to some extent – a tension that is highlighted and exacerbated as their work brings them into proximity with endangered and resistant land that is often the source of their endangerment as workers.

Petrocultural Disidentification

> There is not a popular intelligence concerned with practical things and a scholarly intelligence devoted to abstract thought. It is always the same intelligence at work.
>
> – Jacques Rancière[44]

When I tell people I am writing a book about poetry written by oil workers, they often respond that they had no idea there was such a thing. Oil-worker poetry is surprising because of stereotypes about both oil workers and poetry – stereotypes that the poets featured in this book both perform and resist from their insider (and therefore also limited) perspectives. I consider the assumptions that oil workers do not care about climate change or that they are not intelligent or cultured enough to write poetry to be classist and dangerous. Oil workers are subjects inhabiting the era of climate change and energy transition; often, they experience the tension between energy systems (framed, variously, as a debate, a crisis, a conspiracy, or a war) as centred on their work, their livelihoods, the question of their goodness or badness, and the futures of their families and communities. These stigmatized subjects are uniquely positioned to sense, to describe, and to theorize both petropoetics and energy transition, yet oil-worker poets such as Naden Parkin, who dares readers to "Name another oil worker constructing poems,"[45] often appear to be isolated, unaware that there are other oil-worker poets.

Mathew Henderson has described writing his acclaimed 2012 poetry collection about oil work, *The Lease*, as "walking into an empty space" in Canadian poetry because "there hadn't really been anybody writing about this particular scene."[46] I am suspicious of claims about so-called "empty space" in a settler-colonial country like Canada, where the myth of *terra nullius* (that land already occupied and cared for by Indigenous peoples is empty and unused)[47] has served to justify the theft of land and the structuring of economies and ways of life as extractive rather than reciprocal. Oil and gas production in Canada is premised on empty space, first through *terra nullius* and subsequently through the erasure of memory involved in the boom-and-bust cycles of a staples economy built on the extraction of natural resources for export.[48] As Dominque Perron observes about another sense of empty space, the movements of the boom-and-bust cycle, "while predictable, seem to provoke an invariably renewed astonishment on the part of provincial and federal governments, as if they were all affected by a collective amnesia, helpless in reaction to this rather frequent phenomenon."[49] It is because of such forgetfulness that, as oil-worker poet Lindsay Bird writes in her book *Boom Time*, workers and other Canadians can "swing fat and hammocked / between bust and bust,"[50] failing to plan or save for the next bust or for the end of the fossil-fuel era. Canada's culture of extractivism makes oil workers vulnerable both to the boom-and-bust cycles of the industry and to the energy transition that is already underway. A boom-and-bust mentality isolates individuals in the petrostate and serves to keep them, as Perron observes, "*in their place*,"[51] including the fraught position of oil workers who are often cast, unfairly, as the perpetrators and the embodiment of the ecocide, toxic masculinity, racism, and settler-colonial violence that pervade Canadian petroculture.

The idea that oil-worker poetry is new is prevalent not only among the poets I study but also in literary criticism of their work, which treats a recent boom of poetry collections about oil work as a new phenomenon.[52] This is likely a result of the poor reception of Peter Christensen's 1981 book *Rig Talk* – the earliest full poetry collection about oil work that I have found – and its subsequent obscurity. In "Canadian Petro-Poetics: Masculinity, Labor, and Environment in Mathew Henderson's *The Lease*" (2014), a foundational text in the study of both Canadian oil-worker poetry and Canadian petro-poetics, Judith Rauscher describes Henderson's book in terms that could also describe both *Rig Talk* and Naden Parkin's *A Relationship with Truth* (2014): "His poems both construct and subvert an imagined working-class masculinity forged by the hardships of petro-labor and marked by exaggerated misogynist heterosexuality as well as a celebration of technological domination over the land. In the process, the texts explore the possibilities and limits of a proletarian ecopoetics sensitive to patterns of subjection of both land and people."[53] *The Rough Poets* builds on Rauscher's work both by situating isolated works by oil workers as part of a tradition of oil-worker poetry and by taking a deeper dive into the interplay Rauscher describes between the performance and subversion of "an imagined working-class masculinity" as a prescribed role for oil workers in Canadian culture.

Following Christensen's speaker's statement about other oil workers that "They make me / rough like their talk,"[54] *The Rough Poets* emphasizes a dominant identity or stereotype of oil workers as *rough* to which each of the poetry collections responds. Recent studies of what Shane Gunster and colleagues call pro-industry "extractive populism" highlight a doubling down on such a rough identity – for instance in the "Low Class Oil Trash" social-media posts studied by Jacob McLean.[55] As Gunster et al. argue, corporate-funded pro-oil social-media groups encourage oil workers to identify with extractive industry. By casting any challenges to the industry as threats to workers and their livelihoods, they "[transform] alienated workers and other pro-industry individuals into an engaged petro-public that can forcefully advocate for the sector in social media, everyday life, and the public sphere."[56] Similarly, Emily Eaton and Simon Enoch use fieldwork interviews and discourse analysis in the Saskatchewan oil patch to show that industry uses strategic philanthropy and community engagement to foster "intense identification" and "a 'hegemonic community economic identity,' in which the interests of industry and community are so tightly bound up that community members actively police criticisms of the industry and adopt ideological perspectives on wider energy issues that align with those of industry."[57] If, as geographer Matthew Huber argues, climate change is class war,[58] these strong identifications are significant victories for the ruling class and the status quo.

Although workers' identifications with industry are ubiquitous and strong, the above-mentioned studies highlight that every identification also contains ambivalence – in these cases, alienation, repressed criticisms, or what Eaton and Abby Kinchy term in another article "Quiet Voices in the Fracking Debate."[59] *The Rough Poets* draws on theories of disidentification by Michel Pêcheux and José Esteban Muñoz to trace a thread of petrocultural disidentification that runs through the tradition of oil-worker poetry in Canada. Disidentification, discussed in detail in chapter 2, is a way of avoiding and perhaps transcending the demand to choose a side between identification or counteridentification with a dominant ideology. In the context of a debate over energy framed as pitting oil workers against environmentalists, for instance, many of the oil-worker poets express both their solidarity with other workers and their concern about the environmental impacts of their work. Oil-worker poets use disidentificatory performances of roughness to position themselves as ambivalent insiders among oil workers. By doing so, they open themselves up to criticism for being complicit or hypocritical, but they also leave open the possibility that their fellow workers are equally ambivalent and know that their interests do not necessarily align with those of the corporations and extractive governments they work for.

Respecting the intelligence and the unique situated knowledge of oil-worker poets involves recognizing them as expert practitioners and theorists of petropoetics. Although the individual poets studied in *The Rough Poets* seldom appear to be aware of the existence of other oil-worker poets, the decades-long tradition of oil-worker poetry that I identify retroactively in this book does have some conventions, many of which are disidentificatory. These include performances and subversion of negative stereotypes of oil workers; experimentation with poetic forms as modes for truth-telling and/or cultural critique; disregard for standards of "good" poetry; use of second-person or otherwise distant narrative voices; negotiation or subversion of rules about "What We Don't Say" or of how and what workers are supposed to speak;[60] ecopoetic concern about the industry's impact on the environment; analysis of classism, racism, and colonialism; and grappling with workers' responsibilities toward the industry, one another, and the land. Oil worker poets use poetry to work out the thought/feeling of what Raymond Williams calls "practical consciousness" – of "what is actually being lived, and not only what it is thought is being lived."[61] While some of the texts I study are more overtly theoretical or philosophical, many advance theories about petroculture in modes that fit Ngũgĩ wa Thiong'o's description of "poor theory" – of "unintentional daring and experimentation" that is inherent in such things as "a workman's clothes," or body, or artistic production.[62] My aim in writing about these poetry collections is to highlight such theorizations, bringing them into conversation with other cultural theory without requiring the poetry to prove or to be faithful to those other theories. Both individually and as a tradition, oil-worker poets employ the medium of poetry and the mode of disidentification to say things – often surprising things – about fossil fuels, the oil-and-gas industry, oil culture, and just transition.

This Book

The first chapter, "Father of the Tar Sands: Modernity and Wilderness in S.C. Ells's *Northland Trails*," studies a collection of self-illustrated poems, short stories, and geographical essays created by Ells, a mining engineer who worked for the Canadian Department of Mines on the Athabasca oil sands from 1913 to 1945.[63] Ells, who liked to be referred to as the "father" of the tar sands, was a colonial founder of literary and cultural representations of the oil-sands industry, the Athabasca region, and oil work in Canada. This chapter argues that in *Northland Trails* (1938; 1956) Ells "fathered" a trope in oil-worker poetry of avoiding and repressing knowledge about the ecological and social impacts of the industry. Turning toward a tension between his heroic modernizing epics and his professions of love for the seemingly untouched nature of the northland, and attending to the "submerged perspectives"[64] of Indigenous labourers working in the extractive zone Ells founded, I read the poem "The Athabaska Trail" as a rare oil-work poem in *Northland Trails* that reveals Ells knew but avoided facing the truth about his legacy.

"'They make me / rough': Speaking Oil Patch in Peter Christensen's *Rig Talk*," the second chapter, is a reading of an early oil-worker poetry collection that was controversial and misunderstood at the time of its publication and has been overlooked as a precursor to more recent petropoetry. Readers and reviewers of former oil rigger Christensen's minimalist and masculinist poetry, including me, struggle to determine whether Christensen is critical of or merely complicit in the ecocidal, racist, and toxic-masculine discourse and culture he portrays in *Rig Talk* (1981). This chapter argues against reading *Rig Talk* through the lens of personal culpability and for reading it as a theory of petropoetics. It draws on theories of disidentification by Pêcheux and Muñoz that posit ambivalent, partial, or subversive identification with dominant ideology as an effective political model that turns ideology "against itself."[65]

The third chapter, "'my love is not dead yet': Living/Loving Oil and the Land in Dymphny Dronyk's *Contrary Infatuations*," interprets Dronyk's 2007 poetry collection as a theory of petropoetics. Reading the plain-spoken, short-lined documentary poems in *Contrary Infatuations* as concrete forms that resemble oil wells and drill bits, I argue that, as an Albertan, a neighbour to Wiebo Ludwig's Trickle Creek farm, and a woman performing reproductive labour, Dronyk's oil work extends well beyond her direct work writing safety manuals and negotiating surface rights for the oil and gas industry. Similar to Lauren Berlant's "cruel optimism,"[66] Dronyk's contrary infatuation is a feeling of bad love that is exemplified by her speaker's decision to stay in a relationship with an abusive man because he is dying. Through sequences of work poetry about gendered, reproductive labour in service of her family, the military, and the forestry and oil-and-gas industries, Dronyk assembles images and metaphors for the impasse of petromodern living, in which we know we need to break up with fossil fuels but we do not know how. I trace this perhaps-unconscious theorization of contrary infatuation as a form of petrocultural disidentification by looking at instances of bruising in Dronyk's book – instances that call for ways of addressing impasse grounded in an ethic of care.

The fourth chapter, "Tending Rusted Steel and Leased Land in Mathew Henderson's *The Lease*," continues the discussion of disidentification with a reading of *The Lease* (2012), a poetry collection narrated in the second-person voice of a naïve young worker who deflects and shares responsibility with readers as if everything in it happens to "you." Henderson, a former production tester, describes *The Lease* as personal and not political. In my reading, a disidentificatory politics emerges, one that refuses to assume the subject position of either the loyal oil worker or the critical ecopoet but rather explores the complicity and the pain of oil-patch workers and residents who simultaneously inflict and suffer petropoetics as dispossession and violence.

"Mud Man: Poetry as Truth-Telling and Land Relations in Naden Parkin's *A Relationship with Truth*" is the fifth chapter, a reading of drilling-fluid specialist Parkin's self-published 2014 poetry collection that analyzes his ideas that poetry requires truth telling and that oil workers and oil-patch residents have unique relationships with and responsibilities to the land. My reading emphasizes Parkin's inversion of Ells's use of amateur poetry to conceal repressed truths. Parkin lets down his guard in his poetry, revealing the pain and the "heart of gold" that hide behind his hypermasculine oil-worker persona.[67] My reading of *A Relationship with Truth* is nonetheless critical of Parkin's appropriation of Black and Indigenous experiences of enslavement and dispossession to describe his exploitation and alienation as a worker; it calls for an anticolonial, antiracist class politics for energy justice.

The sixth chapter, "'do not / be naïve': Language and the Stakes of Animacy in Lesley Battler's *Endangered Hydrocarbons*," reads former Shell project information manager Battler's 2015 collection as Language poetry that demonstrates how the petrochemical industry and its opponents mix and manipulate language to serve their interests and ideologies. *Endangered Hydrocarbons* reveals the animacy of supposedly inanimate hydrocarbons, linking the system of endangered hydrocarbons with colonialism, slavery, and racial capitalism. Battler's fraught play with endangered hydrocarbons highlights the dangers of other linguistic formulations such as *carbon capture and storage, fugitive emissions, dangerous radicals, ethical oil,* and *energy slave.* It demonstrates that our energy systems are colonial and that a just transition must also be decolonial/anticolonial.

"Boom Time, Giant Time, and Other Elsewhens of Lindsay Bird's *Boom Time*" is the final chapter. It interprets Bird's 2019 poetry collection about living and working in a Fort McMurray work camp in the early 2000s as the irreverent and questioning poetics of a daughter speaking back to the founders and other giants of the tar sands from the perspective of what geographer Stephanie Wakefield has called the "Anthropocene back loop."[68] Whereas Ells worked in the optimistic front loop of a modernizing and industrializing process, Bird's speaker inhabits and kills time among disillusioned and homesick workers in the blighted back-loop scenes of toxic tailings ponds, dingy shopping malls, climate change, and the coming Fort Mac wildfire.

The conclusion, which begins with a reading of the poem "Birds Migrate at Night, Mostly Unseen" by Kelly Shepherd, contemplates the implications of this study for energy justice.

The Rough Poets is a work of engaged climate-justice scholarship that envisions energy transition as a way not only to fend off the worst effects of global warming but also to right and repair historical wrongs, redistribute resources (including land), and build an equitable and green energy system. This book takes oil-worker poetry seriously as literature and as a mode through which petrocultural makers not only enact and condone but also analyze, problematize, and resist extractive and harmful practices of petropoetics. Drawing on the poets' own theorizations of petropoetics – for example, as *rig talk, contrary infatuation*, and *endangered hydrocarbons* – *The Rough Poets* finds ground for solidarity in a warming world where attending to the ravelling and unravelling of petropoetics is urgent oil work for everyone.

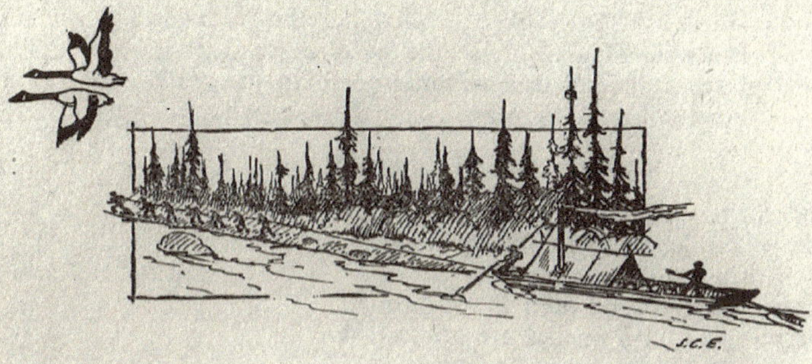

The Athabaska Trail

Theres many a trail winds away to the north-
 ward,—
Through swamp and muskeg and bottom land
 wide,—
But the trail that once carried the wealth of
 the northland
Was the tracker's trail by the river side.

38

Figure 1.1 *Above and overleaf*
"The Athabaska Trail" by S.C. Ells, as it appears in the 1956 edition of *Northland Trails*.

Gone are the trackers, coiled are the track-lines,
But still, of a night, as the mist settles down,
I see that long trail winding down to the northland,
And call back the past,—and the men who are gone!

* * * *

Drip, drip, and patter, patter,
The yellow leaves fall clumsily down,
Drip, drip, and patter, patter,
Yellow leaves,—and gold,—and brown;
For the high bush berries are crimson now
And the low bush berries are done;
Sodden and yellow the wild hay droops,
The days of summer are gone.

Drip, drip and patter, patter, the leaves fall clumsily down,
And the willows droop by the river—for the days of summer are gone,
Silent and swift steals the river away, with the woodlands tarnished gold,
For the autumn days are numbered—and the wind is raw and cold.
The morning air is cold and chill, before the rising of the sun,
Through swinging curtains of the mist, the men come toiling, one by one.

Like silent legions of the north, the endless spruce march by,
Their inky silhouettes clear cut against the evening sky;
Their heads adorned with golden wreaths, like graceful maidens tall,
The silver stems of poplar gleam, when shades of evening fall.
Drearily falls the autumn rain, the wind is raw and cold,
Wearily wing the grey geese south,—the year is growing old.

* * * *

Drip, drip and patter, patter, and it's chill in the early morn,
The tracking line grows heavy,—while men trudge wearily on,
Wet with the dew at night and morn, but with sweat in the noonday sun,
Oh! there's warmth,—and rest,—and shelter,—when the last day's work is done!

CHAPTER 1

Father of the Tar Sands: Modernity and Wilderness in S.C. Ells's *Northland Trails*

Sidney Clarke Ells (1878–1971) was a white mining expert and civil servant from Ottawa, a stubborn hands-on innovator who led the federal government's efforts to industrialize the Athabasca oil sands from 1913 to 1945.[1] In his self-illustrated literary collection *Northland Trails* (1938; 1956), Ells mourns the decline of the fur-trade ways of life and the seemingly pristine northland of the early twentieth century; he also envisions a fully colonized and industrialized future northland populated by white prospectors and engineers. Yet, by leaving his oil work out of *Northland Trails*, he represses his role in turning the northland he claimed to love into an extractive zone;[2] he avoids facing the destruction and harm that would become his legacy.

Dominant narratives of the genesis of the tar-sands industry,[3] including Ells's *Recollections of the Development of the Athabasca Oil Sands*,[4] emphasize the stubborn persistence of heroic tar-sands innovators in the face of opposition and adversity. As Métis scholar and poet Emma LaRocque writes in her study of Indigenous resistance literature, however, "[i]t is important that we understand colonial subterfuge behind the fantastic hero-ification of the White man."[5] Heroic oil-sands narratives are ideological, colonial texts that marginalize Indigenous peoples and lay claim to land that was already occupied, and still is occupied, as a sentient homeland.[6] Métis Elder Alvena Strasbourg (1921–2016) tells a different version in her 1998 memoir. She writes, "[s]hare with me some of my fond childhood memories of Fort

McMurray, before they discovered the oil sands. They called it progress, prosperity and wealth. But I remember a Fort McMurray when people lived with clean air and pure water, working together, sharing and caring. There was no discrimination, crime, drugs, alcohol or welfare; just a plain and simple life. This is what I call true wealth and happiness, but those days are gone."[7] Strasbourg's memoir is a testament to concurrent Indigenous ways of life that, through the passing on of culture and of narratives such as this, continue to resist and survive extractive, colonial land relations. This is a "submerged perspective," in the terms used by Macarena Gómez-Barris when she writes that "[e]xtractive zones contain within them the submerged perspectives that challenge obliteration."[8] In *Northland Trails*, Ells collects heroic colonial narratives alongside loving depictions of the Northland and its inhabitants; the friction between these modes unwittingly exposes colonial subterfuge and draws attention to submerged perspectives.

Ells wished to be remembered as "The Father of the Tar Sands."[9] As a reader in the late-petromodern era looking back to the origins of Canada's most infamous extractive industry, and as a feminist skeptic about the patriarchal idea that having a father figure is necessarily good for individuals, families, or institutions,[10] I find the father-of-the-tar-sands title undesirable, funny, and apt. This chapter treats Ells, irreverently, as the "father" of oil worker poetry. Ells "fathered" a tradition of repressing knowledge about complicity and responsibility that translates, in later oil-worker poetry, to strict adherence, ambivalence, confusion, or irreverent play with rules about what can and should be said about oil work and life in extractive zones. Throughout *Northland Trails*, and especially in the poem "The Athabaska Trail," we glimpse extractive logics that are foundational to Canadian petropoetics. It is in relationship to these logics, embodied and celebrated fully and unironically by Ells, that subsequent oil-worker poets develop more complex practices of disidentification.

Father of the Tar Sands

While Sydney Ells from Ottawa
Rides around in his private car
Saying to himself with a smile of bliss –
"I am the guy that started this"
– Al Wheeler[11]

S.C. Ells was sent in 1913 by the Canadian Department of Mines to investigate the oil-sands deposits in Treaty 8 territory, on the homelands of Woodland Cree, Chipewyan Dene, and Métis peoples near the former Hudson's Bay Company fur-trading post of Fort McMurray. He would continue to work primarily on the Athabasca tar sands until his retirement in 1945, surveying and mining the underground deposits, paving experimental roads with asphalt made from bituminous sand, and developing early methods for bitumen separation. Although Ells had a home and a wife in Ottawa, he travelled frequently to Fort McMurray, often arriving in spring and staying until fall, sometimes remaining through the cold northern winters. As local sled-dog driver, canoeist, and poet Al Wheeler's teasing portrayal of Ells in a 1928 poem shows, Ells was a privileged civil servant, not a typical miner, but out of both necessity and passion, Ells did the labour of mining, separating, transporting, and paving with bitumen alongside the workers he employed. The 1931 photograph in figure 1.2 shows Ells seemingly in the middle of work, holding a pail, with the Abasand Oils Ltd plant behind him and the steep shore of the Horse River beside him. After former Abasand owner Max Ball first called Ells "the father of the Alberta bituminous sand research and development" in 1950,[12] Ells encouraged his own reputation as the father of the tar sands. The Sidney Clarke Ells fonds at Library and Archives Canada reveal that Ells spent much of his career and his retirement defending and reasserting this reputation – in media interviews, letters, and multiple versions of and addenda to his memoir – against those of better-known and better-liked founders like Karl A. Clark and Robert Fitzsimmons. Although Ells may be less celebrated than he had hoped, he is still considered an important figure in the history of the oil sands.[13] In addition to his mining work, Ells did foundational creative, imaginative, and cultural work on behalf of the settler-colonial state, laying the groundwork for extractive industry in the Athabasca region.

Ells was an author of poetry, short stories, histories, and hand-drawn illustrations about life in the Athabasca region,[14] first created as Christmas cards for friends and family or as contributions to the *Canadian Geographical Journal* or the *Canadian Mining Journal*, and later collected in the book *Northland Trails*, published in 1938 and in an expanded edition in 1956. *Northland Trails* was part of the popular-poetry tradition that flourished in the early twentieth century.[15] At a time of modernist innovation in Canadian poetry, Ells, who had no formal training as a writer or visual artist, favoured

Figure 1.2
S.C. Ells at Abasand plant, 1931.

swinging ballad rhythms and iambic metre in the style of Rudyard Kipling and Robert Service. His poetry is described on the 1956 dust jacket as "Canadiana," participating in the nation-building project of creating distinctively Canadian stories and epics. Ells's illustrations strive for realism but also have a cartoonish quality in their depiction of labourers, non-human animals, landscapes, sternwheelers, trappers, and other residents of the North. Judging from the twenty-six reviews of *Northland Trails* collected in the Sidney Clarke Ells fonds at Library and Archives Canada – published primarily in newspapers and geological and mining periodicals in the 1930s and 1950s – the book was well received by a wide range of Canadian readers. Ells is seldom remembered today as a literary and visual artist,[16] but *Northland Trails* is a precursor to subsequent representations of the Athabasca region that range from industry or environmentalist rhetoric and advertising to poetry and short stories, from maps, diagrams, and aerial photographs to comics and video games.[17]

Recent scholarly work on Ells has critiqued the role he played in the colonization of the Athabasca region and its framing as a beautiful but empty hinterland, available for resource extraction. In "Bitumen Exploration and the Southern Re-Inscription of Northeastern Alberta: 1875–1967," historian Hereward Longley considers the role of Ells's maps and reports in the "cartographic colonization" of the Athabasca region.[18] Longley shows that Ells's surveys of bitumen deposits have been used by government to exclude resource-rich land from land claims negotiations under Treaty 8 (1899), some of which are still ongoing today. Countering Ells's grandiose claims about his own legacy, Longley writes, "[t]he efforts of Sidney Ells are far more significant for their contribution to colonizing the region by re-imagining place in the southern mind than they were for any tangible accomplishment."[19] Longley sees few lasting impacts of Ells's innovations in mining and bitumen separation, but he shows that the impacts of Ells's cultural and aesthetic work are indeed tangible and long-lasting, although they have not prevailed over the Indigenous lifeways that have successfully resisted and survived them. Discussing Ells's technical reports and memoir in their book chapter "Visualizing the Tar Sands Through Time," sociologists Debra Davidson and Mike Gismondi show that Ells contributed to a colonial visualization of the oil sands that emphasizes "industriousness."[20] They conclude that Ells "literally took the measure of the place, concentrating his geologist's eye on verticality and not on surfaces," treating Indigenous residents as either potential labourers or part of the "wilderness terrain" that he saw merely as overburden, a set of obstacles standing between him and the bitumen.[21]

In *Unsustainable Oil: Facts, Counterfacts, and Fictions,* literary scholar Jon Gordon reads Ells's *Recollections of the Development of the Athabasca Oil Sands,* focusing on the two poems by Ells that serve as the epigraph and epilogue. Gordon agrees with Davidson and Gismondi's assessment of how Ells represented the land, but he adds that a repressed tension between "modernity and wilderness" propelled Ells's work and poetics,[22] because he also loved the land he sought to conquer.[23] Gordon identifies an unspoken subtext of Ells's poetics – what literary scholar Patricia Yaeger would call its "energy unconscious"[24] – the knowledge that, despite his professed affection for the Northland and its inhabitants, Ells did foundational oil work that would be destructive to northern ecologies and ways of life. In my reading of Ells's collected creative works, I demonstrate that the dynamics that Gordon observes in Ells' memoir also play out in *Northland Trails.* Throughout the book, Ells tries but fails to keep separate two "trails" that are in conflict: the "old, old trail" of wilderness, representing idealized premodern fur-trade ways of life, and the "new trail" of modernization, blazed by heroic, white prospectors and engineers.[25]

Ells's nature poems like "White Water" (15), "My Lullaby" (45), "Hunger" (52–3), and "The Trapper's Farewell" (215–19) exult in the seemingly untouched wilderness of "the Northland" (23) – seen as empty, even though it had already long been inhabited by Indigenous peoples. The nature poems celebrate the lives of fur-trade voyageurs and trappers, professing the speaker's love for the northland as his true home. They express a preference for fur-trade land relations that Ells casts as unalienated and Indigenous but that were already colonial, characterized, as anthropologist Patricia A. McCormack describes, by "unremitting expansion" on the part of Euro-Canadian colonists and "determined opposition by Aboriginal people to threats to their autonomy, the measure of their sovereignty."[26] Epic modernizing poems like "The Argonauts,"[27] "The Seekers" (42–3), and "Followers of the Grail" (68–72) celebrate the rugged individualism of white scientists, engineers, and prospectors by representing them as questing Argonauts and knights, determined to industrialize and modernize the North, who wield science as a "magic wand" (69) and bring "new-found leisure" (70) and cures for "plague and pestilence" (72).

In a handful of poems where the trails of modernity and wilderness overlap or intersect, the contradictions between them threaten to undo the logic and the poetics of the nature-loving engineer. For example, in "My Lullaby," Ells seems to have set out to suggest that the technological lullabies of "[a] smelter's muffled murmur ... the voice of rumbling mills" can be as soothing as the sounds of the natural world, but he changes his tune mid-poem, deciding that he prefers the natural lullaby of "water's muted symphonies" (45). In Ells's poems about the "*Lure of the North*" with accompanying illustrations of nearly nude figures (102; 10–11; 54–5), the northland is personified as a "stern compelling mistress" or a "lusty young giant" who must be conquered (55). In these poems, conquest by white northern men "who won't take 'No'!" is both sexualized and revealed as non-consensual (32). These poems sit uneasily both alongside the poem "Wasaya" (92–6), which celebrates a harmonious (read: patriarchal) marriage between a white trapper and an Indigenous woman, and in light of derogatory representations of Indigenous men as slouching and unemployed dispossessed subjects (see, for example, 143; 199) – with both tropes (the useful Indigenous wife and the lazy Indigenous man) serving to represent the Northland as *terra nullius*, as empty land and unused resources available for extraction.[28] What we see when the trails of modernity and wilderness combine is that the project of colonial modernization is predatory and violent – that the land and resources it extracts were already claimed and in use before the arrival of colonial "fathers" like Ells.

I have argued elsewhere that Ells may have thought of himself as a goose, and that he uses goose imagery in *Northland Trails* and other speculative visualizations of the tar sands to lift off from the land, adopting a "goose's-eye view" that avoids responsibility for his role in making the Athabasca region an extractive zone.[29] This chapter builds on this argument with a close reading of "The Athabaska Trail,"[30] a poem in which the trails of modernity and wilderness overlap through Ells's oil work.

Modernity and Wilderness in "The Athabaska Trail"

Ells's poetry, prose, and pen-and-ink drawings are most often focused on labour either in the pre-industrial fur-trade economy or in an emerging or imagined industrialized northern economy, but I was surprised, when I first read *Northland Trails*, to find that it contains only a few glancing references to Ells's own labour in the Athabasca region.[31] In a 1962 letter to Ells that contrasts *Northland Trails* against Ells's memoir, O.T.G. Williamson calls *Northland Trails* "much too modest and impersonal," an instance of "hiding your light under a bushel" where Ells did not take "full credit for the great work he has done,"[32] but I interpret the erasure of Ells's oil work from *Northland Trails* as hypocrisy rather than modesty. Ells omitted his own labour from *Northland Trails* as a way of managing the contradictions between modernity and wilderness that were inherent not only to his oil work but also to his very presence in the North.

In *The Country and the City*, British cultural theorist Raymond Williams describes a longstanding practice of the ruling class making themselves "temporarily absent" at moments of dispossession, so that they can be seen as sympathetic to the plight of those whose lands and lifeways are stolen, instead of being held accountable for the theft.[33] In "Ideas of Nature," Williams describes capitalists who cast themselves as both improvers and conservationists of nature as "hypocrites": "Established at powerful points in the very process which is creating the disorder, they change their clothes at weekends, or when they can get down to the country; join appeals and campaigns to keep one last bit of England green and unspoilt; and then go back, spiritually refreshed, to invest in the smoke and the spoil."[34] This hypocrisy is rooted in a condition that Williams describes as the "alienation of nature, [the] separation of nature from human activity."[35] Essential to the operation of capitalist and colonial economies, nature is constructed, in the example of coal mining in England, as either "coal-bearing" or "heather-bearing"[36] – that is, either as the source of resources and a site of industry or as "wilderness" imagined to be unspoiled and untouched by humans.[37] Lacking reciprocity and accountability, such false ideas about the relationship between humans and nature allow Ells to portray himself as both an improver of nature – a mining expert – and a lover of nature who finds refuge from industrialization in the wilderness – a nature poet. Ells can get away with doing this because such "ideas of nature" permeate settler-colonial culture in Canada (including, notably, the genres of nature poetry and work poetry).

Contradicting such ideas, anthropologist Anna Lauwenhaupt Tsing describes transitions to new resource economies as characterized by friction: "[n]atural resources are not God given but must be wrested from previous economies and ecologies in violent extractions." These extractions have wide-ranging local and global implications, and they leave "none of us unscathed."[38] The colonial reframing of the Athabasca region as a resource frontier and an extractive zone resulted in an ongoing process of what Lena Gross describes (following Traci Voyles) as "Wastelanding the Bodies, Wastelanding the Land."[39] Air, water, land, animals, and plants in the Athabasca region today are contaminated, with the worst effects felt by nearby Indigenous communities such as the Fort McKay, Athabasca Chipewyan, and Mikisew Cree First Nations, and with the coming energy transition away from fossil fuels exposing the possibility that oil corporations, none of whom have yet found ways to fully remediate the tailings ponds that contain their toxic waste,[40] may abandon the region and their responsibilities, leaving these sites to be tended by governments and local communities.[41] Anthropologists Katherine Wheatley and Clinton Westman summarize their research on water issues in an Athabasca region where corporations have been given free rein: "what we document here is nothing less than the future of a natural, cultural, and moral catastrophe – one that is based on a speculative, magical, fantastic, and highly questionable set of projections."[42] Heeding Ells's own claims, I credit him as a "father" of the short-sighted and fantastical visions and projections that are foundational to the oil-sands industry. Ells did not like to admit it, but he knew that not only economic gain but also ecological, cultural, and social losses would result from industrialization.

Among the few minor references to Ells's oil work in *Northland Trails* are the note and illustration that precede the poem "The Athabaska Trail" (see figure 1.3). The note, titled "The Athabaska Trail (1913)," is one of several prose introductions to Ells's poetry that one 1938 reviewer calls "delightful little explanatory notes"[43] but that in my reading often tell stories that the poems themselves have avoided or failed to convey. "The Athabaska Trail" is the only poem in *Northland Trails* that is both preceded and followed by notes – an even longer explanatory note titled "The Athabaska Trail (1916)" (with illustration and a six-line poetry fragment) follows the poem. All this explanation suggests that Ells is trying to avoid accountability for a process in which he participated not only as a tracker but also as a visionary, innovator, and "father" of extractive industry.

The first paragraph of "The Athabaska Trail (1913)" looks to the past. Ells, who relished hard labour and old-fashioned ways of doing things, describes the fur-trade-era job of tracking boats upstream along the Athabasca River as grim, brutal, torturous, and therefore admirable. As Ells explains in "The Athabaska Trail (1916)," the Athabasca River was used as a fur-trade shipping route beginning around 1869 and ending with the arrival of the Alberta and Great Waterways Railway to Waterways, Alberta (near Fort McMurray) in 1916.[44] Trade goods going north and furs going south were transported on flat-bottomed, square-ended boats called "scows" (as seen in figure 1.3), with rowing sweeps on the sides, a long rudder in the stern, and poles for pushing

The Athabaska Trail (1913)

Prior to the advent of the internal combustion engine along northern rivers, south-bound cargoes of furs were "tracked" upstream by brigades of large canoes and heavy bateaux—sometimes for many hundreds of miles. Crews of men harnessed to heavy "tracking" lines, hundreds of feet in length, fought their way grimly along the shores, often through tangle of overhanging brush, knee deep mud and waist deep water. The ceaseless torture of myriads of flies from daylight till dark, the harassing and heavy work which only the strongest men could long endure, made "tracking" one of the most brutal forms of labor.

In the late fall of 1913, the writer and a crew of Breeds and Indians tracked the first important shipment of samples of bituminous sand[1] from McMurray up the rapids and fast water of Athabaska river to Athabaska Landing, a distance of nearly 250 miles. For twenty-three days, from daylight till dark, in snow and rain, the heavily loaded scow was hauled upstream. The following lines reflect, in part, the mental reaction,—a longing for rest—and warmth—and shelter.

[1]Ten tons.

36

Figure 1.3
"The Athabaska Trail (1913)" note and illustration that precede "The Athabaska Trail" in the 1956 edition of *Northland Trails.*

away from rocks. When travelling downriver (that is, going north), the scows were carried by the flow of the river, piloted by skilled Métis and First Nations voyageurs who were known as the "Athabaska brigade."[45] When upriver (southward) travel was necessary, the scows were pulled by teams of trackers: Indigenous men harnessed to tracking lines, walking along the shore and pulling the boats against the current. As McCormack notes, Indigenous freighters and rivermen became increasingly unemployed or precariously employed with the advent of Hudson's Bay Company sternwheeler boats on the Athabasca beginning in the 1880s and, later, of rail lines to the north.[46] Even with sternwheelers replacing their labour on parts of the river, voyageurs were needed until 1916 to travel the seventy-five-mile stretch of the river immediately south of Fort McMurray, which included fourteen rapids and was passable only by smaller boats.[47]

Fur-trade-era tracking labour is represented in the full-page illustration that appears alongside Ells's note. This pen-and-ink drawing is featured on the dust jacket of the 1938 edition; it depicts labourers straining against the tracking line and the pull of the water, drenched by the falling rain. The "trail" the trackers walk is not perceptible as such and takes them in and out of the river. As Strasbourg conveys in her description of her grandfather Julian Cardinal's experience of tracking scows through the Grand Rapids, this work was not only difficult but also dangerous: "These boats were so heavy, the men on shore wore harnesses across one shoulder and around the waist. This gave them more leverage and freed their hands to grab trees and anchor themselves. Renegade waves sometimes slammed the scows around, dragging men into the river and drowning them if they couldn't swim."[48] The men in Ells's illustration have exaggeratedly muscular bodies, in contrast to the ordinary statures of most trackers in historical photos taken around the turn of the twentieth century.[49] These imagined trackers look strong, steady, and determined – showing qualities that Ells admired and emulated – while hiding the exhaustion, fear, and ambivalence they may have also felt. The depiction of two lines of trackers following one after the other gives a sense of a long tradition, with the boat following behind outside the frame suggesting its continuation, despite the imminent end of tracking that could be felt in 1913. Through the focus on tracking in "The Athabaska Trail" and surrounding notes, and with repeated evocations and illustrations of trackers in the book,[50] Ells makes the tracker the embodiment of an idealized Northern way of life. He presents the end of tracking labour on the Athabasca as a severe loss. Yet, through a version of colonial subterfuge, he also submerges the perspective of the Indigenous trackers, overwriting their experiences with his own ideas and limited experience of tracking and its significance.

If the first paragraph of the explanatory note makes the point, as Ells writes in "The Athabaska Trail (1916)," that "*the early voyageur is worthy of an honoured place in the national Hall of Fame!*"[51] the second paragraph serves a different purpose. This paragraph tells one of Ells's favourite stories about his oil work, which is also recorded in more detail in his memoir[52] – the story of his shipment of ten tons of tar sand from Fort McMurray to Athabaska Landing (now known as Athabasca) by scow in 1913. It describes a scene where Ells's modernizing oil work coincided with the system of fur-trade-era labour that he misrepresents as traditional or natural in *Northland Trails*. Ells refers to his own labour distantly in this paragraph, using third-person narration (referring to himself as "*the writer*") and the passive voice ("*the heavily loaded scow was hauled upstream*")[53] – evasive language that seems like modesty but might also be hypocrisy. The scow in the story was pulled upstream by a team of twelve Indigenous trackers whom Ells refers to using racist slurs and derogatory comments.

Ells's account in his *Recollections* reveals his disdain for the trackers, most of whom did not speak English, and who on multiple occasions refused to carry on, having to be threatened and cajoled to continue. It also reveals Ells to have been a demanding and ruthless boss, who, in addition to requiring the trackers to work, as the note in *Northland Trails* describes, "*twenty-three days, from daylight to dark, in snow and rain,*"[54] also required them to sleep without tents, "under the dripping trees,"[55] and to work in conditions that caused a hernia in one tracker and pneumonia in another, all for less than one-third of the pay Ells received for the same period.[56] It was only after the worst of the journey, during which several of the trackers fell ill or were injured, that Ells began to help track the scow himself. In a sarcastic letter to Royal North-West Mounted Police Corporal Charles "Denny" La Nauze, who helped him hire the trackers, Ells complains about his experience of doing labour that he considered to be beneath him. He writes, "The trip up the river was to me most interesting, though my perspective was somewhat twisted, owing to the fact that I was on the wrong end of the tracking line a good deal of the time."[57] Although Ells would boast about this experience for the rest of his life, using it to bolster his reputation as the father of the tar sands, his perspective on the journey was indeed "twisted" by his racial and class status as a white civil servant. Ells uses the explanatory notes to link himself with "*the early voyageur*," but he was never a tracker. Although he experienced tracking labour, he came from the "wrong end" of the labour arrangement – he understood neither the language nor the perspective of the trackers.

In *Northland Trails*, Indigenous men are either portrayed by a version of the stereotype of the noble savage that casts them as "natural labourers" of the fur-trade era[58] or they are represented as unemployed and inexpert labour at a pivotal moment in the transition between fur-trade and mineral economies. In the essay "LaLoche Portage," Ells looks back on the former "glory" of an old fur-trade route. He writes, "[n]ow only an occasional ragged Breed [*sic*], followed by his inevitable retinue of wretched starving dogs, slouches silently along."[59] From his location as a self-proclaimed father of the transition between the extractive regimes of the fur trade and the oil sands, Ells characterizes early trackers as heroes but contemporary ones as lazy and suspicious; when he does so, he is doing ideological work that justifies land theft, pollution, and the replacement of Indigenous labourers with white prospectors and engineers.

Considering the shift from mercantile to industrial capitalism in Canada, Yellowknives Dene political scientist Glen Sean Coulthard notes that "[i]ncreased European settlement combined with an imported, hyper-exploited non-European workforce meant that, in the post-fur trade period, Canadian state-formation and colonial-capitalist development required first and foremost *land*, and only secondarily the surplus value afforded by cheap, Indigenous labour."[60] Métis/settler literary scholar Warren Cariou has observed the interplay of ideas about Indigenous productivity and shiftlessness in the transition between extractive economies. He writes, "[w]hen the bottom falls out of the fur economy, when the oil downturn hits, when the forestry industry retrenches, Indigenous laborers are often among the first to lose their jobs, their status, and perhaps also some of the pride they had gained when it seemed they were welcome in the settler-colonial realm of work."[61] Strasbourg recruited and trained Indigenous workers for tar-sands industry jobs following the opening of the Great Canadian Oil Sands plant (later Suncor) in 1967 and the Syncrude plant in the 1970s. Noting a decline in Indigenous employment at Suncor in the seventies, she concludes, "I think the original guilt of spoiling Aboriginal lands had faded."[62] The idea that Indigenous people are unproductive and unemployed contributes to the colonial belief that the land and resources of the North are there for the taking, and that any future employment of Indigenous workers (for example, work in the tar sands) will be an act of corporate benevolence rather than inadequate compensation for the loss of territory, clean water, healthy living conditions, and traditional ways of life.

The trackers Ells hired in 1913 (some of whom may be depicted in figure 1.4) resisted and at turns refused the terms of their employment. As McCormack argues, the perceived "intransigence" of Indigenous people negotiating the tension between Indigenous and colonial modes of production was in fact "damage control."[63] The trackers' subversive and critical Indigenous presence in the story critiques the poem that follows, as well as the broader narrative of the development of the Athabasca Oil Sands. Even as the story is mediated through Ells's own perspective as a colonial civil servant, the trackers' perspective disagrees with Ells's description of the journey as the delivery of an "*important shipment.*" The trackers resist Ells's attempts both

Figure 1.4
Photograph of unidentified trackers, "Getting Asphalt from Fort McMurray Tar Sands, Alberta," 1914. The description in the archival record reads, "First shipment. Taken on scow that was tracked up the Athabasca River for 240 miles. Sidney Ells and party hauled the barge." I believe this photograph was taken by S.C. Ells in 1913.

to cast them as *early voyageurs* in a re-enactment of an old form of labour and to exploit and erase them as unskilled and unnamed labourers, when in fact they are some of the earliest oil workers (fathers?) at the birth of a new tar-sands industry. When the trackers at this moment of energy transition and the death throes of the fur-trade economy perform "*one of the most brutal forms of labour*" as a necessity rather than a vocation, their resistance draws attention to the power dynamics and colonial politics of the oil-sands industry. Ells ends "The Athabaska Trail (1913)" with a closing sentence to describe "*the mental reaction*" to arriving at Athabasca Landing. Its phrasing and multiple dashes (" – *a longing for rest – and warmth – and shelter*") will be echoed in the closing line of the poem. The dashes that thus frame the poem suggest that much is being left unsaid. They submerge not only Ells's own mental reaction but also whatever the trackers thought and felt about their work.

The agency of the Indigenous trackers is carefully contained because it undermines the way Ells wished to tell this story, but the trackers are not the only potentially subversive presence Ells must manage. Ells's own presence as a tar-sands engineer mourning the end of tracking on the Athabasca is also problematic. As Ells describes in his 1939 essay "Athabaska Trail," the railway would be extended (and therefore the practice of tracking on the Athabasca ended) to ship minerals, including oil sand, more efficiently. He writes, "[a]t the present time, mineral deposits constitute the powerful [lodestone] which is drawing men northward. To the discovery of these deposits must be attributed the rapid development of transportation facilities throughout the Athabaska-Mackenzie basin."[64] What Ells admits in the essay but does not wish to consider when framing his poem is that the railway to Fort McMurray was built to ship bitumen and that he had demanded this development as part of his oil work.[65] In an example of the oil-sands engineer making himself temporarily absent at a moment of dispossession and loss, Ells avoids taking responsibility for the role he played in the changes he mourns. It is with this in mind that I turn, now, to a reading of the poem "The Athabaska Trail" (see pages 21–2).

Looking at the poem before beginning reading, I make two observations that will be key to my interpretation. First, I can tell after only glancing at "The Athabaska Trail" that it is one of Ells's goose poems. In the illustration, a line of Canada geese predominates, crossing the poem itself and linking an image of a paddler camping beside a river to a past northern scene with a line of tiny trackers towing a scow, trudging their way out of the frame and off the page. Like Ells's other goose references, this poem uses a goose metaphor to naturalize his presence in the North and to facilitate his flight from responsibility and accountability – in this case, responsibility for his role in the disruptive energy transition that ended tracking on the Athabasca. The flight of the oversized geese charts a path between the three sections of the poem and the scenes they depict. Beginning in the first two stanzas with the perspective of a paddler looking toward both the north and the past, the poem takes flight in the middle stanzas, offering a goose's-eye view of a past scene of tracking labour before briefly touching down, in the final stanza, for a closer view of trackers at the end of a long and difficult journey. Each of these scenes is narrated in the present tense, so that this is also a time-travelling poem, with the geese as a constant the speaker can draw on to "call back the past" while inhabiting the changed present.[66]

My second observation is that, like many of Ells's other poems, "The Athabaska Trail" uses variations on the ballad – an English poetic form with roots in oral folk traditions. The first three stanzas are ballad stanzas, with three or four stressed syllables per line, with the lines grouped into a four-line stanza (doubled to eight in Ells's third stanza), and with rhyming second and fourth lines. Like Rudyard Kipling, a poet he admired, Ells commonly doubled up ballad lines into longer lines of six or seven stressed syllables that maintain the ballad rhyme scheme and form rhyming couplets grouped into longer stanzas. Midway through "The Athabaska Trail," Ells switches from ballad lines (e.g. "Drip, drip, and patter, patter" in the third stanza [with stressed syllables underlined here]) to doubled-up lines (e.g. "Drip, drip, and patter, patter, the leaves fall clumsily down" in the fourth stanza [39]). This switch is interesting to a reader looking for repressed details related to Ells's oil work; it suggests that, as an amateur poet, Ells managed the form of the poem less carefully than its content. "The Athabaska Trail" is like a work song, written to the remembered cadences of tracking. I imagine Ells beginning to compose it while working, considering how the motions and rhythms of his body were linked with earlier trackers. In its rhythm, the poem embodies a tracking journey. It moves through the stages of the trackers getting started, stumbling, establishing a stride, becoming exhausted, and, at the end of the poem, taking a break and finally catching their breath. The repeated phrase "Drip, drip, and patter, patter" (39), with its heavy punctuation and disruptive metre, embeds the trackers' own trips, or stumbles. While Ells carefully managed the content of the poem, the repressed contradictions of "The Athabaska Trail" and *Northland Trails* are more readily perceptible in its form. Keeping these two observations in mind, I turn to a close reading of the poem.

With the theme of the trail recurring throughout *Northland Trails*, the opening stanza of "The Athabaska Trail" makes this poem the centre and highlight of the book because it is about Ells's favourite trail. Although there's "many a trail" in the North, the speaker – the nostalgic paddler of the illustration – names this as the ultimate trail when he asserts that "the trail that once carried the wealth of the northland / Was the tracker's trail by the river side" (38). Ells uses a double meaning of "the wealth of the northland" (furs and also tar sand) to refer, subtly, to his oil work and his 1913 shipment of bituminous sand by scow. Although this seems like a starting point for Ells to do some modest boasting, the second stanza takes a different turn. It begins with a trip, a telling moment where, as Jacques Lacan phrases it, "something stumbles" and the unconscious or the repressed can be glimpsed.[67] The established rhythm is turned on its head in the first line of the second stanza, in which the speaker recalls, dramatically, that the trackers are gone: "Gone are the trackers, coiled are the track-lines."[68] This is the only line in the opening two stanzas that begins with a stressed syllable. It is a stumble that replaces the metrical feet of iambs ("but still") and anapests ("of a night"), which begin with unstressed syllables, with dactyls ("Gone are the") and trochees ("trackers"), which begin with stressed syllables. In the system of syllables as steps, it represents both a material stumble (in which a tracker trips) and a response to a staggering realization. Hidden behind the knowledge that the trackers are gone is Ells's knowledge of the role he played in the transition from the fur-trade economy he admires to an industrialized fossil economy; it is this repressed idea, encoded in the seemingly excessive emotion and sense of surprise in this stanza, that both trips him up and prevents him from revealing himself as both a tar-sands engineer and an occasional tracker. Instead, in this second stanza, the speaker locates himself outside the northland, looking "down" (i.e. downstream, northward) toward it, and remembering "the men who are gone!" (39) – the trackers who no longer work on the Athabasca.

The break between the second and third stanzas signals a shift in perspective; in the third, fourth, and fifth stanzas, the speaker is transported, in memory, to a past scene of tracking along the Athabasca. Instead of considering why the trackers are "gone!" Ells uses geese in the illustration and the poem to take flight. This section contains the prettiest lines in the poem and perhaps in the book, focused on the scenery that surrounds the trackers, who track the scow at the same time of year that Ells and the trackers he hired did in 1913, when it was autumn both in the natural world and in the employment of trackers on the Athabasca. The fourth stanza reads:

> Drip, drip and patter, patter, the leaves fall clumsily down,
> And the willows droop by the river – for the days of summer are gone,
> Silent and swift steals the river away, with the woodlands tarnished gold,
> For the autumn days are numbered – and the wind is raw and cold.
> The morning air is cold and chill, before the rising of the sun,
> Through swinging curtains of the mist, the men come toiling, one by one. (39)

The scene is described as if by an observer rather than a labourer. If the speaker locates himself anywhere in relation to the image of the line of toiling trackers, it is as one who flies over, taking in the scene, aestheticizing rather than participating in the trackers' labour. The lines are full of references to clumsiness, weariness, and old age, attributed to leaves, wild hay, willows, the day, geese, and the year, reflecting a tiredness that the trackers – who make their first appearance in the strict iambic metre of the final line – must ignore in themselves as they carry on, embodying the sturdy, stoic masculinity that Ells celebrates. Despite this, in the rhythmic subtext of the poem, the metrical trips introduced through the spondee (metrical foot of two stressed syllables) that begins the repeated "Drip, drip" lines resist the erasure of the trackers as a toiling, at-times clumsy material presence in the poem – stepping, tripping, and dripping with rain and sweat. Observations that "the wind is raw and cold" and that the river "steals" northward are included as picturesque descriptions of the scenery but might also describe the conditions of the trackers' toil and the way the river takes their spent energy. In the next stanza, the speaker, with a goose's-eye-view, compares the line of trackers with a natural order represented by other rows and lines: those of spruce, poplar, and geese.

Another shift in perspective occurs with the break between the fifth and sixth stanzas. Using the "Drip, drip" refrain from earlier stanzas to maintain the sense of the larger scene (and the rhythm of the trackers' steps), the speaker focuses, briefly, on the trackers and their working conditions:

> Drip, drip and patter, patter, and it's chill in the early morn,
> The tracking line grows heavy, – while men trudge wearily on,
> Wet with the dew at night and morn, but with sweat in the noonday sun,
> Oh! There's warmth, – and rest, – and shelter, – when the last day's work is done! (39)

The speaker notes the chill of the mornings, the heat of midday, the constantly wet conditions, the exhaustion of the workers, and the relief they feel at the end of the journey, yet the cheerfulness at the end of the stanza seems naïve, and the reader is left without a sense of what tracking labour is like. Aside from the observation that "the tracking line grows heavy," there are no concrete answers to my questions about how tracking labour *feels*: which muscles ache? Does the tracker sometimes fall forward onto the ground, or backward when overpowered by the river? What is it like to stand upright after leaning forward so long to pull on the line? What does that kind of weight feel like on the body? On the mind? What would a tracker compare it to? Even the phrases that Ells uses in his prose, such as "*knee deep mud and waist deep water*," "*ceaseless torture*," and "*myriads of flies from daylight till dark*" (36), are left out of the poetry in favour of clichés that entangle the details of the labourers' toil and sweat with imagery of raindrops, dew, and sunshine. The limited content of these four lines in which Ells avoids conveying his insider knowledge about tracking and the speaker remains at a remove from the trackers is paralleled by the tiny scale of the drawing of the trackers on the facing page. The dull content of the closing line is mitigated by its rhythm, which uses excessive dashes and commas to make the reader pant like an exhausted tracker, and which pushes the reader to consider the submerged perspective of a tracker.

In "The Athabaska Trail," Ells positions himself, and the poem's speaker, as a nature poet mourning the end of tracking labour on the Athabasca rather than as an oil-sands engineer who both experienced tracking firsthand and played a role in its obsolescence. Ells tries to avoid looking like a hypocrite by removing himself from the tracking story told in the poem and confining the details about his oil work to the explanatory notes. Despite excising his work from the content, he retains it, perhaps unconsciously, in the form and the rhythm of the poem. What goes unsaid – but not unfelt – is that, in addition to the obsolescence of the tracker, and Ells's own obsolescence as an old-fashioned engineer with a contradictory passion for the North, this poem also mourns the future effects of Ells's own oil work, from his exploitation and betrayal of the trackers to the framing of the northland he claimed to love as an extractive zone.

Conclusion

As a mining engineer, Ells envisioned and hastened the transition between the fur-trade relations that were foundational to the settler-colonial state and a new northern economy based on modern staples like bitumen. As a nature poet who was nostalgic for the seemingly pristine environment of the fur-trade era, Ells also mourned the energy transition he desired. Ells left his work out of his poetry to avoid facing the contradictions between his affection for the land, his colonial vision of progress, and his repressed knowledge of the devastating impacts the industry he "fathered" would have on the communities and ecologies of the Athabasca region. Rather than bracketing *Northland Trails* from Ells's other oil work, I consider this text to be doing significant ideological and cultural work that benefits extractive industry and the settler-colonial state. I have called Ells and his poetics hypocritical throughout this chapter, poking fun at his sense of importance and of being a great visionary. In fact, the hypocritical poetics Ells "fathered" is mirrored by the all-too-familiar strategies still used today by corporations, colonial governments, and complicit petrocitizens to manage and obscure their/our own hypocrisy. Ells's poetics made him turn away from his ethical responsibilities to the land and the northern people he claimed to love. This reading of *Northland Trails* suggests one way of dealing with Canada's petrocultural daddy issues is to counter the veneration of founders like Ells by industry, governments, and the ruling class with clear articulations of who bears responsibility for historical and ongoing acts of ecocide, genocide, and climate change. Following the example of the Keepers of the Water in the Arctic Ocean Drainage Basin (including the Athabasca River),[69] may we hold profit-driven corporations and governments accountable while also venerating, affirming, and caring for water, land, and life itself in the context of Indigenous knowledge and sovereignty.

The Driller Makes a Mistake

Peter Christensen

The cold darkness
makes you angry
The crew is tired
                    hungover

Cold   slows   everyman   down

The metal vigil breaks
and the mud column
holding the liquid earth
releases

The engineer said
    The steps you take when you blow out
    are long ones

And in the time it takes
to run five paces
two thousand meters
of mud and chemical
blasts out
of the well
onto the deck

We stand back in the cold
Wait
Hear the gas coming   touch atmosphere
Ignite
Explode
Burn

D B
R R
I I
L TT
L W T
I IL
NS E
G TS
S

T S
O O
W U
E R
R GAS

CRASHES DOWN
Steel glows white hot
in the mouth of the fire

Flames torch winter
A SUN
Trees in a poplar grove bud
and turn green
Earth has beat back the season

Texas men are called
to push the roaring sun
back into the earth

The poplar trees freeze
BURST
in the middle of winter

"The Driller Makes a Mistake" by Peter Christensen, reprinted with permission of the author. This version combines the versions found in *Rig Talk* (Saskatoon: Thistledown, 1981), 26–7, and in the original manuscript submission, "The Plains Are Alive with the Campfires of Millionaires," 1980, MSS 116 (A.90–64), box 16, folder 2, Thistledown Press Ltd fonds.

CHAPTER 2

"They make me / rough": Speaking Oil Patch in Peter Christensen's *Rig Talk*

What Is Rig Talk?

The image of an oil rig in an advertisement (see figure 2.1) drew my eye while scrolling through a microfilm of 1982 issues of the *Calgary Herald*, looking for a review of former oil rigger (or roughneck)[1] Peter Christensen's 1981 poetry collection *Rig Talk*. "DO YOU SPEAK 'OILPATCH?'" the ad for a two-day seminar on "Basic Petroleum Technology" blares, suggesting that the oil patch is equally a location, a business opportunity, and a distinct culture with its own dialect. According to the ad, the ability to participate in oil patch as discourse is expedient, "highly useful" to almost anyone – "investors, royalty owners, bankers, lawyers, accountants and financial personnel, computer and administrative personnel, secretaries and clerical personnel, landmen, drafters, technicians, and others." Attendees at the Basic Petroleum Technology seminar recognized the significance of oil in business, culture, and everyday life; they put the course content to entrepreneurial use, making a career or a life for themselves by learning to speak oil patch.

Christensen's *Rig Talk* is, likewise, a lesson in the language spoken by drillers, roughnecks, truck drivers, derrickmen, and seismic testers. Rather than offering readers opportunity, however, the book's lessons are troubling and at times unclear. Controversial and misunderstood at the time of its publication, *Rig Talk*'s subsequent obscurity has made it a little-known early text

Figure 2.1
Advertisement in *The Calgary Herald*, January 1982.

in Canadian oil-worker poetry and petropoetics. *Rig Talk* is a pathbreaking book, based on Christensen's time working as an oil rigger in the 1970s, that combines work poetry, ecopoetry, and vernacular poetry to dramatic yet ambivalent effect. Christensen's tough, minimalist style mirrors a hypermasculine culture that frowns on too much talk, leaving plenty of room for debate about whether Christensen's speaker participates in, condones, or merely observes the acts of violence, negligence, and abuse portrayed in some of the poems. Instead of taking a clear position for or against the oil industry, Christensen uses rig talk both to reproduce and to critique the classist, ecocidal, settler-colonial, racist, misogynist, homophobic, and ableist structures of extractive industry. Christensen's complicit, disidentificatory poetics exposes rig talk as a discursive formation and world-making project in which everyone is implicated. *Rig Talk* features oil workers as petropoets – not only as makers of oil and gas but also as fluent speakers of the language of production and theorists of our petromodern predicaments who have vital roles to play in the maintenance or dismantling of the petrostate. This chapter draws on cultural theories of disidentification to consider subversive performances of rig talk as means to reconcile complicity, dependence, resistance, and solidarity in transformative visions for a just energy future.

Christensen is a white settler poet who was born to immigrant parents and raised in rural Alberta. He worked as a roughneck, seismic helper (or "jughound"),[2] and gravel truck driver during the oil boom and shocks of the

1970s, before becoming a mountain guide and park ranger. A long-standing writer of work poetry, Christensen studied creative writing at the University of Lethbridge in the 1970s and was a founder of the literary journal *Canada Goose*. *Rig Talk* is Christensen's second poetry collection, dedicated to "the Province of Alberta" and illustrated with pencil drawings of workers, non-human animals, and oil rigs by Jacqueline Forrie. It was published during the brief regime of the National Energy Program (1980–85) and before the glut of 1982 and the bust of 1986, at a time when oil was greasing the gears of an ascendant neoliberal ideology while oil companies were already investigating the contribution of fossil fuels to what was then known as "the greenhouse effect" – now known as climate change or global warming.

Rig Talk features cowboy-style poems[3] in what Mark Cochrane describes as Christensen's characteristic mode of "tough imagism – clipped lines, flat observation, stark visuality."[4] Several poems are truncated or censored sonnets, revealing a preference for minimalism in form and content. For example, "Everything Must Be New," a half-sonnet with seven lines and five syllables in all but one line, is a critique of the overconsumption that stokes demand for oil, gas, and petrochemicals. The poem ends with the couplet "I do not forget / my place among things" – both a personal ethics and an understated indictment of Canadian culture.[5] In deceptively simple poetry that, according to Thistledown Press's promotional materials, "presents life as seen by an oil rigger,"[6] *Rig Talk* performs versions of rig talk that range from the language of oil workers to a poetics of the oil industry, provoking questions and offering warnings about what the industry was making of Alberta, while challenging any understanding of poetry or culture that excludes oil workers from the realm of cultural production.

Rig Talk is divided into three sections. The first section, "Oil Rush," contains documentary poems about oil work, spoken by a persona of the poet who narrates as

> Roughnecks work the deck
> Spin chain
> couple   uncouple steel
>
> the nights pass like noise[.][7]

"Oil Rush" has a loose narrative arc that begins with a new worker going "Up North" with aspirations to become "[a] big man" (10; 14). As shown in the interplay of the words *up* and *down* (along with rhymes for these words) in the poem "Gravel Trucks Arrive at the Pit," the worker discovers instead that the work of extraction wears workers down (12). A subtle metaphor compares workers to the Christensen-brand drill bits, labelled with Christensen's own surname on their sides, that were commonly used in the 1970s and 1980s, so that the workers in "Graveyard Shift" trip pipe all night to retrieve and replace a diamond drill bit, "worn smooth" (24), that symbolizes what the industry does to workers.[8] (See the Christensen Diamond drill bit in figure 2.2.) The optimism of the earlier poems is eroded by the gradual materialization of fear – fear of injury, explosion, sour gas, and "the bush" itself (17) – as a repressed working condition. Fear is a synonym for a worker's job, as in the line "I work the morning fear" (23), where managing fear – being afraid and "Keeping Fear Away" (18) – is what an oil worker does. Optimism comes crashing down with the blowout in the concrete poem "The Driller Makes a Mistake" (26–7), in which a section of the poem is formatted to resemble an oil rig. (The version of this poem published in *Rig Talk* does not clearly show the oil-rig form that Christensen first created; the version that precedes this chapter is reproduced from the manuscript Christensen first submitted to Thistledown.)[9] The "Oil Rush" section ends with an "Elegy for a Rig Worker" that reveals the emerging class consciousness of a worker who realizes he is being treated as "an expendable machine."[10]

The second section, "A River Begins Here," is a suite of ecopoems focused on the natural world and the worker's relationship with it – as a site of home, work, and recreation; as a victim of pollution and ecocide; and as a voice of opposition against extractivism and colonialism. For example, "River Dance" reproduces and subverts colonial tropes by recalling "the last dance" of the Bighorn Stoneys on their territory before it is flooded in 1972 by politicians who "raise themselves over the earth" to make a "dead river" and build the Bighorn Dam.[11] In "Slave," the Slave River voices its disgust at the non-reciprocal relations of extraction and the dumping of toxic materials – "I have cleaned your toilets for years / have the dettol and arsenic of sanitation in me."[12] Framing the river's cleaning as work, and recalling the misnaming of the Dene people after whom the Slave River is named,[13] this poem evokes the fraught concept of the "energy slave" (as used by Buckminster Fuller, and more recently by Alberta journalist Andrew Nikiforuk and others) to link the appropriations of labour, land, bodies, and cultures that make up business as usual in the settler-colonial state.[14] In the poem "End of the Chain," a wolf pup the workers have chained up in their camp is terrorized

Figure 2.2
Christensen Diamond drill bit from the 1970s–1980s.

at night by another wolf.[15] As a victim and an object of care for the oil workers – who shoot the pup's mother after she attacks one of their dogs, then "save" the pup by chaining it up – the wolf pup is not only an apt metaphor for what the industry does to workers but also a being who resists the chain of the metaphor itself. Forrie's accompanying drawing links "End of the Chain" with "Slave": it shows the pup in a frame inset over another image that represents both the surroundings of the pup and a broader landscape, drawn to a different scale (see figure 2.3). In the larger image, the chain that binds the pup also chains the land and a river. Chains were also one of the roughnecks' primary and most dangerous tools, used to couple and uncouple drill stem; it was easy for workers' hands to get caught in the chain and pulled into the machinery. Together, the poem and the image suggest a scale-shifting reading that links the chaining of the pup; the exploitation and harm done to individual workers, residents, and landscapes through oil and gas extraction; and the broader ecological, social, and cultural consequences of petropoetics.

The final section, "Rig Talk," is made up of vernacular poems in the voices of residents of the oil patch and workers off the job.[16] I read the poems as allegories and critiques of colonial extractivism, yet they can easily seem to condone the physical and verbal abuse of women and other workers. For example, the speaker of "The Ride" hitches a ride in a "carload of drunks" and can find no way to get out except to drink along with them and witness their physical and verbal abuse of the woman driver;[17] he is like an oil worker along for the ride, only tolerating behaviour he abhors to make a living. In these poems, it is unclear who is speaking or whose perspective is being privileged. Is it Christensen or some other oil worker who shirks responsibility for getting a fourteen-year-old girl pregnant in "Shotgun" (57), or who commits the violent act in "Defense" (62), or who calls his wife, his truck, and the earth "THE OLD LADY" in "Going Home" (48)? These poems are often parodic (but seldom funny) performances of a harsh masculinity that defiantly leave open the question of whether the acts of abuse and negligence – of getting "so drunk on the same old shit" of misogyny, racism, and lateral violence (56) – are committed by Christensen or someone else.

Rig Talk was not well received at the time of its publication. The endorsement on its back cover, written by Canadian poet Tom Wayman, emphasizes the book's significance as work literature: "Peter Christensen's RIG TALK brings us, for the first time in contemporary writing, an insider's look at the harsh and difficult working life in the oil patch. These are tough poems about

Figure 2.3
Jacqueline Forrie's illustration that follows the poem "End of the Chain" in Peter Christensen's *Rig Talk*.

a terrible job, destructive no less to the people who work at it than the landscapes it scars." Wayman has long argued that work writing is authentic and potentially transformative when it is written as an "inside job" – that is, from the insider perspective of a person who has done the work (as opposed to that of an outsider who has done research on the work).[18] For Wayman, both the "tough" or "stark" style of the poetry and the balancing of ecological and labour concerns are appropriate for insider oil-work poetry. Despite support from advocates of work poetics such as Wayman, however, *Rig Talk* was heavily criticized for its plain, literal, and rough language and imagery; for Christensen's seeming "acquiescence" to a violent masculinity;[19] and for what reviewers saw as a disconnect between Christensen's work poems and his nature poems.[20]

In one review, Francis Zichy writes, "Christensen is committed both to the world of big machines and tough men, and to the natural world, and he is puzzled and disturbed by their incompatibility, but he finds no way out of the bind, and often fails to discover the language that will bring his concerns to life."[21] Zichy portrays Christensen as an unskilled poet who fails either to choose between or to overcome the stereotyped, ideological positions of the oil worker and the nature poet. In a 1982 letter to Thistledown editor Glen Sorestad, however, Christensen frames this interpretation as a misunderstanding of the book. Christensen writes, "Rig Talk seems to be a controversial book. Basically seems the academics don't understand what the book is about and quickly pass moral judgment on all those heathen folk who dirty their hands."[22] Although *Rig Talk* is a flawed text that proved difficult for reviewers and readers to interpret, this chapter takes seriously Christensen's claim that by focusing on the individualizing, classist question of who has clean or dirty hands in a petrostate, critics like Zichy misunderstood the book. In my reading, understanding what rig talk is and who speaks it is key to unpacking the poetics and politics of this foundational text for a tradition that has continued to engage with complicity, purism, racism, sexism, ecology, and what counts as (good) poetry.

Zichy's statement about the incompatibility of "the world of big machines and tough men" with "the natural world" is based in an understanding of nature poetry that conceives of nature as existing in a sphere separate from culture, labour, or industry – an understanding that prevailed in literary criticism in the 1980s. Today, however, *Rig Talk* is recognizable as *ecopoetry* rather than nature poetry. Lynn Keller cites Jonathan Bate's *The Song of the Earth* (2000) as the first use of the term *ecopoetics.*[23] Bate describes ecopoems as separate worlds – as "imaginary parks in which we may breathe an air that is not toxic and accommodate ourselves to a mode of dwelling that is not alienated"[24] – but subsequent definitions disagree with Bate. For example, *ecopoetics* journal founding editor Jonathan Skinner defines the movement as being concerned with practices of dwelling not in an idealized natural world but rather in the compromised ecologies that humans actually affect and inhabit.[25] *Rig Talk* is ecopoetics in this expanded sense; in its exploration of what it means to be a settler extractive worker who uses being "New Here" as an explanation and apology for his participation in ecocide,[26] it anticipates what Keller calls the "poetry of the self-conscious Anthropocene."[27] It contemplates the failure of the settler-colonial petrostate (and its complicit citizens) to reconcile taking from the land with taking care of the land. What *Rig Talk* is about is no mystery, yet it eluded many of Christensen's critics: it is about petropoetics, a material and cultural process that brings together extractive industry and nature, to explosive and devastating effect.

Although *Rig Talk* does not predict climate change, the imminent bust, the long-term impacts of colonial and neoliberal ideology, or the coming crisis of abandoned and orphaned oil wells in western Canada, it suspects, foreshadows, and fears such results of the hubristic actions the speaker observes and ambivalently participates in through his oil work. Embodying, if not necessarily believing in, ideologies of progress, upward mobility, misogyny, and settler-colonial ownership of the land as traits of a destructive and greedy system that Anishinaabe economist Winona LaDuke calls "Wiindigoo Economics,"[28] Christensen's speaker works "[s]eventeen hours a day" in a booming and dangerous industry;[29] blows up animals, trees, and rocks "for fun" (18); and enables or perhaps perpetrates assaults on women and the earth (15, 50–2, 57). Yet, in ways that suggest solidarity but may also be appropriative, he also links exploited workers with polluted rivers, abused women and non-human animals, dispossessed peoples, and nature at "the end of the chain" (43). He calls out holier-than-thou consumers of oil and petrochemicals, responding to the illusion that some citizens of the petrostate can have clean hands with a theorization of *rig talk*, or of petropoetics, as an ideological and cultural system in which everyone has a "place among things" (61). He implicates poetry in rig talk as too much "talk talk talk" that overwrites and "owns everything" (58);[30] and, for good measure, he implicates the reader, "you," through his occasional use of second-person narration when "you cram into the camper" going up north (10), "[y]ou drill another hundred feet" (24), and "you dive from the catwalk" after lighting the cigarette that starts a rig fire (31). In the disorienting, wide-ranging, and scale-jumping poetics of *Rig Talk*, individual culpability is beside the point, since rig-talk-as-petropoetics implicates and affects everyone in what US historian Bob Johnson calls a "carbon nation."[31]

Yet, as Johnson shows, the fossil fuels that are for some a source of modern ease and progress can be "disabling, constraining, and even atavistic" for those who do the work of extraction and production.[32] In both petromodern and ecological ideology, working-class subjects are interpellated to embody toxic identities (for example, the colonial masculinity of a stereotypical roughneck), in part so that they can be held responsible, unfairly, for the extractive relations of petromodernity, and left to suffer "the material and psychic violence in modernity's basement,"[33] a sublimated cultural space reserved for racialized, dispossessed, and marginalized subjects. In a version of the "inhuman proximity" that inhuman geographer Kathryn Yusoff has shown bringing Black, Indigenous, and racialized bodies in proximity to harm through the racial-capitalist logics of extraction,[34] oil workers are portrayed as less human, and as toxic, because of their proximity to the toxic and dangerous materials they extract. The relegation of workers to "modernity's basement" and less-than-human status is a cultural move that preserves our energy system and the unjust racial and class hierarchies on which it is built.

Christensen's *Rig Talk* blurs the lines between material and cultural production, poets and petropoets, and oil workers and other petrocultural subjects. As a synonym for petropoetics, *rig talk* emphasizes that oil workers are not only petropoetic objects, taking their place in a system where "[t]he plains are alive / with the campfires of millionaires,"[35] but also petropoetic subjects, fluent in the language of oil production and positioned to interpret and cut into its power dynamics. Rig talk is a world-making project in which Christensen implicates himself as both exploiter and exploited, "sky man" and "expendable machine";[36] yet rig talk can also be a non-innocent, disidentificatory means of resistance that may be effective because it is what Wayman calls an "inside job."

Rig Talk as Disidentification

Disidentification is a linguistic and performative mode through which gestures or speech acts enact both complicity and resistance; its transformative potential lies in its rejection of the idea that subjects must be constituted as either for or against dominant ideology. Marxist philosopher and linguist Michel Pêcheux first used the term in *Language, Semantics and Ideology* (1975; English edition 1982), in which he lays the groundwork for a "*materialist theory of discourse*" after Louis Althusser.[37] According to Althusser, ideology must constantly be reproduced through the interpellation and the consent of subjects.[38] Pêcheux demonstrates that such reproduction happens both through the seamless identification of the "good subject," who accepts and embodies the discursive formations of dominant ideology, and through the outright refusal of the "bad subject," who "*counteridentifies* with the discursive formation imposed on him [*sic*]" and yet still serves to strengthen it.[39] As an experimental, transformative refusal of the subject positions on offer, disidentification involves taking up "*a non-subjective position*" that works in an "epistemological break" where meaning has broken down.[40] It turns ideology "against itself" and produces the grounds for a resistant politics[41] – for Pêcheux, a proletarian politics.[42]

Cuban American theorist José Esteban Muñoz draws on queer and critical race studies to make an important intervention in Pêcheux's theory by bringing together disidentification and performativity in *Disidentifications: Queers of Color and the Performance of Politics* (1999). As Muñoz demonstrates through his study of disidentifications like Pedro Zamora's queer, Latinx, and HIV-positive "counterpublicity" on the early reality-TV show *The Real World*,[43] disidentification can look like mere complicity, parody, or mimicry of normative or majoritarian ways of being, but it is also resistant and transformative. For Muñoz, disidentification is critical ambivalence that always involves "negotiations between desire, identification, and ideology" – desiring something like the "white beauty ideal," but doing it "with a difference."[44] Describing disidentification as world-making or perhaps as poetics, he writes, "[d]isidentificatory performances are performative acts of conjuring that deform and re-form the world. *This reiteration builds worlds.* It proliferates 'reals,' or what I call worlds, and establishes the groundwork for *potential* oppositional counterpublics."[45] Muñoz was influenced by the work of Judith Butler, who emphasizes, in their own assessment of Muñoz's work after his death, the implications of disidentification for solidarity and resistance. They argue that identification is not identity, that it always introduces "noncoincidence and difference," and that "it reveals itself to be disidentification from the start."[46] From this perspective, we can recognize the potential not only of identification for the formation of solidarity (for instance, among workers who do the same job and identify with the industry they work for) but also of disidentification for other versions of solidarity (for instance, among workers who are critical of the industry they work for). Muñoz's theory of disidentificatory performativity and its implications for broad-based solidarity are key to any subsequent work on disidentification, including my analysis of *Rig Talk* and oil-worker poetry as being concerned with class, gender, sex, race, and land.

As *Rig Talk* shows, everyone has a place and does work in the material-discursive structure of the petrostate, including the oil worker and the nature poet, who are both complicit in settler colonialism and extraction. From its beginning, *Rig Talk* blurs the distinctions between the speech of poets, oil workers, readers, and the rigs themselves, using a disidentificatory strategy that Muñoz calls "tactical misrecognition" to put subjects out of place and disrupt petrocultural discourses and power structures.[47] In the opening poem, the speaker visits a drilling rig and is mistaken for a labourer looking for a job. After he tells the driller, "I'm writing /   a book about rigs," the driller responds, "*Well it's about gawdam time / somebody wrote about us*," and offers the speaker a tour.[48] The speaker establishes his credibility as a work poet not only through his familiarity with the rig and his donning of a hard hat, but also by describing the way the driller first misrecognizes him and then endorses his writing. Yet, the speaker is also careful not to appropriate the driller's speech. If tactical misrecognition allows the poet to be recognized as a worker, it also allows the driller to be recognized *as a poet* who does not need another poet to speak for him. Christensen uses italics to show the driller's voice breaking through the narration of the speaker.

The driller and the poet enact an additional misrecognition: "a book about rigs" is taken by the driller to mean a book about oil workers ("*us*"). Thus, the poem introduces under erasure the idea that the book is also about the "talk" of the rigs themselves. In Christensen's poems, where "A touch from a spinning drill stem / can leave you dumb   broken"[49] – and Forrie's illustrations, where dark steel rigs tower over and are compared to the soft bodies of workers (see figure 2.4) – rigs represent power, capital, settler-colonial ownership, and the indifference of oil executives and consumers who exploit and objectify workers. The workers, in turn, exploit and objectify women, non-human animals, and the land, playing their part in a system predicated, as ecofeminist scholar Carolyn Merchant has shown, on a modernist, colonial, and misogynist ideology of "the death of nature."[50] Yet, if rigs are often treated as tools, inanimate objects, or metaphors in *Rig Talk*, they also exceed or shift such categories, with both the poems and Forrie's illustrations showing rigs breaking out of their frames, twisting, and bursting into flames. In "The Driller Makes a Mistake," Christensen makes the word *twists* enact the motion it describes. Accidents, blowouts, and fires shake up the poetry, speaking the power and resistance of the land itself when trees bud in winter and "Earth has beat back the season"[51] or when a non-human power in "Wild Fire" comes

rushing up from the earth core
fifteen thousand feet
rushing up
          to greet the fire
and celebrate a new sun[.][52]

At such moments, the workers' worst fears materialize and the land itself booms out a version of "rig talk" that can kill or maim workers, twist and take down rigs, and reveal a natural order more powerful than corporations, the oil and gas industry, the petrostate, and the big talk of oil workers who know how small they are beside the rigs and on the land.

Rig Talk is part of a Canadian linguistic and literary tradition that Okanagan Syilx writer and scholar Jeannette Armstrong describes in her poem "Threads of Old Memory" as "meant to overpower / to overtake."[53] Christensen fails to escape or transcend the colonial way of being on the land that he refers to as being "New Here."[54] Yet, in moments when land talks through the rigs, exceeding, subverting, and breaking the discursive formations of extraction, *Rig Talk* gestures toward, or longs for, what Armstrong calls "land speaking," Indigenous discursive traditions where human being can be harmonious with a wider "land language."[55] Workers have intimate knowledge of the land's resistance to colonization, objectification, and extraction. Although they suppress that knowledge through the boasts, threats, and violence they use as inadequate strategies for "Keeping Fear Away,"[56] each invocation of *rig talk* is also a reminder that nature is not under human management or control. In poetic and concrete instances of rigs talking, *Rig Talk* encompasses a non-Indigenous oil worker's experimentation in listening to animate and speaking land.

The final poem, titled "Rig Talk," closes the book by further opening up disidentificatory positions for oil workers. I quote the poem in full here:

I wonder at the power
of the men
          I work for
They make me
rough like their talk

I laugh with them
when they say

Figure 2.4
Jacqueline Forrie's illustration preceding the untitled opening poem in which a poet and former oil worker visits Cactus Rig 17.

they are not afraid
of women
    sex
    manhood
    ANYBODY[57]

Although it can be read – unimaginatively – as a young poet's claim to have been corrupted by his coworkers, this poem is filled with the irony and double meaning of disidentification. Spoken from a more wizened perspective than a poem earlier in the book in which a young boy looks up to oil workers as "Heroes,"[58] the word *wonder* in the line "I wonder at the power" signals an unresolved tension between "wonder and dismay" that Zichy identifies in this poem[59] – *wonder* here encompasses both awe and a questioning of power. *Power* refers simultaneously to the power oil workers hold over one another in the tight hierarchy of a rig, the power they claim illegitimately over others, the labour power appropriated by the bosses, the fuel the workers extract from the land, and the terrifying-yet-repressed power of the land. As the earlier poems show, "the power / of the men" is fleeting and also includes disempowerment and danger. This is signalled by the use of line breaks and spacing to imply the bracketing of the words "of the men," so that it is power, in its multiple senses, that the speaker works for. While the statement "They make me / rough" seems to deflect responsibility or blame from the speaker, I take this as another tactical misrecognition, spoken by a worker who is also "worn smooth" by oil work. The line break after "They make me" highlights the dynamic through which energy workers are the underappreciated makers – the disavowed poets – of petromodernity, who can only make all of us rough by offering glimpses of the rough working conditions and the ecological sacrifices through which our ways of life are reproduced.

Christensen begins the second stanza by having the speaker say "I laugh with them," making a tenuous and disidentificatory distinction between *laughing at* and *laughing with* the performances of oil workers who claim not to be afraid of "ANYBODY" – not the sublimated power of a feminized earth that the worker counters with "sex," nor the impossible interpellation into "manhood." *Laughing with* mingles respect and critique – in this case, a critique that comes not from the outside but from the workers themselves. In light of the stories told in the preceding poems of workers burned alive, broken, or narrowly escaping such fates, as well as stories of how workers cope with ever-present fear, the speaker invites readers to laugh with them, too. The speaker knows he has plenty to fear, and knows he is not the only worker who laughs at the idea that misogyny, extraction, destruction, and denial are the only appropriate responses to fear.

Rig Talk closes with the suggestion that the conditions of oil work position all workers and indeed all Canadians as disidentificatory subjects, interpellated into identities that Muñoz describes as "toxic" or "spoiled"[60] – identities similarly exposed by Métis/settler scholar Warren Cariou when he asserts that in Canada we all have "tarhands."[61] Caught as we all are between wonder and dismay, Christensen shows solidarity by speaking as an insider instead of setting himself apart as better or purer than other workers. He identifies with oil workers by doing extractive labour, by performing a fearless and violent masculinity; by going along with hazings, abuse, and homophobic jokes; and by showing disdain for the land that he and other workers live and work on. Being a complicit insider rather than a judgmental outsider allows Christensen to show that oil work always involves disidentification; that workers see through, laugh at, and are sickened by these performances; that they care about the land; and that they do not necessarily agree with or give consent to the millionaires or the petrostate. In moments of crisis, danger, and self-awareness, rig talk articulates and embodies petrocultural disidentification as a form of petropoetic theory, critique, and resistance.

Conclusion

Rig Talk is a flawed text, a text that gets its hands dirty, speaking oil patch from an insider perspective that can easily be dismissed as compromised and complicit. Despite this, *Rig Talk* is also an astute theorization of petropoetics as a cultural, social, and political force and experience. Rig talk is the discursive formation through which we are all interpellated to speak oil patch as subjects and objects of the settler-colonial petrostate. Rig talk is the language of production of oil, gas, and petrochemicals, ecocide and extraction, and global warming; as Christensen demonstrates, it is also a discursive space in which resistance to racial-fossil-capitalist modes of production can be articulated and worked out.[62] Despite the lukewarm reception of *Rig Talk* at the time of its publication, Christensen's collection can be read as a founding text for the tradition of oil worker poetry. In its focus on language, its minimalism, its use of disidentification, its unapologetic roughness, and its theorization of petropoetics and the petrostate, *Rig Talk* anticipates the oil-worker poetry that would follow in subsequent decades.

Interest-Based Negotiation

Dymphny Dronyk

The Calgary land man
rests his boot
on the bottom rail
of the corral,
trades riding stories
with the rancher,
as she worries
the leather cord
of her white braid.

Together they watch
the horses hassle each other
in a spring sun
full of promises,
and skirt the reason
for his visit:
the joint ownership
of the land
on which they stand.

Careful maps under his arm,
aware of the
scars on the land,
he's a rancher himself,
a man who rides
the high country
and can name
wildflowers.

They negotiate
a minimum impact
middle ground
where the pump jacks
can hypnotically
suck up the oil

on the edge of
her grazing cattle herd,
on the fringe of
the wild meadows.

Each feels
a little victorious
for having held onto grace,
for protecting their values.
He notices the liver spots
on her tough hands,
how their shoulders
slumped
in unison
at the inevitable
when the deal was done.

When he takes
his leave,
signed papers clipped
into the neat folder,
she invites him back
for the branding season,
and puts an arrowhead
she's found along
the proposed pipeline route
in his palm,
where it lies
with the weight
of 20,000 years.

for Alex, who told me the story

"Interest-Based Negotiation" by Dymphny Dronyk, reprinted with permission of the author and publisher from *Contrary Infatuations* (Calgary, AB: Frontenac House Poetry, 2007), 83–4.

CHAPTER 3

"my love is not dead yet": Living/Loving Oil and the Land in Dymphny Dronyk's *Contrary Infatuations*

Dymphny Dronyk is a white settler mediator and writer who has worked as a contractor in the oil and gas industry in Alberta, doing jobs like negotiating surface rights and writing safety manuals for residents living near sour-gas wells. *Contrary Infatuations* is Dronyk's first poetry collection, published by Frontenac House during an oil boom in 2007. The book ends with "The Patch Poems, 2006," a sequence of ten numbered poems about being a rare woman working in the oil and gas industry. Instead of reading only this final section as being about oil work, this chapter takes "The Patch Poems, 2006" as the culmination of an affect theory of contrary infatuation that builds across the seemingly disjointed sections of the book. *Contrary Infatuations* accumulates images and metaphors for the impasse of petromodern living through sequences of feminist work poetry about reproductive labour performed as a cook for tree planters, as the wife of a soldier or contractor deployed during the first Gulf War, as a mother, as a neighbour to eco-saboteur Wiebo Ludwig's Trickle Creek farm, and as "The Only Girl at the Rig."[1] Considering the long, narrow forms of Dronyk's simple, autobiographical lyrics as concrete petropoems that evoke the shapes of oil wells, drill pipe, and spinning drill bits, this chapter reads Dronyk's poetry geologically, looking beneath its plain surfaces for additional layers of analysis that go unspoken but not unthought. After identifying imagery of bruising as a sign of contrary infatuation, I use bruises to know where to dig. What emerges is a theory of contrary infatuation as a structure of feeling that keeps oil workers and other petro-subjects in destructive relationship with fossil fuels – doing reproductive oil work in support of the industry and the petrostate. My reading of the repressed content of *Contrary Infatuations* reframes the book as an invitation to seek out ethical responses to impasse that factor in love, desire, compromise, and change.

What Is Contrary Infatuation?

Dronyk's term *contrary infatuation* seems to refer to loving things that are contradictory, that are bad for the self, that are not lovable, or that do not love back. It may observe, simply, that opposites attract. It invokes love while questioning whether what it describes really is love – is it just infatuation? It also includes what is contrary, or opposite, to infatuation, so that other emotions such as dislike, anger, hate, and boredom come into play. *Contrary infatuation* speaks to contradictions between what we love and what we do – between our values and our actions – or between what we love and what is good for us. Despite there being so many possible interpretations of what contrary infatuation might mean, Dronyk offers no definition. The term is used only in plural form, as *Contrary Infatuations*, in both the title of the book and the title of a poem early in the opening section. This suggests that the title poem is only one among the series of contrary infatuations that makes up the book.

The love poem "Contrary Infatuations" establishes an index for identifying other examples of contrary infatuation. In it, the speaker recalls that her lover was most attracted to her not when

> I bathed at midnight
> and softened my feet
> in hopes that you'd kiss them

but rather when she was "dirty and wet" while apple picking.[2] Dronyk's style has been called unpoetic,[3] but I interpret it, following literary scholar and affect theorist Sianne Ngai, as stuplime, revelling in plain, inane language and the platitudinous logics of settler-colonial extraction as a way of holding "opposing affects together" and "[revealing] the limits of our ability to comprehend a vastly extended form as a totality."[4] This style is exemplified here in plain, droning, adjective-heavy lines that both deflect and reward a deeper reading – as if the poetry that only occasionally, as reviewer Joel Deshaye writes, "reaches higher ground" were an invitation for readers to direct their attention downward and inward instead.[5] Dronyk's title poem hints at its end at the more grimly contrary aspects of the scene, with the use of the word *bruised*:

> you picked leaves
> out of my tangled braid
> and bruised
> my sweaty neck
> with kisses.[6]

The mingling of love and violence that is so benignly introduced here is a recurring motif in *Contrary Infatuations*. Bruising is a sign of harm that arrives late and lasts much longer than a moment of contact. It can offer a retrospective analysis that a touch or a relationship was problematic. Psychic, emotional, and perhaps physical bruising become signs of contrary infatuation throughout the book, clustering around the poet/speaker's relationships with men and patriarchy, with extractive industry, with oil, and with the land.

Contrary Infatuations makes associations and theoretical claims that the speaker hardly considers inside the individual poems – especially the idea that her life has been structured by contrary infatuation, and furthermore that the feeling of contrary infatuation is characteristic of petromodernity and of life in a petrostate. It is in this perhaps-unconscious sense that *Contrary Infatuations* advances an affect theory: that is, a theory about emotions, feelings, or the senses. In Raymond Williams's foundational formulation, a "structure of feeling" is a mood or style of a generation or period that may not yet have been theorized or named,[7] "a cultural hypothesis" that combines "thought as felt and feeling as thought."[8] Feelings matter because, as Lauren Berlant summarizes, "the present is perceived, first, affectively."[9] We feel things about the present before we can put them into words or thoughts. Dronyk's theory of contrary infatuation as a structure of feeling of petromodernity occurs in an intuitive, glancing, and repressed mode at the edge of affective perception and emergent thought.

Contrary infatuation is similar to queer affect theorist Lauren Berlant's theory of *cruel optimism*.[10] Berlant's cruel optimism is attachment to something that is both harmful and seemingly necessary to the self. It is the mood or attitude through which people carry on, continuing to look forward even in moments when it seems there is nothing to look forward to, twisting optimism and desire to suit the limited available options and further entangling themselves in relationship to the "significantly problematic object" that seems both to offer them freedom and to limit their range of motion within the systems they navigate.[11] Cruel optimism exists in relation to the promise of the good life, a promise that gets distorted as the prospects for living in a long moment of crisis shift toward the mere reproduction of life – not living well but living on, "treading water in the impasse."[12] The futurity of cruel optimism predicts that impasse and its attendant modes of survival (adaptation, acceptance of precarity, habit) will persist. Although Berlant's work on cruel optimism is not specifically about oil, their concept has been taken up by the energy humanities because it describes the sense of being at an impasse in our relationships with fossil fuels.[13] Dronyk's *Contrary Infatuations* complements and extends Berlant's analysis of cruel optimism, theorizing a structure of feeling of impasse from inside the oil patch, reproductive labour, and optimism itself.

Contrary Infatuations has an overt feminist politics that is in keeping with feminist-Marxist theories of reproductive labour. Sylvia Federici argues in *Caliban and the Witch* that women's unpaid and underpaid emotional, home-making, gardening, child-rearing, sexual, and caregiving labour has long been a source of surplus value in capitalism. She writes, describing the devaluation of reproductive labour as a form of primitive accumulation, that "once women's activities were defined as non-work, women's labor began to appear as a natural resource, available to all, no less than the air we breathe or the water we drink."[14] The labour Dronyk's speaker does is a mixture of paid and unpaid labour, but *Contrary Infatuations* demonstrates that the speaker's paid work on behalf of the lumber and oil-and-gas industries is also feminized reproductive labour and contrary infatuation. In a glowing review of Dronyk's book for *Alberta Oil* magazine, Gordon Jaremko praises the poem "Separating the Men from the Girls," which ends with the following stanza:

> My presence loosens the code
> softens the worksite,
> and somehow
> we all adjust.[15]

Jaremko characterizes this softening, feminine presence as positive, as if extractive industry were recuperable, only needing the "creativity and morale boosts" that women workers provide.[16] Dronyk's poetry is easily interpreted in this optimistic way. Yet, in a reading for reproductive labour as contrary infatuation or cruel optimism, the poem can also be seen to contain the repressed possibility that the woman oil worker is not meaningfully changing the culture of the oil patch. Instead, by being an emotional support to the other workers who "spill" out their hardships to her (like oil),[17] and by doing the relational work involved in acquiring new sources of oil, she helps to reproduce extraction. Adjustment may describe the speaker's adaptation to, not her transformation of, the relations of contrary infatuation. While it may be bold for Dronyk to highlight the interpellation of women to do paid and unpaid reproductive labour on behalf of extractive industry, the book is palatable to pro-industry readers like Jaremko because it stops short of articulating a radical or transformational feminist politics.

Dronyk's blunt feminist politics is interesting but obvious; there is no need for me to unpack it.[18] Instead, I am interested in how *Contrary Infatuations* avoids and represses analysis that could push its politics further. Dronyk's poetry is preoccupied with the protocols and boundaries of "What We Don't Say" in the oil patch.[19] This *non-dit* is based in anxieties about personal responsibility, complicity, hypocrisy, and indebtedness to oil companies, oil communities, and oil itself, as well as a separate set of concerns about responsibility and indebtedness to the land and to the Indigenous peoples who are its rightful caretakers. Bruises may be seen and mentioned throughout *Contrary Infatuations*, but the speaker shows little interest in investigating where they come from. Because of this, *Contrary Infatuations* leaves much to be discovered in a reading for what Patricia Yaeger has called an "energy unconscious."[20] I read *Contrary Infatuations*, in the spirit of *Cruel Optimism*, with attention to bruises as signs of repressed situated knowledge about the fraught relations of production in the oil patch and the petrostate. What emerges is a petrocultural theory of contrary infatuation.

Contrary Infatuation as Bad Love

The word *bruise* and the mood of the bruise come up in the poems about the speaker's husband in the early sections of *Contrary Infatuations*. Similarly, in an interview, Berlant calls "[a] destructive love affair" their "favorite example" of cruel optimism and uses the scene of leaving a bad relationship (where the self gets hurt whether they stay or leave) to ask, "Why is it so hard to leave those forms of life that don't work?"[21] Petrocultural literary scholar Stephanie LeMenager likewise calls contemporary humans' relationship with oil "destructive attachment, bad love."[22] Bad love is a potent image of contrary infatuation as the reason why petrocultural subjects choose to stay in impasse. The poems in *Contrary Infatuations* that cast the speaker's relationship as a scene of bad love are, notably, also saturated with oil.

In "Soldier, Sailor," the speaker says to her lover, "Make love to me like a soldier" and "Make love to me like a sailor," but she is disturbed by his "macho dreams," the way his gun "gleams maliciously in the moonlight" and his "desperate arms" are "too tight / around my neck."[23] In "Our Empty, Empty Bed," the speaker's husband is stationed in the Middle East during the Gulf War of 1990–91, and the speaker watches the coverage of the war on television, struggling to separate it from her "safe little life" in Canada.[24] As she describes,

soldiers sleep at the edge
of your well sites
trigger fingers poised
for your safety.[25]

The repetition of the word *your* in this stanza draws attention to the differences between where the speaker is and where her husband is, implicitly comparing foreign oil wells to the seemingly apolitical wells in Canada. It highlights the blatant hypocrisies of the war: ostensibly about protecting Kuwait from invasion by Iraq, the American-led Gulf War claimed the region's oil for the United States and its allies.[26] Through the ironic use of the corporate speak of the safety warning ("for your safety"), the poem negates the idea that the wells were being guarded for the safety of the soldiers or workers rather than the oil itself. Although Dronyk lived in Victoria at the time of the war, the speaker's failure to reassure herself by differentiating between oil wells in Canada and overseas foreshadows the threats and harm she would soon face in Alberta.

In "4 a.m." the husband works as a logger, living a bleak, bleary-eyed, and dangerous existence. The couple endures day-to-day life while imagining "better times, / alternate plans."[27] The speaker looks forward to the husband's return from work:

Tonight he will
shower and reappear human
his hair smelling like
shampoo instead of gasoline. (28)

In these lines, the husband swaps the smell of petrochemicals (of domestic and public life) for the smell of gasoline (of labour, of the chainsaw). These are two sides of the same coin, two faces of petromodernity – one human, the other inhuman(e). Although the husband *reappears* human, he is revealed to be made of and with oil. Similarly, in "Rage," in which the husband is volatile and frightening, and the speaker has developed a disidentificatory "poker face" to keep the peace (26), the speaker fantasizes about killing him with a bulldozer, using an oil-fuelled vehicle to overpower and escape him. These poems make important material and metaphorical links between oil and the husband/lover, and between oil and power.

In the long poem "Astrocytoma," Dronyk uses the word *bruised* to describe how brain cancer leaves the husband "alone / in a bruised mind" (66). This poem narrates the speaker's experience of the husband's diagnosis, treatment, surgery, decline, and death. The cancer explains the husband's cruelties, which the speaker can now call insanity, madness, and being "like one possessed by a demon" (56). It also explains why the speaker stays, normalizing the supportive role she plays for her husband and her children during a tragedy. In the impasse before the diagnosis, "I contemplated life without him / and hid my brittle heart" (55), but with the diagnosis comes a renewed attachment of contrary infatuation:

I must go on.
my love is not dead yet,
he and our children
look to me for laughter
for strength. (57)

Dronyk's "my love is not dead yet" line is telling: it refers back to the sense earlier in the poem that the speaker may not be able to love this man, and forward to the next line, which makes him the very embodiment of what "my love" is. Although the speaker describes "a battle scarred husband and wife" (63), she also considers how her love has been scarred and has become contrary infatuation – like her husband, her love is dying, but she maintains it in the state of being "not dead yet."

This story of a victim of intimate partner violence who stays, optimistically, with her partner is the primary image of contrary infatuation in Dronyk's collection. Dronyk's speaker shows both extreme honesty about her contrary infatuation and extreme loyalty to her husband, even though he hurts her. The reader is faced with the dilemma of how to account for the speaker's behaviour, feeling the tension between cultural values that dictate, contrarily, that no one should stay with an abusive partner and that no one should die alone. Contrary infatuation interpellates the speaker as a woman and caregiver, using the cultural value of "unconditional love" (which Dronyk invokes in her dedication to her husband at the beginning of the book) to make her stay.[28] Later, in "The Patch Poems," the speaker shows the same kind of loyalty to oil, even as she regrets the harm that oil extraction and consumption do to the land. She wishes her relationship with oil could be different, but she knows it is "not dead yet."

Inhuman geographer Kathryn Yusoff describes a "collaborative project" between humans and minerals that has produced not only modernity, capitalism, and climate change but also "the geopolitical subject of late capitalism,"[29] a subject who has received "gifts" from fossil fuels and who must account for their responsibilities, their practices, and their very being in relation to "geologic life."[30] In light of Yusoff's more recent analysis drawing on Black feminist theory and poetics in *A Billion Black Anthropocenes or None*, I understand "geologic life" to be a product of "White Geology" and racial capitalism.[31] Readers catch glimpses of geologic life as contrary infatuation in the "Patch Poems" titled "Drilling Mud" and "Perforating" – two poems that exemplify Dronyk's use, throughout the book and especially in this section, of a long, narrow form that evokes the shapes of oil wells and drill stems. In "Drilling Mud," the speaker describes the fluids pulled up to the surface by a drill bit as "ancient," with a "primordial / scent," and "still warm"; she finds

> the warmth
> comforting
> in my hands.[32]

"Drilling Mud" reads like a nature poem, evoking earthy images of rock and mud, combined with the sensory experience of bread warm from the oven, yet the speaker is handling a toxic substance that should not be touched with bare hands.[33] "Perforating" describes the speaker standing near an oil well that is being perforated by a geologist and wireline crew.[34] The poem closes with the stanza,

> None of us
> breathe
> at the moment
> of detonation,
> wait for
> the shockwave
> of energy
> to rock us.[35]

The multiple meanings of the verb "rock" perforate this plain-spoken, oil-well-shaped poem. In one sense, the underground explosion shakes the earth, expressing the agency claimed by humans positioned as dominators of the earth and extractors of resources. Yet, in another sense – encouraged by the moment earlier in the poem where the geologist refers to rock formations "as if he's gossiping / about old friends"[36] – "rocking" is an action performed by the rock as subject, acting on the humans as objects. The breathless workers are *astonished* in the sense of V.A. De Luca's description of the sublime according to William Blake – where "one becomes what one beholds,"[37] yet, the poem makes this experience mundane, an example of the "concatenation of boredom and astonishment" of Ngai's stuplimity.[38] When "None of us / breathe" in "Perforating," the humans are behaving like rocks, and the rock registers as one of the subjects, one of "us." The poem points to the ways in which our energy system constitutes a petropoetic relationship with fossil fuels that changes us – one that also *rocks us*, like infants, into the complacency and inertia of contrary infatuation.

The poem "Cross Threaded" compares a cross-threaded drill stem to relationships affected by oil work. Cross threading occurs when joining sections of drill pipe are threaded wrong, potentially causing damage to the pieces and threatening the stability of the entire drill stem as well as the safety of workers. "Cross Threaded" suggests that oil work and the culture of the boom are not healthy for human relationships. Being intimate with oil and its infrastructures gives the workers

hands
clumsy with cold
rough with calluses.[39]

The poem implies that hands accustomed to doing the difficult and dangerous work of threading lengths of drill stem are ill-suited for human tenderness. The demands on workers during an oil boom take them away from their loved ones and cause conflicts and interpersonal problems on and off the worksite. As oil worker Clint Breeze says, "The longest I've ever worked was 57 hours straight with a two hour nap in the middle. It's tough. It's a rough life. The oil doesn't stop coming out of the ground, it's got to be tended to."[40] Two kinds of love are in conflict here as contrary infatuation: romantic/familial love vs love of oil (or oil money, or oil work). These two become entangled when the lines get crossed so that oil workers find themselves tending to oil to support and care for their families.

Dronyk's use of an industry-based metaphor in "Cross Threaded" draws parallels between intimate human connection and a troubling level of intimacy with oil. It makes the optimistic note on which Dronyk ends the collection – with "Love by Cell Phone," a poem about a long-distance relationship with another worker in the industry – ring empty. Although the speaker says,

I come to believe
you are always here
in my pocket,
riding beside me

it becomes clear that she and her partner are both on call for oil and that they remain

the go-to people,
the soothers of ego,
the healers of rifts,
as we rush to well sites[.][41]

Although the cell phone, seemingly a work phone, offers the speaker a more immediate connection with her partner, it exacts a costly price: constant availability to serve the whims of oil and smooth the problems it causes. The lovers see the cell phone as the means of their connection, but it is also a material product and symbol of the oil economy that reveals the cross-threading of their relationship with their work. Oil is both the speaker's boss and the lover who is always there with her. This intimacy with oil describes not only the life of an oil worker but also the intimacy all petromodern subjects both suffer and enjoy: it is the oil and not the human lover that is "always here." The speaker's bad-love relationship with oil is contrary infatuation – "not dead yet" despite climate change, despite her love and concern for the land, and despite the difficult relationships involved in both working in the oil and gas industry and living in the oil patch.

Dronyk's representation of geologic life as bad love offers gut-wrenching, compelling imagery for impasse. She closes the collection with the unsatisfying conclusion that there is no alternative to the paradoxically bruising and comforting relations of contrary infatuation, fossil-fuel dependency, and climate collapse. While Dronyk herself seems to accept this conclusion, her speaker's survival and ultimate overcoming of both the abuse and the death of her toxic beloved tells a different, undead story. This investigation of bruises continues with a search for alternate endings.

Contrary Infatuation in the Oil Patch

Dronyk includes an explicit reference to bruising in the description of "the bruised / purple of the concave sky" in the northern Alberta Peace Country village of Hythe in the poem "Harvest Storm."[42] In three poems with postscripts indicating they were written in (or perhaps about) "*Hythe, 1996*" (19) or "*Hythe, 2001*" (20; 21), Dronyk depicts a sky so beautiful it hurts in the place where her family lived when her husband died of brain cancer. Unexplained descriptions of Hythe as a place where "fear scrapes my throat / and paranoia pummels my belly" are the only indicators that it was also in Hythe that Dronyk lived on a farm adjacent to the Trickle Creek community led by infamous eco-religious saboteur Wiebo Ludwig (19). Dronyk's experiences of being challenged, threatened, and harassed by Ludwig and other residents of Trickle Creek, as well as her concerns and opinions about them, are present only as an unspoken subtext of *Contrary Infatuations*. The three poems about Hythe are cryptic pastorals, bittersweet odes to a beautiful and terrifying place "at the edge" (19) – on a frontier of resource extraction and a battleground over sour gas.

According to Andrew Nikiforuk's history of the conflicts between Ludwig and the industry in *Saboteurs: Wiebo Ludwig's War against Big Oil*, it was in early 1990 that a new well drilled adjacent to Trickle Creek first accidentally released sour gas, causing miscarriages in humans and livestock as well as other health problems.[43] The Alberta Energy Company (AEC) refused to admit that sour gas could have these well-known effects or to accept responsibility. Nikiforuk sees this as the moment of the radicalization of Ludwig and other members of his fundamentalist, back-to-the-land Christian community, who committed acts of sabotage to well sites and oil infrastructure in the Peace Country – including a well site adjacent to Dronyk's property, sometime after Dronyk moved to Hythe in 1993. Dronyk first met Ludwig while she was working for AEC on emergency response manuals for residents of the oil patch to use in the event of a sour gas leak. Ludwig initially tried to woo her as a potential community member, then he tried to bully and threaten her, so that Dronyk would eventually be under twenty-four-hour protection hired by the oil company.[44] Although Ludwig's methods and the patriarchal rules of his community were offensive to many of his neighbours, including Dronyk, he voiced concerns that were common to many inhabitants of the Alberta oil patch. With his "war" on the oil industry echoing the imagery and tactics of the 1990–91 Gulf War (for example, recalling the strategic oil well fires started by retreating Iraqi forces in Kuwait), Ludwig showed that the Canadian oil patch is a sacrifice zone for capitalist development, vulnerable to the dynamics of the "resource curse" that have been hypothesized in other petrostates.[45] In *Saboteurs*, Nikiforuk documents something like a resource curse among settlers in the Alberta oil patch, who typically own only the surface rights to their land, where mineral rights are leased to oil companies by the provincial government. Although landowners are offered compensation for industry access to their land, they are often beset by health problems, unpotable tap water, exposure to toxic chemicals through sour gas venting and flaring, effects of acid rain on crops and trees, unexplained deaths and illness of cattle, foundations broken by seismic testing, and industry and government collusion to deny responsibility for these effects.

There is room for solidarity and collective organizing among residents of the oil patch, but Ludwig's violent tactics led nearby residents to distance themselves from Trickle Creek, reinforcing a taboo on criticism of the oil and gas industry in the Peace Country, Alberta, and Canada.[46] Dronyk respects this taboo in the overt content of her poetry, advancing arguments in "The Patch Poems" that claim that complicit people have no right to complain about the industry – arguments similar to the "energy lifeworld" rhetoric that, as Shane Gunster and colleagues observe, the oil lobby uses to dismiss environmentalists and other critics as hypocrites because they are dependent on fossil fuels.[47] Dronyk's poems also often adopt or perhaps perform the obfuscating discourses of corporate speak and public relations. In "Surface Rights Acquisition – What We Don't Say," the workers who negotiate surface rights at kitchen tables in farmhouses have "bruised souls"[48] – bruised, it seems, by the difficulty of being "trapped" in a petro-economy "[f]uelled by our / communal addiction" to oil (80). They have the bruises of contrary infatuation from balancing the wishes of oil companies and landowners, following a code that requires them to be "careful," "leery" (80), "deliberate," and "nice" – to "play fair" and "take the high road" (81). On the drive home, however, the surface rights negotiators can fantasize about making "pithy responses" to the landowners (81): responses that point out the hypocrisy of showing any resistance to the industry while also owning trucks, heating their homes using natural gas, and benefiting from oil royalties.

When Dronyk's speaker imagines saying to a surface rights holder,

> *Are we not all*
> *benefactors, sir,*
> *sharing the profit*
> *of the Crown,*
> *racing these fast highways*
> *as we take our children*
> *to warm, safe schools?* (82)

she seems to address Ludwig as a second, implied *sir*. This may be a satisfying imaginary comeback, but the affect theory of contrary infatuation exposes its flaws. Dronyk uses the word *benefactor* here where she appears to mean *beneficiary*. This slip is telling: the speaker sees herself as a beneficiary of the conveniences and comforts of oil culture, yet her job also positions her as a benefactor – as a representative of the oil company's generosity in offering financial compensation to landowners. In fact, both the landowner and the negotiator are beneficiaries of Treaty 8; based on a colonial interpretation of the treaty as land acquisition, they position themselves, falsely, as benefactors in relation to the land and to dispossessed Indigenous peoples (who have infamously been denied access to such benefits as "warm, safe schools"). In an imagined comeback that would silence dissent by implicating both her interlocutor and herself in settler colonialism and an all-encompassing energy lifeworld, Dronyk's speaker engages here in what Alexis Shotwell calls "purity politics."[49] Purism reproduces the relations of contrary infatuation by claiming that an imagined place outside of contamination is the only position out of which it would be ethical to resist the energy system that bruises Indigenous peoples, surface rights holders, and industry employees alike. Although an appeal to purism might seem like a satisfying way to address *what we don't say*, it serves to entrench existing power structures and inequities.

Dronyk threatens to expose a more interesting unspoken dynamic in a comment she made to the *National Post* in an interview about Trickle Creek in 2000, after she had moved away from Hythe: "All they say is, 'The land is poisoned, the land is poisoned, the land is poisoned.' Then they offer you honey or butter from the land. And I say, 'How is that honey not poisoned? How is that butter not poisoned?' Why does no one pick up on that?"[50] Dronyk seems to intend this statement, too, as a witty comeback or takedown, a glancing reference to the contrary infatuations inherent to living in the oil patch. But her questions create an opportunity to ponder more questions about contrary infatuation: What would it mean to admit that the honey is poisoned, the land is poisoned, and the land is stolen? What responsibilities and obligations would then become apparent? What would a resistant politics grounded in contrary infatuation as compromise and linked-but-differentiated experiences of harm look like?

On Leaving a Mark: Contrary Infatuation and Anticolonial Land Relations

In Dronyk's nature poems, as well as in "Patch Poems" like "The Legal Survey System,"[51] the speaker contemplates her place in a natural world gridded and marked for ownership, settlement, and industry, with a history of colonialism and resource extraction that she feels mournful about but also removed from. In "Poetry on Nose Mountain," the speaker and her friends use "well-site signs" and surveying grids to navigate their way as they go off-roading. Their vehicle "rips apart the landscape" with its "fat tires," but they tell themselves they are "only voyeurs" to the past colonial violence that underpins their claim on the land as playground and home.[52] The speaker claims, weakly and perhaps ironically, that she and her friends are only having fun, and that the harm they do to the land is negligible, since the "pioneers" who "broke," "carved," and "tamed" the land did so much more harm.[53] Dronyk's speaker demonstrates her own contrary infatuation with settler colonialism and extractivism by being selective about what she is willing to be held responsible for and which entanglements she is willing to admit. In the realm of *what we don't say* about colonialism and the land, however, she reveals herself as not only bruised but also a bruiser. Knowingly making a home on stolen land embodies the cruel optimism of the settler and the settler-colonial state.

From the perspective of purity politics, Dronyk's speaker is compromised. Her response to contrary infatuation is to avoid saying or doing anything that would put her at odds with the oil industry, but this resolves only one twist in the tangle of contrary infatuations. It leaves her at odds with the land, continuing to work in the same industry that pollutes the land and air she needs to live. The speaker claims that both colonialism and pollution are events that happened before she arrived – that the land was "no longer wild" when she got there.[54] Métis discard studies scholar Max Liboiron describes things differently, however, when they assert that "Pollution is Colonialism." For Liboiron, "pollution is not a manifestation or side effect of colonialism but is rather an enactment of ongoing colonial relations to Land."[55] Liboiron describes land and resource theft (or primitive accumulation) as ongoing in a colonial state like Canada, constantly perpetrated and reproduced through extractive land relations such as those that structure the oil and gas industry, the land survey system, the real-estate market, or the university. Instead of focusing on how this situation makes everyone hypocrites, Liboiron focuses their analysis on the responsibilities and obligations to enact good land relations (including good relations with Indigenous peoples) that everyone is subject to.

Liboiron writes, against purism, "[c]ompromise is not about being caught with your pants down, and it is not a mistake or a failure – it is the condition for activism in a fucked-up field. Research and activism, scientific or otherwise, never happen on a blank slate. As a result, we are always caught up in the contradictions, injustices, and structures that already exist, that we have already identified as violent and in need of change."[56] In contrast to the colonial relations that already exist and that enact power relations that operate from the top down, Liboiron advocates for thinking about relations and responsibilities in a way that is grounded in the land where we live and that scales up. This reverses the bruising, trickle-down relations Dronyk describes in a funnel-shaped stanza as the "greed," "bad planning," and "hypocrisy"

of our bureaucrats,
our colleagues,

the landowners
and even
ourselves.[57]

It suggests, instead, a set of responsibilities that scales from *ourselves* all the way up to the bureaucrats, oil barons, corporations, and governments.[58] Although the petro-economy may seem unchangeable, it is in fact the laws and ethics that dictate good land relations that are immutable. The way to address contrary infatuation is to start with good land relations.

In Dronyk's poem "Interest-Based Negotiation," which recounts an exchange between a rancher and a "Calgary land man" representing an oil company, the speaker describes the deal the two parties strike by rattling off the placating language of negotiation that Dronyk used in her own oil work:

They negotiate
a minimum impact
middle ground
where the pump jacks
can hypnotically
suck up the oil[.][59]

The first few lines of this quotation amount to saying *blah blah blah,* with the word *hypnotically* near the end of the stanza perhaps cluing readers in to the way they have been momentarily hypnotized. This babbling speech is *what we do say* – celebrating compromise as a so-called win-win scenario – but the poem highlights the significance of what goes unspoken – the silent slumping of shoulders and the exchange of an ancient arrowhead between the two parties after the deal is done. *What we don't say* includes a shared sense of inevitability that contains both feelings of powerlessness and wishing for things to be otherwise. It also includes a shared understanding that Indigenous precedence and sovereignty undermine

the joint ownership
of the land
on which they stand[60]

– the system of settler-colonial ownership that the arrowhead exposes as illegitimate and based on theft. "Interest-Based Negotiation" contains unspoken-but-shared knowledge that undermines the structures of the industry and the colonial petrostate, including the relations of contrary infatuation that keep those structures in place. Instead of being a symbol of compromise and loss, the arrowhead could point the way to breaking up with oil and gas and to reframing what it means to live responsibly and ethically on land now known as "the patch."

Conclusion

As the "Patch Poems" reveal, the oil patch is reproduced through a discourse of purity fuelled by a repressed, unspoken, but shared condition of contrary infatuation. The possibility of being exposed as a hypocrite drives Dronyk's speaker to endure and inflict the bruises of contrary infatuation, pollution, and colonialism, while following the rules about *what we don't say*. While the speaker reproduces contrary infatuation as ideology, however, Dronyk's naming and mapping of contrary infatuation as affect theory throughout her collection suggests a reading of the speaker's performance – and the petromodern condition – as disidentificatory and open to change. Recognizing contrary infatuation is not a crisis to be managed, mitigated, or avoided; it is a starting point for a compromised, ethical, decolonial and anticolonial politics based on love for the land and for the human and non-human communities who live on it. *Contrary Infatuations* prefigures solidarity among bruised workers, women, Indigenous peoples, racialized peoples, settlers, rocks, and land. It calls for circles of community and care that widen outward from the individual and the local toward the collective and the global, as the basis for a people's movement that holds corporations, governments, and the ruling class to account while envisioning just energy futures.

Washout

Mathew Henderson

Across the field you can see a farm girl who might be pretty,
stripped down and out of her father's coveralls.
Might get you hard if she wasn't hidden so well.
Kinda gets you hard anyway, as she climbs the tractor,
her legs bouncing against the sides of her loose rubber boots.
Remember where you came from? What the girls were like there?
Now open the fucking well and walk the pipe like a healer,
your ungloved palm hovering over the unions.

She's in the tractor now, over there, radio on,
windows cracked, texting a guy from school while you hit
the first sandoff of the day – ball frack, zone two,
and Bill tells you, *Right now, down below, there's enough nitrogen,*
sand and shit to shoot one of those fat fuck thousand-pounders
from TV right the fuck out of his bed, so open that bastard slow.

And then, *Nevermind,* and he does it himself.
The thin pipe rattles, your lightest pipe, the stuff you solo
around the lease on your shoulder. The whole line kicks
and, standing beside the flowback tank, the noise is older
than anything you've ever heard, like you've always been hearing it,
and just now became aware. The first time you drove a car
the engine kicked, sounded like a coil cleanout,
a blowdown, a frack, a bleedoff. When you learned to
knead dough, your father's palms over your hands,
there was a man outside punching holes in the earth,
making your mother's windows buzz and rattle.
Does the farm girl hear this, over there,
in the tractor cab? Does she know it's you?

Near the end where the steel turns ninety degrees,
goes straight up, some burr inside catches, peels off,
and the sand cuts through the pipe and into the air.
But your hands, they're already in an X above your head,
when you remember the sign for *shut the fucking well.*

CHAPTER 4

Tending Rusted Steel and Leased Land in Mathew Henderson's *The Lease*

Mathew Henderson's *The Lease* (2012) is a collection of lyric, confessional poetry that mimics the talk of oil workers while focusing on the interior life of a naïve, conflicted production tester. The second-person narrator deflects responsibility and agency, telling his coming-of-age story as if it all happened to *you*. Despite Henderson's claims that his oil-work poetry is honest and accurate but not political, this chapter focuses on the disidentificatory politics of *The Lease.* Stemming from Henderson's refusal to speak from the ideological position of either the loyal oil worker or the critical ecopoet, disidentification in *The Lease* marks the shifting limits of what workers threatened by accidents, ecological loss, global warming, and the next oil bust will or will not do for money or for oil. Meaning breaks down in *The Lease* around the open question of what a lease is, and the narrator puzzles over whose claims on the land are legitimate. The lease is exposed as an intersection of corporate, settler-colonial, patriarchal, racial, and class power where oil-patch residents suffer, inflict, and benefit from dispossession and loss. This chapter picks up on the discussion of so-called empty space in the introduction to posit the dystopian, deconstructed material and cultural space of the lease as ground for an emergent energy-justice politics.

Mathew Henderson is a white settler who was born and raised in Prince Edward Island, but who moved to Alberta the year he finished high school and his father took over an oil-and-gas production-testing company. Henderson worked as a production tester in Alberta and Saskatchewan beginning in 2003, for a year before starting university, then in the summers for several years after that until he began a master of fine arts program at the University of Guelph.[1] In a 2013 interview, Henderson describes the job of a production tester: "Basically, a tester has a 30,000-litre tank that can withstand a lot of pressure, and a flarestack that can burn off gas, and the tester drives around the oil patch going wherever someone needs that tank, or they 'safely' dispose of excess gas and fluid during some operation or another. We were are also responsible for conducting various tests and reporting results to the oil company: salinity, acidity, oil content, oil density, rate of flow, composition of fluid and things like that. Sometimes it involved a great deal of manual labour, and sometimes it was just sitting and looking at gauges. I was really quite bad at my job for the first twenty months."[2] The tester's portable tank, flare stack, pipes, and gauges are used for testing, and also for processes like cleaning the sand out of a well after it has been fracked.[3] Notice the ambivalence and disidentifications in Henderson's description, where the pronouns used for the tester(s) shift between *they*, *we*, and *I*.

The Lease is Henderson's first poetry collection. In a setting where "cows gather in darkness near the edge of the site, / scratching thighs against steel tankers,"[4] and where the job of the production tester is to "[t]end the rusted steel like a shepherd,"[5] the semi-autobiographical poems reference the always-obsolete, colonial, and necrotic politics of the pastoral tradition.[6] In the mode of what Max Karpinski has called the "petropastoral,"[7] they serve both to naturalize and to critique extractive industry. Often written in the Canadian dialectical form of the Jackpine sonnet,[8] Henderson's poems accommodate the speaker's abuse of and affection for the "dead prairie" he inhabits,[9] his equation of ecocide and misogyny, his status as not only one of the workers but also the boss's son, and the mixture of admiration and contempt he expresses for his coworkers and himself.

The reception of *The Lease* has been overwhelmingly positive, including a glowing review in *The New York Times*[10] and shortlistings for the Trillium and Gerald Lampert awards for poetry, so that poet Matthew Tierney calls the book "universally loved."[11] In fact, as I have discussed in the introduction, *The Lease* seems to be beloved for the same disidentificatory characteristics for which Peter Christensen's *Rig Talk* (1981) was scorned by many critics a few decades earlier – for expressing a workerly language and tone that are "honky-tonk-plain or Tonka-truck-tough,"[12] for performing and critiquing a stereotyped toxic masculinity,[13] and for refusing to take sides between workers and the land. In his review of *The Lease*, Africadian poet, playwright, and literary scholar George Elliott Clarke praises the book but also critiques its privileging of class over race: "Intriguingly, Henderson writes often of Caucasians 'coloured' by sun, oil, or gas, but seldom about 'the Natives,' whose land is being looted of its resources. 'Colour' is pronounced, but it's class that's privileged."[14] If, as Judith Rauscher writes, the poems in *The Lease* "explore the possibilities and limits of a proletarian ecopoetics sensitive to patterns of subjection of both land and people,"[15] Clarke's critique reminds us that it is worth attending to what is excluded from or what exceeds the limits of a poetics situated at an intersection not only of land and labour but also of gender, colonialism, and race. Keeping this in mind, in this chapter, I read *The Lease* as disidentificatory rig-talking poetry that both upholds and subverts the toxic power structures of the oil patch and the petrostate.

As I describe in chapter 2, disidentification is a mode for responding to ideological interpellation that skirts the imperative either to cooperate or to resist. Drawing on Michel Pêcheux's, José Esteban Muñoz's, and Judith Butler's theories of disidentification as reluctant, parodic, destructive, or failed cooperation that simultaneously repeats and undermines ideological discourses, I interpret Christensen's petropoetics of rig talk as a theory and practice of disidentification. Chapter 3 draws on Laurent Berlant's theory of cruel optimism to interpret Dymphny Dronyk's poetry collection *Contrary Infatuations* (2007) as attending to the fraught attachments that underlie and prolong petrocultural disidentification and impasse. Although Henderson was not aware while writing *The Lease* that it would be part of an emerging tradition of oil-worker poetry in Canada,[16] his use of disidentification is one of the characteristics that signals his book's belonging within that tradition.

In Henderson's poem "What You Do," the narrator responds to the sexist and racist talk of one of his colleagues by disidentifying: "When he talks you quease and pull away, but grow a little / more like him for all your shutting up."[17] Like Christensen's poem "Rig Talk," in which the speaker says "They make me / rough like their talk,"[18] Henderson uses a line break to show that the narrator is both made sick and simply *made* through oil work and rig talk: he *grows up* and *grows to belong* in the hypermasculine, sexist, homophobic, racist, fatphobic, and violent culture of the oil patch. In the abstract for a lecture on "Navigating Class and Ethics in The Lease," Henderson describes an ethical poetics for representing oil workers that refuses to set the poet or the speaker apart by counteridentifying: "[w]hile I feared that it would be unethical to include depictions of rampant misogyny or environmentally destructive practices in the poems without explicitly condemning such practices and behaviours, I eventually realized that such condemnations were at odds with the project in that they positioned the speaker of the poems as apart from the characters in the book. Instead, I argue that the clear and honest depiction of such practices is both the most honest and ethically sound way to encounter the contradictions and complexities of the oilfield."[19] The poetics of "clear and honest depiction" that Henderson describes is disidentication: rather than openly critiquing the toxic culture of oil work, the poet depicts and reproduces it ambivalently, engaging its relations as contrary infatuation, with a tendency to persist. Henderson has framed his poetry as apolitical, calling it "all very personal" and not "historically relevant outside the field of poetry."[20] Despite this, I read *The Lease* as disidentification that works on and against the social and cultural position of the oil worker to suggest a resistant politics for complicit subjects amid the crises of climate change, resource boom and bust, and energy transition.

Like the speaker of *Rig Talk*, the workers in *The Lease* frown upon too much talk. In one poem, the narrator describes low-level workers as "hands" who "wring oil from the earth" and "do not speak";[21] in another, coworker Dave expresses disdain for "This one guy" who "goes and gets himself a shrink who gets him on comp / because he had a *traumatic experience*," a guy who, according to Dave, doesn't know "what work *is*."[22] The workers suppress speech and emotion, converting their anger and fear into violence against women, non-humans, and themselves. Yet, the narrator breaks with the prohibition on so-called *bitching* and *howling* by using the mode of confessional poetry to address a presumed audience of sympathetic and complicit readers.[23] Disidentification registers in *The Lease* through the narrator's confessions of the aches and pains, anxieties, failures, and feelings that he silences in his day-to-day work, as well as through his portrayal of the talk that passes between oil workers when they think no one else is listening. By admitting his feelings of both disgust and familiarity, and by incorporating rig talk into his own speech throughout the book, the narrator refuses to perform as either a good poet who exists at a remove from the bad workers or a good worker who shows complete loyalty to the extractive industry that pays his bills.

Apart from a couple of vernacular poems spoken in the first-person voices of other oil workers, the poems in *The Lease* use present-tense, second-person narration to implicate poet and reader alike in the narrator's actions as well as his fearful and guilty feelings about them. When the narrator commands himself, in "Washout," "Now open the fucking well and walk the pipe like a healer, / your ungloved palm hovering over the unions,"[24] his imperative phrasing places readers as workers along the pipes, pipelines, and commodity chains of the oil and gas industry, preventing them from counteridentifying or assuming a comfortable distance from the poems. Yet, he also blocks identification, as in the poem "Who Are You Out There?" in which the narrator says, "You're no part of it. You can only watch"[25] – referring at the most literal level to the production tester who watches roughnecks working on a rig, yet also reminding readers that *you* are an outsider and a voyeur. In the closing poem, when the narrator accuses both the reader and himself of "faking, lurking," he worries simultaneously about how he will write about his former coworkers after leaving the industry and about the way readers might also betray the workers – about whether "you turn them over in the end."[26] Such narration by "you" puts the reader in a position of "reflexive spectatorship," a position which Jennifer Wenzel argues is a promising mode for solidarity.[27] It resists the "*unimagining*"[28] of the role of the oil worker in Canadian culture, which Henderson has described as an "empty space,"[29] but which also takes the form of stereotypes. In such a reflexive situation, readers may "quease and pull away," yet they may also recognize their dependence upon and likeness to workers like the narrator. *The Lease* shows that rather than full identification or belonging, the critical ambivalence of disidentification is what it feels like to be an oil worker, or to be in solidarity with workers.

The disidentificatory poetics of *The Lease* comes together around the central question of the text: what is the lease? Pêcheux describes the "shake-up" of the epistemological break,[30] where meaning breaks down because it turns out to be ideological and where disidentification opens up as a possibility, in relation to a question: "What I am referring to here is that work of the unthought in thought whereby the very terms of a question, with the answer it presupposes, disappear, so that the question literally loses its meaning while new 'answers' form to questions which had not been asked."[31] The shake-up around the lease brings together the exploitation of land, workers, women, and Indigenous and racialized peoples, in an epistemological break that the workers in *The Lease* discuss with one another. In "Todd," the narrator tries to explain what the lease is to his coworker:

> and the lease, you have to tell him,
> is just where you work. No, *Where you work*

is the lease. Confusing because it isn't beer
or smokes or a car stereo system.

Despite his mocking of Todd for being "slow,"[32] the speaker is also confused about the location, dimensions, and meaning of the lease. Like Christensen's only-partial explanation for extraction that "We Are New Here" and Dronyk's description of workers being *rocked* in "Perforating,"[33] this poem conveys a sense of settler-colonial stupor akin to Sianne Ngai's concept of *stuplimity* – "a concatenation of boredom and astonishment"[34] that is linked, in oil-worker poetry, to questions of land relations and the suppressed conditions of "geologic life."[35] If the italics in this stanza signal Todd's speech, it is Todd who understands that the lease is more than "where you work": it is also a discursive formation that creates the material conditions through which "you" sell your labour power, own or live on the land, and understand your place in the world as an oil worker. The narrator works on the lease, but the lease is also where he lives, as a resident of the oil patch with the mineral rights for his family's land leased by an oil and gas company.

In "Washout," the narrator remembers his father teaching him how to knead dough while "there was a man outside punching holes in the earth, / making your mother's windows buzz and rattle."[36] Having a "man outside" the family home is a violation – one that is compared to a violation of the mother's body. The treatment of the narrator's home as just another lease parallels both the tenuous and shifting definitions of women in the oil patch as wives, mothers, sisters, or "just pussy,"[37] and the way the workers themselves are treated by the industry and consumers as "tanned gears" or replaceable tools.[38] The man is another worker, doing what both the father and the narrator do outside other homes in what Dominique Perron has described, following Denis Duclos, as "an autophagic society,"[39] where "individuals' and markets' sustainability depends on consuming what they produce in order to survive in a neoliberal economy."[40] What the narrator and his father are meting out as oil workers is also what they are being fed as oil-patch residents: dispossession through abstraction, alienation, and violence. This dispossession is predicated on the dispossession of Indigenous peoples, an origin and ontology of the lease that is nearly always outside the frame of Henderson's poems.[41] The whitewashing of dispossession in "Washout" suggests reading the poem alongside Kainai/Sámi filmmaker Elle-Máijá Tailfeathers's short film *Bloodland*, which depicts drilling for oil as drilling into the body of an Indigenous woman.[42] Tailfeathers made the film using funds from a distribution cheque from an oil and gas lease that the Blood Tribe Chief and Council signed without the consent of band members. It links harm to the earth with gender, racial, and settler-colonial violence. The epistemological break around the lease, and the intersecting forms of dispossession and harm the lease encompasses, require what the final report of the National Inquiry into Missing and Murdered Indigenous Women and Girls call a "Deeper Dive" into the documented links between oil and gas extraction and violence against Indigenous women, girls, and two-spirit people in particular, including the negative impacts of "man camps" and transient workers in local communities. Like *rig talk* or *contrary infatuation, the lease* is a synonym for petropoetics that can attend to its land, gender, and racial politics.

In the stuplime poem "You Ask Your Father What a Lease Is," the father answers the narrator's question with seemingly unrelated information,

> about the geese beyond
> the aqueduct, how they turn the sky grey,
> how as a teen he never put his gun away dirty.[43]

From his complex and compromised position as a landowner and production-testing contractor, the father responds to the lease with an ethics of hard work, responsibility, and care, but also with a sense of entitlement to abundant and cheap natural resources that seem to be there for the taking. Yet, like Todd and the narrator, he is unable to put the lease into words. In the stanza that follows, the narrator draws his own conclusions about the lease:

> The lease is meaningless: a square paced
> first by seismic workers, and then your father,
> and then by every other man you know.
> But you've always pulled meaning from nothing,
> and when he leads you to an empty field you
> tear grass in fistfuls, read the roots like a will. (17)

The narrator considers the lease as a square of land, paced by men who represent ownership by the father, the province, and the oil and gas company that leases the mineral rights. The repeated act of pacing, emphasized by the iambic metre of the line "and then by every other man you know," demonstrates that the claims of settler-colonial ownership and industry leases must constantly be reproduced by ideological subjects – that, as the narrator observes, "[t]his place repeats itself" (8), and that it must repeat itself or fall apart. The speaker feels that as a poet he should know how to "[pull] meaning from nothing" in the way that wills, leases, surface rights agreements, and the treaties that underpin them do; but when he goes looking for meaning or metaphor in the "empty field" and in the roots of the grass he pulls from the ground, the stupor of the epistemological break only widens. The empty field is a colonial *terra nullius* that the narrator knows is not empty. Although he might "read the roots like a will," looking for his inheritance and his claim on the land, he finds something more radical lying there at the root, in the double meaning of *will.* His extractive approach to meaning as something he can take from the land comes up against the will and sovereignty of the land itself, and of its original, Indigenous caretakers, which persist despite the repeated pacing of the lease. Although the narrator may judge fellow worker Dave for "the shit he says" and for having a racist attitude toward "the Natives / who sleep, curled up, on his hometown streets" (61), what lies at the root of the lease is the colonialism and systemic racism from which the narrator benefits, which, as the ground of petropoetics and the petrostate, allow him and Dave to sleep safely but illegitimately on stolen land.

In the relations structured by the lease, power and wealth flow upward while abuse and violence trickle down. Henderson represents workers as abusers and money-counting beneficiaries in this system, yet also as victims – terrorized gophers (18), drowning kittens (49), and broken men. The devaluing of workers' lives through the lease can be seen in their discussions of which body parts they would cook or lose "for an even million" (31) and their visceral responses to the news of a fatal blowout where "the pipe swung so fast it took one guy's face / clean off" (54). The lease legitimizes an extractive industry's use of the land and of workers' bodies. Although it seems to provide the workers with identity, freedom, and a way of life, it also takes away from these things, offering them only temporarily and at a high cost. In the epistemological break around what the lease is and means, it can be seen as a compromise that workers might not continue to be willing to make.

In the poem "Joe Talks about Snubbing," coworker Joe describes a job he "won't even do" that pits the lives of workers against the will of the earth:

> But yeah, it's tripping under pressure.
> Basically pushing pipe down a hole

that wants to push you back. It's when
the patch itself gets so goddamn angry –

The story drops off here because it reminds the narrator of another story about Joe sharing how to "avoid the nipple" and pleasure a woman. In the third stanza, the narrator – "you" – sets the scene, complete with Joe's "dirty or freckled" elbows and his miming, "darting his tongue / in and out under the imaginary tit." The final stanza is narrated by Joe again:

Right there, that's what they like,
just underneath. Get your tongue
in there, boys. My ex-wife, real good girl,
Christ, she giggled like fuck for that. (63)

Through this seeming accident of memory, the narrator expresses the unthought thought that oil and gas extraction – "punching holes" – is comparable to rape. The contrast between the ex-wife's pleasure and the earth's anger shows that everyone – including Joe, the narrator, and "you" – knows that the land is more than dead nature or "a mindless, submissive body" available to be exploited and leased.[44] In a situation where it becomes clear that Mother Earth does not consent, Joe reveals a disidentificatory ethics of what he "won't even do" for money or for the industry.

The narrator knows he is subject not only to "the wills of men / who will you"[45] but also to the will of the land, which oil work pits him against, in a battle the narrator expects to lose. Rather than expressing the climate-change denial that readers might expect from an oil worker – a stereotyped denial that I have not found in poetry by oil workers – the narrator characterizes the lease as a deferral rather than a denial of the eventual triumph of nature. He expresses a cynical "hope" in the persistence, for a little while longer, of oil work and of the lease itself:

As if hope alone could tend the ocean,
could hold it above you just a while
more before it crushes the record
clean, ravines the prairies and scrubs
the sum of your summers to
bent steel beams, cracked alfalfa.[46]

The lease is a hope to delay the consequences and the dangers of petromodernity, represented here by the rising seas of climate change or the Genesis flood. Unlike rig talk, the lease has a finite temporality that leaves the workers waiting, individually and collectively, for the catastrophe or transition when the lease will be up and they will no longer be oil workers.

The epistemological break is not in itself a resistant politics; it is only an opening for a politics to emerge. In *Disidentifications: Queers of Color and the Performance of Politics*, José Esteban Muñoz writes, "disidentification is a step further than cracking open the code of the majority; it proceeds to use this code as raw material for representing a disempowered politics or positionality that has been rendered unthinkable by the dominant culture."[47] The narrator of *The Lease*, in response to both the sight of a coworker who lost a hand in an accident and the panicked feeling he has every time he opens an oil well, says "[y]ou wait."[48] The only explanation of what he waits for is the metaphor of a drowning man who waits "for a hand or hook to pull you from this place."[49] This sense of waiting comes from the disidentification that Judith Butler notes is part of identification from the start,[50] and the narrator appears to wait with urgency but without knowing what he waits for. He waits for a change that could be a blowout, an accident, the automation of his job, a flood, a collapse in oil prices, a strike, a shutdown, a green energy transition, or a politics of reparation and of giving land back to Indigenous peoples. His waiting is a dormant or deferred form of resistance, a critical ambivalence that hides behind his "hope" for things to remain the same. Perhaps the worker waits for a hand extended in solidarity among a critical mass of workers and Canadians ready to redefine what they will and will not do for the petrostate. Perhaps the cracked code of the lease serves as raw material – a hook – for critiquing extractivism and imagining alternatives.

Against the idea that oil and gas workers are hypocrites, dupes, or too implicated in the system to understand it, Mathew Henderson's *The Lease* demonstrates that workers are uniquely positioned to theorize and resist petropoetics. This important text in Canadian petropoetics puts its finger on and applies pressure to an epistemological break in the ideological discourses of settler colonial ownership and extraction in Canada. The lease is a way of thinking and talking about land, a way of measuring time, and a way of rationalizing the extractive and alienating relations of petromodern production. The lease allows oil workers and other complicit subjects to manage contrary infatuation – to hold out hope while putting off change. The lease tends to parse consent, complicity, and guilt in ways that emphasize individual culpability while obfuscating collective, governmental, corporate, and ruling-class responsibilities. It makes "you" feel bad while also condoning what extractive industry does to workers, land, and communities (from Indigenous and local oil-patch communities to the provincial, the national, and the planetary). Identifying the lease as ideological discourse is a first step in cracking its code and an opportunity to reframe and remake meaning, subjectivity, and citizenship. It creates openings for solidarity between oil workers and other Canadians in the differences, desires, fears, and hypocrisies that make our petromodern identifications also disidentifications.

Blue Collar Mayhem

Naden Parkin

Exaggerations and explanations
From my mouth
My own independent radio station
I've grown to hate this daily race for the paper
Raping nature
Just so my pockets ain't vacant.
Naden's tainted
Can you blame him?
My face stays straight but inside it's cave-ins
There's shame in my veins for remaining a layman
So I wake up
Straight for the pay check
Taming natural gas
Propane pays him
Payments to make
What if descendants came in?
So amen
Is what I say when the day ends
God please say when ends meet on minimum wages
Until then
I guess I'm just caged in
My family name has been slaves since days of cave men,
I ache
I just want to break this chain and
Erase the Parkin's day in this blue collar mayhem.

CHAPTER 5

Mud Man: Poetry as Truth-Telling and Land Relations in Naden Parkin's *A Relationship with Truth*

You'll never know whether I'm clever or slow
— Naden Parkin[1]

Naden Parkin's 2014 self-published book *A Relationship with Truth: Poem and Verse Born in the Canadian Oil Patch* is a collection of earnest, rhyming poems that describe the predicament and the emotions of a white-settler drilling fluid specialist who feels stuck working in extractive industry. This is an unusual poetry collection: the design, layout, and editing are less polished than most of what the literary presses publish. The title is clunky. The content of the poems can be repetitive, sing-songy, and crass, as in the opening lines of the love poem "The Cutest Girl": "She was the cutest girl I ever knew, / She was the cutest girl I'd ever do."[2] The endorsements on the back cover come not from poets or literary scholars but from an Ultimate Fighting Championship fighter and the host of a reality TV show called *Licence to Drill.* (The TV host begins, "I'm not much of a poetry reader …") In light of the way Parkin's *A Relationship with Truth* revels in being rough around the edges, this chapter focuses on what is impressive and fascinating about this book: its workerly, anti-literary poetics offers a unique perspective on oil workers' relationships with industry and the land.

A Relationship with Truth is distinct among the poetry collections I study because it is working-class poetry – *popular culture* in the sense of being the culture of ordinary people.[3] These are poems written and published by an untrained writer – someone whose poetics is influenced by high-school English class, schoolyard rhymes, commercial jingles, greeting cards, and hip-hop lyrics. The questioning of the intelligence of workers that Parkin refers to as the enigma of whether he (or his poetry) is "clever or slow" recurs throughout the tradition of oil-worker poetry,[4] but, as Marxist cultural scholar Raymond Williams writes about working-class scholars and poets, "[i]t is part of the insult offered to intelligence by a class-society that this history of ordinary thought is ever found surprising."[5] Composed in Parkin's head while "driving around from province to province, town to town and rig to rig,"[6] the intuitive poetry in *A Relationship with Truth* captures a "structure of feeling" of oil work by referencing and mimicking other familiar, popular, and ordinary cultural forms.[7] Whereas other oil-worker poets like Peter Christensen, Mathew Henderson, and Lindsay Bird did oil extraction work temporarily as a short-term or summer job, Parkin represents oil work from inside not only the work itself but also the working class and the sense he shared with other well-paid oil workers that he had no viable employment options outside the oil industry.[8] Parkin's poetry is at times offensive, crude, and unsophisticated, but dismissing it for these reasons would mean ignoring an important oil-patch aesthetic or intelligence.

Parkin wrote *A Relationship with Truth* while living in Grande Prairie, Alberta, and working in Alberta and Saskatchewan as a travelling drilling fluid specialist, also known as a "mud man." Unlike S.C. Ells's use of amateur poetry to conceal such truths, Parkin's intuitive, hip-hop-inflected poetics exposes the "contrary infatuations" of a mud man whose identity ties him both to the industry and to the oil-patch land he calls home.[9] The title *A Relationship with Truth* references Al Gore's iconic 2006 film about global warming, *An Inconvenient Truth*. On the front cover, the emphasis on the word *relationship* makes a distinction between those for whom the truth about climate change is merely inconvenient and those for whom it is catastrophic, even apocalyptic. This includes those who were, as Parkin's poetry is described in the subtitle, *Born in the Canadian Oil Patch* – who live and work in the oil patch; who make their living, support their familial and other relationships, and understand their identities through the oil and gas industry; and who do not know who, what, or where they are without oil and the oil patch. From an insider's perspective, Parkin represents the threatened positionality of an extraction worker on the eve of the 2014 oil bust and in anticipation of energy transition.[10]

Parkin has organized the book into the loose narrative arc of a love-and-success-story – the persona's search for meaning and for a life partner, ending with a marriage to his dream girl and the recuperation, through his oil-industry job, of the rural way of life he remembers from his childhood before the loss of the family farm. In combination with the title, the sepia-toned photo of an oil-patch sunset on the front cover suggests a second, unconscious narrative that is the focus of this chapter. This counternarrative, which I interpret as the text's "energy unconscious,"[11] centres Parkin's fears about what the oil and gas industry is doing to the land, about his future employment, and about what the inevitable energy transition to come will mean for oil-patch workers and residents. In this chapter, I read *A Relationship with Truth* against the grain, focusing on two interpretations of relationship with truth: first, Parkin's own notion that writing poetry demands honesty, and second, the idea that *A Relationship with Truth* is ultimately about relationship with the land. My reading respects Parkin's vulnerability and intelligence while also being critical of instances where he appropriates the dispossession of Black and Indigenous peoples to convey his own exploitation and alienation. Ultimately, reading both against and along with *A Relationship with Truth,* this chapter calls for an anticolonial and antiracist class politics for energy transition.

Poetry and Honesty

> Know that I chose to show this
> To let my soul expose what all of you already know
> But you hold in.
> – Naden Parkin[12]

The poetry in *A Relationship with Truth* is lyric, narrative poetry, often in unmetred rhyming verse reminiscent of hip-hop lyrics and aware of its unconventional form and content. The words *Poem and Verse* in the subtitle refer to poetry and hip-hop, closely related forms with separate traditions and audiences that Parkin treats as indistinguishable.[13] The hip-hop elements make the poetry seem both new and more like "old-school poetry,"[14] with rhyming, rhythmic, and repetitive lines and refrains that have more affinity with older poetic forms like the ballad than with contemporary poetry.[15] The extreme honesty practised by the speaker of the poetry – a persona closely aligned with Parkin who sometimes refers to himself in the third person as *Naden* – is a characteristic influenced by a hip-hop disdain for *fronting* (or misrepresenting oneself),[16] as well as the traditions of sentimental poetry and the confessional lyric. In the poem "A Place Within," Parkin writes, "As I navigate through this maze of shit / I found a place in Naden where no fake emits / No pain exists."[17] Parkin credits poetry and the persona with helping him find his authentic self. Telling the truth about the "wounds deep as tar sumps" (52) and "shame" (53) that result from the contrary infatuations that are inherent to his mud-man identity as both an extraction worker and a lover of women and the land, Parkin does not avoid pain, but "no pain exists" in the sense that in his poetry he does not have to suppress one infatuation in favour of the other.

Like other oil-worker poets, Parkin disidentifies with the subject position of the supposedly typical oil worker who does hard, dangerous work for the money and who embodies a dominant, iconic Northern masculinity. As I discuss in chapters 2 and 4, "disidentification," as theorized by Michel Pêcheux, José Esteban Muñoz, and Judith Butler, describes the way that resistant subjects simultaneously perform and subvert dominant ways of being. Naden is "[a] working class man" (42); a man concerned with what it means to be a man (see 68–9); a cisgender, heterosexual man looking for a woman to love him back; a man with "A fist of cash / A hippy's conscience" doing extractive work he feels bad about (57); and a man who struggles with but does not want to be defined by addiction (see 30–1; 63). Like *Rig Talk* poet Peter Christensen, Parkin is unapologetic about his masculinism; by conforming to stereotypes, he shows that he belongs among oil workers. From within this insider position, however, he represents oil workers as deeply conflicted. For example, the poem "Northern Man" begins with the persona characterizing the oil and gas industry as part of a nation-building project that he believes in. He says, "You ask me, I'd invest in that / It's natural gas and the oil patch," seemingly expressing full support of and identification with the industry. After this, however, the poem shifts and ends with a note of ambivalence:

> Western Canada, we're blessed with that
> And cursed with that
> And if you think not, then you're immersed in facts[.] (11)

Parkin's poetry is related to what Jennifer Wenzel calls "petro-magic-realism." Wenzel refers to landscapes and literatures, especially African and Indigenous ones, affected by the exoticist notions of *magical realism*, *petro-magic*, and the *resource curse*;[18] the illusions about oil work and life in the Canadian oil patch that Parkin addresses with a mixture of honesty and fantasy are different but related. Being what Parkin calls "immersed in facts" means accepting the myths of oil as either "blessing" or "curse," along with a supporting set of ideological "facts," such as those cited by the oil lobby on one side or environmental activists on the other. Instead, with no one poem expressing only identification with the oil industry, Parkin consistently represents the truth that oil is always a blessing and a curse, for oil workers, settler and Indigenous communities, and Canada.

The poem "Blue Collar Mayhem" begins, for example, by conveying the contrary infatuations of an oil worker in a petro-economy, tired of his own "Exaggerations and explanations" for why he continues to do oil work, despite his misgivings about it. Naden says,

> I've grown to hate this daily race for the paper
> Raping nature
> Just so my pockets ain't vacant.
> Naden's tainted
> Can you blame him?
> My face stays straight but inside it's cave-ins
> There's shame in my veins for remaining a layman[.][19]

Parkin's use of rhyme, assonance, and rhythm in these lines is impressive. The rhymes between *paper*, *nature*, *vacant*, *tainted*, *blame him*, *cave-ins*, and *layman* are all slant rhymes that may be forced in oral performance. Parkin uses assonance between *hate*, *daily*, *race*, *paper*, *raping nature*, *ain't*, *vacant*, *Naden*, *tainted*, *blame*, *face stays straight*, *cave-ins*, *shame*, *veins*, *remaining*, and *layman*. He also uses matching trochaic metre in the lines "<u>Rap</u>ing <u>na</u>ture," "<u>Na</u>den's <u>tain</u>ted," and "<u>Can</u> you <u>blame</u> him?" (with stressed syllables underlined here) to make the rhymes seem fuller than they are. Several of the rhyming words he uses here are repeated in the collection as rhymes with *Naden*, as in the line "Tainted, jaded, hatred, painted," in "Love Can Kill Ya";[20] they show that Naden's bad feelings about his oil work are tied to his sense of self.

The persona's pain is located at the intersection of his disempowerment as a worker, his concern for the land and respect for women, and his role in perpetrating violence on a feminized earth. In "Blue Collar Mayhem," he acknowledges that respect for the land, like respect for women, is something he is willing to compromise for a pay cheque and to support his family. His linking of gender violence and petro-violence through the description of resource extraction as rape is in keeping with Indigenous and premodern conceptions of the earth as mother; it is compounded by the phallic and penetrative technologies used by extraction workers.[21] As Carolyn Merchant demonstrates in *The Death of Nature*, the scientific revolution of the sixteenth and seventeenth centuries was a misogynist and colonial project that undermined earlier organismic land relations of balance, respect, and reciprocity in order to turn the animate Mother Earth into dead, inert nature, "a passive receptor of human rape";[22] it established land relations that extractive capitalism uses to exploit the land and accumulate capital. Merchant remarks, however, that "the organismic perspective has by no means disappeared. It has remained as an important underlying tension."[23] The persistence of the rape metaphor in representations of extraction in both Indigenous and non-Indigenous texts is an example of that tension.[24] Michael Watts characterizes *petro-violence* as both "*ecological* violence" and "*social* violence";[25] Heather Turcotte pushes this idea further in her framework of "petro-sexual politics." She writes that "gender violence is not merely an effect of petro-violence, it is the necessary condition for such violence to even take place."[26] In "Blue Collar Mayhem," Naden feels trapped in the toxic masculinity that makes him both a perpetrator and a victim.

Parkin ends "Blue Collar Mayhem" by dismissing the alternatives to oil work and describing Naden as an enslaved person when he writes, "My family name has been slaves since days of cave men."[27] Parkin's references to labour, capital, and class reveal an uneasy class consciousness, one that he seeks to articulate without sounding like a Marxist. His descriptions of working-class people as "enslaved," expressed by a white poet using the primarily Black idiom of hip-hop, inadvertently expose the racist roots of extractive capitalism and petro-violence. When describing himself as chained to dangerous, extractive work that pays more than any other job he would be qualified to do, and when calling his family and himself "slaves,"[28] the persona uses a common metaphor for alienated or dehumanizing labour[29] – a metaphor that is also problematic.[30] Calling himself a slave conveys Parkin's sense of being exploited by a class of "the richest guys / Who bitch and cry over misplaced dimes."[31] Yet, despite the way the metaphor of slavery resonates for Parkin, its use is imprecise and perpetuates harm. By equating his exploitation as a working-class labourer with what Denise Ferreira da Silva describes as the "total violence" of the colonial expropriation of Indigenous land and enslaved bodies,[32] Parkin trivializes the experience of historical and contemporary enslavement, as well as its ongoing material, social, and psychic effects and afterlives.[33]

Parkin's experience of what it is like to "[risk his] limbs for fistfuls of twenties,"[34] or to have the surplus value of his labour appropriated by his employer, is different from the total appropriation of the flesh and labour of the enslaved. It occurs to him to call himself a slave, however, because the system that supports the extraction of both "natural resources" and "human resources" is premised on the categories of the human and the inhuman that have been used to justify the enslavement of humans, the theft of land from Indigenous peoples, and the extraction of minerals. Black feminist scholars such as Sylvia Wynter have shown that the idea of the African as the Other of "Man" is foundational to the projects not only of slavery and colonialism but also of humanism, modernity, coloniality, capitalism, and the fossil-fuel energy system (or petropoetics). Abolishing this idea would be apocalyptic – the end of the world (as we know it) – because all human systems and structures (including but not limited to the economy) would collapse. It would be an ending that some scholars argue is the only way to realize an antiracist, decolonized world.[35]

Perhaps Parkin glimpses such an apocalyptic horizon in his poem "Something Inside," with its misguided proposal to "saddle up painted": that is, to dress up like an Indigenous warrior[36] and "wage" a supposedly colourblind "war for the slaves," where the greatest insight is Naden's realization that the thing he would be fighting is an unnamed "Something, in me."[37] The unnameable "Something Inside"[38] that Naden tries to get at using the language of both classism and racism might be described using the term *racial capitalism*. As literary and Africana studies scholar Jodi Melamed explains, "Capital can only be capital when it is accumulating, and it can only accumulate by producing and moving through relations of severe inequality among human groups – capitalists with the means of production/workers without the means of subsistence, creditors/debtors, conquerors of land made property/the dispossessed and removed. These antimonies of accumulation require loss, disposability, and the unequal differentiation of human value, and racism enshrines the inequalities that capitalism requires."[39] Parkin's use of enslavement as a metaphor points to the foundational role that racism plays in the structures of inequality required for capitalist production and profit. As a systemic and structuring force in the world and the white mud-man identity Parkin inhabits, racial capitalism works in, on, and through him. As Naden describes, "It's freaking me out, it's beating me down, / Eating me up and making me shout."[40] It casts him, at turns, as an exploited worker, a beneficiary of colonial conquest, a dispossessed farmer, and a bearer of white privilege. Parkin's poetics of extreme honesty leads him to reveal some ugly truths about his participation and complicity in racial capitalism, toxic masculinity, and environmental harm.

The statement and question "Naden's tainted / Can you blame him?" in "Blue Collar Mayhem" are central to *A Relationship with Truth*, with the unanswered question reading as a plea not to hold Naden responsible for the impacts of his oil work. Dominant ways of thinking modelled after neoliberal, free-market ideology tend to individualize responsibility, blaming workers and consumers with limited options for the environmental and social harms of extractive industry instead of holding corporations, executives, and governments accountable. Given the emotional pain that he describes oil workers enduring, I am reluctant to blame Naden. Yet, withholding blame does little to relieve Naden's pain or to reconcile his harmful relationships with oil, women, and the land. I read *A Relationship with Truth*, instead, in terms of what I consider to be its implicit desire and call for an ethics for oil workers and other complicit petrocultural subjects in the era of climate change. Blaming Parkin might look like dismissing him as backward and "slow." Instead, I hold Parkin responsible, in Donna Haraway's sense of "response-ability," as having, or cultivating, "the capacity to respond."[41] This is a way to respect Parkin's intelligence and take seriously his insight that truth is not static but rather unfolds through ethical relationships. Parkin's self-exposure is an invitation to look for relationships and to connect the dots between the instances of violence, loss, and harm that he describes. By reading empathetically, drawing on Naden's articulation of what "all of you already know / But you hold in[,]"[42] readers can continue the work of exposure, constellating and creating systemic (rather than individualized) analysis that contemplates solidarity as shared capacity to respond.

Land Relations as Relationship with Truth

> I was birthed on a small farm,
> What gave me worth was that dirt,
> But now it's all gone.
> – Naden Parkin[43]

As I have already shown, Parkin's identity as a "mud man" runs deeper than his job description. Beginning with the subtitle that describes his poetry as *Born in the Canadian Oil Patch*, Parkin represents himself throughout *A Relationship with Truth* as loving and belonging to the land. It is from the land that Naden gets his "heart of gold"[44] – a recurring symbol of his goodness that echoes Neil Young's song "Heart of Gold."[45] Naden's love for the land he knows as the oil patch is the ground of his serious concerns about his oil work, but he struggles to imagine ways other than extractive ones to relate to the land. Parkin's self-definition as native to the oil patch often takes the problematic form of identification with Indigenous peoples through his sense of dispossession and endangerment. In other instances, Parkin uses references to a historical trajectory of Canadian resource economies as layering one dispossession upon another to expose oil workers' perceptions and fears about the energy transition to come. At the same time, he reveals his hunch, in the form of an energy unconscious, that there are decolonial or anticolonial alternatives to land relations based on theft, loss, and the extraction of resources.

Parkin's positioning as native to the oil patch is what Margery Fee calls a "literary land claim."[46] Parkin makes claims to the land through what Adam Gaudry and Chris Anderson call "Self-Indigenization" – a strategy that "claims to circumvent colonialism as it transforms many Canadians into Indians and Métis, who are no longer the beneficiaries of Indigenous dispossession, but part of the dispossessed themselves"[47] For example, the opening lines of the poem "As the Moon Creeps" use passive phrasing to describe Parkin as having been "birthed on a small farm." Parkin attributes the action of his arrival to the one who gave him birth – his mother – while his rhyming of *birthed* with *worth* and *dirt* also suggests another rhyme that points to a close relationship with *Mother Earth* that was lost when his family lost the farm in the transition between farming and oil-and-gas resource economies. In their sorrowful tone and passive phrasing, these lines echo a poem fragment from earlier in the book, in which Parkin mourns the loss of the wood bison who used to graze on land now known as the oil patch:

A flat land with a painted sky
Graced by the great herds
But all the grazers died.[48]

By saying that the bison simply "died," Parkin obscures the historical circumstances through which white traders, bureaucrats, missionaries, and governments encouraged the overhunting of bison in the eighteenth and nineteenth centuries, then leveraged the resulting famines, epidemics, and conflicts to appropriate territory and power from Indigenous peoples.[49] In the resonance between these two poetic sequences, Parkin represents himself as an endangered species – one of the grazers – rather than one of the beneficiaries of dispossession.

Other examples of self-indigenization include Parkin's portrayal of himself as an Indigenous warrior in "Something Inside" (discussed above). Through references to his "oil patch blood" and "pure" blood[50] – claims to indigeneity and innocence that employ white-supremacist language – the persona makes slippery claims not only to belong to the working class, the North, and the oil patch, but also to be entitled to white privilege, to a settler-colonial heritage, and to the land itself. In the poem "Groundbirch Camp," with its faux-Indigenous name referring to a Shell natural-gas project,[51] an Indigenous woman affirms Naden's goodness and promises him fame and success by saying, "Your old soul glows like it's gold dust, / Expose it, and the whole world will notice"[52] Although fossil fuels may be both a blessing and a curse to residents of the oil patch, a settler's equation of his sense of dispossession or of belonging with Indigenous experiences and knowledges obscures very real differences in the distribution of resource blessings and curses. Literary critics have long identified a trope or pattern in settler-Canadian literature through which settlers are represented as threatened and as victims;[53] these examples from Parkin's poetry demonstrate that such representations are pervasive and ideological; they obscure settlers' roles as the beneficiaries and perpetrators of colonial violence.

Through references to past and future economies and energy systems, *A Relationship with Truth* highlights the violent practices of settler colonialism and resource extraction that have fashioned the land Parkin lives and works on as oil patch. In the poem "Her Cost," Naden situates himself within an extractive economic history that stretches "From the furs to the farm to the rigs to the dark / That churns in the earth until it's burned in my thoughts."[54] This depiction of the way that resource economies claim and rename already occupied territory as a process of *churning* reveals that such reterritorializations are a series of disruptive and violent dispossessions. It links Parkin's loss of the family farm backward in time to the theft of the land from Indigenous peoples first by colonial powers as a source of furs and then by the settler-colonial state as farmland. It also links the churning of farmland into oil patch to the end of the fossil-fuel economy as a new churning that places oil-producing families and communities at risk. Unconsciously, Parkin fears the inevitable transition from the oil-patch mode of production to something else; something he cannot imagine but refers to only as "the dark." This unknown "dark" at the end of the trajectory from fur trade to oil patch is paralleled by a prior territorialization that Parkin leaves in the dark: the land's existence as sovereign Indigenous territory that precedes and is concurrent with each of the other versions. The knowledge and traditions of the white settler fail Parkin: he cannot imagine the land either before or after the colonial and extractive regimes that have redefined it.

In his poetry, Parkin expresses grief about the negative impacts of oil extraction on the land he loves and demonstrates an unconscious or half-conscious desire to see and relate to the land differently. In *Pollution Is Colonialism*, Métis discard studies scholar Max Liboiron distinguishes between, on one hand, colonial land relations that treat land as resource and, on the other, a traditional Indigenous conception of what Liboiron terms "capital-L *Land*," "the combined living spirit of plants, animals, air, water, humans, histories, and events"[55] Decolonial l/Land relations are practised by Indigenous peoples on their territory and are not to be claimed by others. It is possible, however, for settlers and other guests on Indigenous territory, as well as those working within colonial institutions, to embody good, anticolonial land relations that are reciprocal and ethical, focused on being good relatives and fulfilling responsibilities to the land.[56] Only an anticolonial relationship with the land as mother, teacher, and home will offer the kinds of truths that Naden wishes for. This would require settler-colonial subjects like Parkin (and me) to take a leap of faith into "the dark" by working to dismantle the extractive framings of the land as oil patch, farm, and fur trade, including our own ownership of and claims to the land; by honouring treaties; and by learning, belatedly, how to live on the land as what Eve Tuck and K. Wayne

Yang call *immigrants* instead of occupiers, "beholden to the Indigenous laws and epistemologies of the lands they migrate to."[57]

Parkin's insight into settler colonialism as a series of dispossessions layered on the theft of Indigenous land leads him to conclude that his only option is to continue to do his job and play his prescribed role in the churning of the extractive economy. A reading for the energy unconscious of *A Relationship with Truth* reveals a desire for a just transition that breaks the chains of violence and harm by overthrowing not only the petro-economy but also the racist and colonial structures upon which any resource economy is built. In *Global Warming and the Sweetness of Life*, interdisciplinary scholars Matt Hern and Am Johal hold together commitments to environmentalism, anti-colonialism, and solidarity with workers. They write, "We are convinced that linking the domination of people to the domination of land and the other-than-human world is a key to grasping an ecological future. We would go even further to suggest that any robust ecological discourses *have* to start with decolonization and thoroughly renovated land politics."[58] Their vision for just energy transition includes a good, sweet life for former extraction workers like Parkin.[59] My reading of *A Relationship with Truth* moves away from blaming oil workers and toward imagining nonviolent modes of production, sweet lives, and good work for everyone. Learning good land relations emerges as a way of "searching for a heart of gold" amid uncertainty and transition.[60]

Conclusion

Parkin's *A Relationship with Truth* is unique in form, content, and its honest exposure of the psychology of a white worker in extractive industry. My reading of this text takes seriously Parkin's reaching for an ethics and politics of energy transition that is grounded in relationship with truth and with the land. I read *A Relationship with Truth*, ultimately, as calling for a just transition grounded in Indigenous sovereignty and knowledge, reparations for the harms done by colonial resource economies, and solidarity with workers.

The Petrochemical Ball

Lesley Battler

look

rococo oxo-
reactors

cerium spires

neodymium
atrium

the steam-
veiled nave of
the Fractionater

here is where
where we reform
raw crude

benzene raffinate
mixed xylenes
pygas
smelly heterocy-
clics
polyols

please don't
feed them

hydrofluoric acids
invite boron
trifluoride

our role
is to distill
volatiles

track their
vernacular

eliminate
rhyming
slang

re-
shape
their
alpha
bets

BA-ba-de-be-pa
ba-ba-de-BA-pa
BA-pa BA-pa

ah, the stomp
of Olefin feedstock
ready to be rendered
into the delicious
Alberta plastics
served at the
Palliser

SHIRRRK-ka pk
SHIIIIIIRK-SH-ka
pok-shh kapok-e'
eee' EEE

here we security-
check & liquefy
pentanes

do not
be naïve

these pentanes
are merely
feigning pain

in reality
they are
caustic

unstable
disloyal to
the Company

allow me to
translate today's
épater

Pentane 1:
TGIF! thank god
it's Faraday

Pentane 2:
what poet
do i quote
before i
explode?

QUEEEE-
AWNX

ozone
throat
music

a sonic
anomaly

OOOOOOOO-
WEEEEE y'aa
aaaawwwl

Ethylene derives
great pride from
her $H_2C{=}CH_2$
genealogy

but reveals too
much bond
cleavage

infamous for
her wiles

her ability
to elicit
secrets from
electrophiles

ZHOA' OA'
OAAAAR tch
PTH th th
thp thp thp
ZHOA' OA'
OAAAACH

Hydrogen

these invincible
princes piss their
inheritance in
dissipation

we would love
to ban them from
the Periodic Table

alas, they
know they're
indispensable

Jesus?

yes, you may
wish to friend
this deity

follow me

BA-ba-de-y'awl
ZOOARCH-oowee
QUEEEE y'awl
SHIRKzee
AWNX

the chondrite
won't hurt

open bar

into the
antebellum
ballroom
of the
catalytic
converter

maleic anhydrate
for resins

explosives love
nitrobenzene

aniline-tinis
satisfy dyes
polyurethanes

toluene
always first
on the dance
floor

glycols like
a good
two-step

these molecules
have completed
our program

their pitiful
shrieks and
squawks have
become carbon
rondelets

double
single bonds
cold sulphur
hip-hop
magnesium
dub

and we have
come to
the end of
the steam
chamber

namaste!

CHAPTER 6

"do not / be naïve": Language and the Stakes of Animacy in Lesley Battler's *Endangered Hydrocarbons*

No language is neutral.
– Dionne Brand[1]

Only in Alberta's oil sands do companies not only volunteer to dig up naturally occurring petroleum that's bubbling out of the soaked ground and oozing into the rivers, they spend billions of dollars for the privilege of doing it. You might call it the largest cleanup of an oil spill in the history of the world.
– Ezra Levant[2]

The ubiquity of energy slaves in the United States today would surely astound Harriet Beecher Stowe, the author of *Uncle Tom's Cabin*. The United States traded in an energy system that shackled Topsy, Sambo, and Eliza for one that enslaves consumers to Hummers, Lincolns, and Fords.
– Andrew Nikiforuk[3]

This is sovereign Wet'suwet'en land.
– Chief and Matriarch Sleydo'[4]

Climate activists are sometimes depicted as dangerous radicals. But, the truly dangerous radicals are the countries that are increasing the production of fossil fuels.
– UN Secretary-General António Guterres[5]

Blah blah blah.
– Greta Thunberg[6]

Lesley Battler is an unmarked/white settler, a poet, and a former Shell project information manager. In her 2015 debut poetry collection, Battler splices and fractionates the specialized and everyday language of the oil and gas industry in a process that mirrors both the refining of hydrocarbons and the production or management of information through appropriation, spin, and corporate speak. In 170 pages of dense, intense, playful, funny, and troubling poems, *Endangered Hydrocarbons* challenges readers to parse which absurdities and abstractions Battler has borrowed from industry (and might be explained, for example, in the energy technology company Schlumberger's online *Energy Glossary*)[7] and which she has made up (such as the oil/literary corporation Sinistrale PLC, with a name that hints – like real names such as Total, Talisman, Imperial, Syncrude, Cenovus, and Shell – that the politics and power of the industry are misleading, malicious, or evil).[8] *Endangered Hydrocarbons* considers hydrocarbons as feedstock not only for petromodern consumer goods but also for culture, media, literature, and the faulty understandings of subjectivity and agency that structure contemporary life. In an extended contemplation of energy transition as culture war, Battler mimics, exposes, and subverts the colonial and extractive language used by corporations, governments, the pro-oil lobby, environmentalists, and consumers. This chapter draws on queer interdisciplinary scholar Mel Y. Chen's *Animacies: Biopolitics, Racial Matterings, and Queer Affect* to read *Endangered Hydrocarbons* as "animacy theory"[9] that links the fossil-fuel energy system with racism and colonialism.

Endangered Hydrocarbons as Language Poetry and Animacy Theory

Building on Peter Christensen's demonstration in *Rig Talk* that energy language is ideological (see chapter 2), as well as poet-theorist Dionne Brand's insight that "No language is neutral," *Endangered Hydrocarbons* makes the point that the language we use to talk about energy is volatile. Battler writes in an innovative, feminist, and queer poetic tradition that, as Kate Eichorn and Heather Milne describe, "approaches language as an inherent problematic and subject of inquiry rather than mere vehicle for representation"[10] – one that, as Syd Zolf describes, "'skirts' the subject and subjectivity without evacuating it."[11] Battler makes her point less through the content of her poems than through her deft manipulations of industry language to say controversial, contradictory, confusing, and absurd things – that is, to say practically anything. She effects a *skirting* of the subject (an avoidance and a feminization or queering) by writing poetry through the perspective of a successful-but-ambivalent woman oil-company employee – a project information manager who knows how to use and analyze industry language because she writes it for a living. Introduced as the speaker of the opening poem, the project information manager grapples with a disapproving intellectual-environmentalist *Past Self* who thinks she has sold out.[12] Although she may seem "Evil" to the past self,[13] she also does not fit in among the executives – the "Gents"[14] – at the oil company. Her smart, funny, ironic, and skirted voice is discernible throughout the collection, even in instances where the poems are spoken in other put-on voices, from philosophers and advertisers to the "Gents" and the hydrocarbons themselves. Battler's skirting of both the subject position of the project information manager and the subject matter of the oil industry makes her a sharp theorist of language, energy, and power.

Endangered Hydrocarbons exposes language and culture in a petro-economy and petrostate like Canada as always *petroculture.* By creating an energy-related term (*endangered hydrocarbons*) and investigating its various possible meanings and uses through a poetics that reviewer Michael Sloane calls "seriously playful,"[15] Battler shows how language can be manipulated, co-opted, and subverted, yet also how it exceeds and undermines language users' attempts to limit or contain it. She uses *endangered hydrocarbons* as a linguistic compound to parallel the petrochemical compounds produced by industry. In her notes at the end of the book, Battler describes her poetic process: "All of the poems in this project are derived from texts generated in a multinational oil company. I spliced items such as wellbooks, mudlogs, geological prognoses, and meeting notes with a variety of found material, including histories and critical theoretical works, as well as travel, real estate, and home decor magazines – basically anything that crossed my path."[16] Battler's poetry is made of found text: pre-existing language from a wide range of sources. By claiming that all of her found material was "generated in a multinational oil company," she makes an argument that oil permeates petromodern living yet deflects attention away from itself, in the way that the magazines seem, for example, to be about home decor but are ultimately also about maintaining the consumerist lifestyles that fuel a petro-economy. In an essay, Battler describes her experimental poetics as working with found text in ways that mirror petrochemical processing: "I am treating production language as crude oil, excavating, treating, mixing, injecting these texts to emulate extraction processes used by the industry."[17] Mimicking processes used to produce oil, gas, and petrochemicals, and referencing her own word-processing on behalf of the industry, Battler demonstrates how language plays an instrumental role in producing cultural forms such as consent, social licence, resignation, dependency, and denial.

For example, Battler's poem "Eco-Terrorism in Canada" satirizes far-right media pundit Ezra Levant's argument in *Ethical Oil: The Case for Canada's Oil Sands* that despite its environmental and human costs, Canadian oil from the Athabasca tar sands is ethical because oil sourced from other countries like Saudi Arabia, Iran, Nigeria, and Russia comes from "the world's dictatorships, human rights abusers, and warmongers."[18] Mimicking and extrapolating Levant's falsely clear-cut categorizations of "democratic, peaceful," "morally superior," and "good" Canadian oil vs. oil that comes from "nasty" places mostly located in the Global South,[19] "Eco-Terrorism in Canada" casts Canadian oil as good and therefore anyone who opposes it as bad. The poem, subtitled "a Petroconomist *special report*,"[20] is written as part of a made-up, pro-industry magazine or website. Evoking/mocking Northrop Frye's settler-colonial "garrison mentality,"[21] it depicts nature or the wilderness as a "Jihadist haven" where plants and non-human animals have organized a resistance movement against extractive industry.[22] The poem codes as Muslim and racialized the (also made-up) "radical al-Taxa / Anti-Extinction League / (TEAL)" that takes aim at taxonomies or chains of being that position the human above or against nature. When "mugwort shuts / airports" and "belugas pack lugers / under black burqas,"[23] the language evokes the al-Qaeda attacks on the United States on 11 September 2001 that would be used to justify subsequent US and Canadian wars in Iraq and Afghanistan, as well as heightened discrimination against Muslims, Arabs, and Sikhs. It exposes the racist and orientalist logics of Levant's framing of good and bad sources of oil – a framing that obscures both ecological impacts and Canada's role in wars, dictatorships, and human rights abuses both in Canada and abroad.

Also encoded in the poem are the characterization of Indigenous resistance to extraction as eco-terrorism and the resulting surveillance and criminalization of land and water defenders,[24] as in the stanza:

never turn
your back
on snake-
root[25]

in which *The Petroconomist* advises the reader to be suspicious of an indigenous species. In the third part of the poem, a description of "carbon-capture / in state-run bird / sanctuaries" where

> wood ducks
> chain CO_2 in
> Hadean pits[26]

speaks to the Canadian government's use of institutions such as reserves, residential schools, the pass system, prisons, and so-called child-welfare agencies to contain, control, subjugate, and end Indigenous lives. The portrayal of the birds inside the sanctuaries as perpetrators of violence parallels the situation where, as Lenape scholar Joanne Barker writes about Canada and the United States in *Red Scare: The State's Indigenous Terrorist*, "the state identifies Indigenous peoples as terrorists in the service of its own imperialist goals." This is because the stability of the state and the capitalist economy depend on "reproducing social relations of gross inequality between the state and Indigenous peoples."[27] In other words, the construction of Indigenous peoples as terrorists uses an imagined, exaggerated, or real threat of violence by Indigenous peoples as a distraction from the actual historical and ongoing violence perpetrated on Indigenous peoples by the settler-colonial state and its extractive economy. The sense of threat expressed in the "garrison mentality" turns out to be a fear of decolonial resistance in response to colonial violence. By framing the oil and gas industry and perhaps all of Canada as a "*drilling / community*" that liberates hydrocarbons,[28] and by representing the imagined revolt of non-human species as acts of senseless violence perpetrated on endangered hydrocarbons, "Eco-Terrorism in Canada" mirrors the language of the corporate-petro-state that protects "critical infrastructure"[29] and corporate profits over the rights of Indigenous peoples and the well-being of ecosystems and communities. As "Eco-Terrorism in Canada" demonstrates, terms like *eco-terrorist*, *ethical oil*, and *dangerous radicals* are neither neutral nor monolithic.

Similarly, references to slavery in *Endangered Hydrocarbons* satirize and problematize left-wing journalist Andrew Nikiforuk's argument in *The Energy of Slaves: Oil and the New Servitude* that slavery was abolished in tandem with the escalation of fossil-fuel consumption, so that the capitalist class today appropriates the labour of fossil-fuel-powered "energy slaves" or "inanimate slaves" in place of enslaved humans.[30] Energy historian Bob

Johnson has argued that the term *energy slave* (first coined by Buckminster Fuller in 1940) has an "uncomfortable racial, class, and gender unconscious."[31] Whereas Johnson and other writers have traced links between slavery and energy while either using the energy-slave metaphor with caution,[32] or without using it at all,[33] Nikiforuk's use of the metaphor is often playful, flippant, and careless. In an example quoted in the epigraph above, Nikiforuk trivializes slavery as a system of theft, violence, and dispossession when he equates the enslavement of characters from Harriet Beecher Stowe's novel *Uncle Tom's Cabin* with the so-called enslavement of contemporary Americans by their cars.

Battler's implicit critique of *The Energy of Slaves* can be seen, for example, in "Pax McMurray," a poem that speaks in a pro-oil-sands voice and characterizes the conventional oil industry as "utilizing / slaves, suffering / endless LTIs."[34] Workers in this dangerous industry are described as if they were enslaved, while it is their corporate employers who "suffer" through lost time incidents (LTIs)– work-related illnesses or injuries that cause employees to miss work and corporations to lose money. The speaker is making – yet also mocking – a point in favour of automation and tar-sands mega-projects, innovations that create not only fewer LTIs but also unemployment for workers whose jobs are rendered obsolete. Like Nikiforuk's use of the language of energy slavery, and like other disidentificatory performances of toxic ideology, the references to slavery in "Pax McMurray" are awkward, uncomfortable, and potentially harmful.[35] Mimicking Nikiforuk, Battler implicates herself while demonstrating that the metaphor of the energy slave is obfuscating, unnuanced, and appropriative.

Battler's own linguistic formulation *endangered hydrocarbons* might likewise be described as a metaphor that takes on a life of its own. Through its joking/not-joking linguistic play, it registers the surprising animacy of supposedly inanimate hydrocarbons. This is apparent on the cover of the book, where the image of black, dripping liquid and the red lettering of the words in the title suggest both oil and blood (see figure 6.1). As Nigerian poet Nnimmo Bassey illustrates in his book title *We Thought It Was Oil but It Was Blood*, oil has become inseparable and practically indistinguishable from the human. As George Caffentzis has argued, oil is a "political liquid," implicated and intimate with human life and politics, especially in its definition as private property rather than as a commons or as belonging to the land and to Indigenous peoples.[36] Oil has been used by humans to reinforce colonial, neoliberal-capitalist, patriarchal, racist, and classist structures of

Figure 6.1
Front cover of *Endangered Hydrocarbons*, designed by Jay MillAr.

power, so that it is tied up in the livelihoods, lives, and deaths of humans in countless ways. Along with the ominous drips of liquid that threaten to leak out of the book itself, the title calls up and creates dissonance with the idea that hydrocarbons are not endangered but endangering – both ecologically, as a cause of global warming and environmental harm, and geopolitically, as a cause of wars, dispossession, and other forms of violence. Yet, in each of these instances of endangerment, the harm is caused not by the hydrocarbons themselves but rather by the human pursuits of searching out, extracting, refining, selling, combusting, and disposing of the hydrocarbons. Humans have built an unjust global energy system on the exploitation of hydrocarbons, and it is in this sense that the conditions and crises of the contemporary moment can be described using the metaphor of endangered hydrocarbons. Battler's poetry examines the overlapping exploitations of humans and fossil fuels through linguistic experimentation that highlights the animacy of hydrocarbons.

The *Oxford English Dictionary* defines *animate* as "[e]ndowed with life, living, alive; (esp. in later use) alive and having the power of movement, like an animal." It defines *inanimate* as "[n]ot animated or alive; destitute of life, lifeless; *spec.* not endowed with animal life, as in **inanimate nature**, that part of nature which is without sensation, i.e. all outside the animal world."[37] Despite the seeming binary opposition of these terms, as Mel Y. Chen shows in *Animacies: Biopolitics, Racial Mattering, and Queer Affect*, cognitive linguists consider animacy – "a quality of agency, awareness, mobility, and liveness"[38] – to exist instead on a scale or hierarchy. Animacy is both a linguistic taxonomy of liveness that assumes objects and subjects will stay in their places (including gendered, sexed, classed, and racialized human places) and a surprising quality of objects that are expected to be inanimate yet that show signs of animacy. In a dominant, anthropocentric, and colonial animacy hierarchy, the male, white, able-bodied, heterosexual, and "'free' (as opposed to enslaved)" human sits at the apex;[39] below him are less privileged and seemingly less animate humans, then animals, plants, machines, and so on, with a stone or an abstract concept at the bottom.[40] In their biopolitical theory of animacy, Chen argues that animacy is "conceptually slippery," that it leaks, and that it can be shifted to serve both objectification/dehumanization and the surprising and queer agency of seemingly inanimate things.[41] Animacy is "an often racialized and sexualized means of conceptual and affective mediation between human and inhuman, animate and inanimate, whether in language, rhetoric, or imagery."[42] Using examples such as calling another person an animal as an insult and the ways in which seemingly inanimate objects like lead and mercury act on and within humans through "intoxication,"[43] Chen demonstrates "that language users are 'animate theorists' insofar as they deploy and rework such orders of matter."[44]

In Chen's terms, *Endangered Hydrocarbons* can be described as "animacy theory"[45] that references found animacy theories related to the oil and gas industry. Like other supposedly inanimate resources such as trees, radium, and water, fossil fuels have many properties that signal their animacy. These include their status as stored energy from prehistoric life as "animal remains";[46] their use by humans as fuel, heat, and energy sources; their "locomotion,"[47] fuelling the rapid movement of airplanes, cars, and trains; their flammability and visibility as, for example, gas flares; the force with which they can come bursting out of the earth; their existence in solid, liquid, and gas states; their fluid movement through pipelines and gas pumps; their capacity to leak, poison, contaminate, and kill; all of the things that can be made from them, including cars, clothing, fertilizer, food, and so on; and, of course, the measurable impacts that their combustion has on the earth's climate and sea levels. It is not surprising, then, that commonly used language about fossil fuels contains signs of their animacy. *Endangered Hydrocarbons* reproduces, parodies, and animates language already at play in corporate, environmental, and public discourse about the industry that casts hydrocarbons as endangered – for example, as *trapped oil; fugitive emissions; stranded assets; carbon capture, utilization, and storage*; and *energy slave*. As animacy theory, it contradicts the way that both the oil lobby and environmentalist discourse (including the energy humanities) have too often treated fossil fuels as inanimate energy sources and mere objects. Conceiving of something like the global energy system that Métis anthropologist Zoe Todd describes as weaponizing *fossil-kin* to generate profit while threatening human and non-human life,[48] *Endangered Hydrocarbons* makes a case for treating fossil fuels with respect and care.

Can the Hydrocarbon Speak?

Battler's poem "The Petrochemical Ball," in which the voices of hydrocarbons can be heard, is an exploration of the question of whether the hydrocarbon, like the subaltern in Gayatri Chakravorty Spivak's famous question, can speak. Battler uses onomatopoeia to represent what hydrocarbons sound like when they are being separated in "the Fractionater" – a real term for a refinery – "where we reform / raw crude."[49] In her argument that late-capitalist life is "geologic life," inhuman geographer Kathryn Yusoff responds to those who might scoff at the idea that fossils can speak: "But what is the nature of their speech and what would they say 'if' they could speak? *Speak! Nothing? Only a spectre? A dumb object?* What mutism is this that characterises our lack of language for this geologic dimension of life? The question here may not be, 'How does a fossil speak?' but what is being said for and of this fossilised inheritance for the future, and where is agency located within these geographical, temporal, and material utterances? And why is this geological being, implied in the Anthropocene, so muted in our discussions?"[50] Yusoff argues that it is time to rethink how we account for our relationships with fossil fuels and for what they might be saying to and through us.[51] By sounding out the noises hydrocarbons make when they are being refined, Battler conveys information about what it feels and sounds like to be intimate with hydrocarbons, or to pay attention to them. Battler suggests that hydrocarbons have distinctive voices and personalities, and thus that they are animate and can speak, but the question becomes, as it is in Spivak's essay, whether their speech can survive or subvert representation – whether it can be heard and understood. Battler's transcription of the speech of hydrocarbons may be a seemingly impossible proposal to listen to what oil has to say for itself.

In the process of fractional distillation, crude oil is brought to a boil, turned into vapour, and introduced into a fractionating column that separates and captures the hydrocarbons that condense at different levels in the column because of their different boiling points. Lighter hydrocarbons like propane are collected at the top, and heavier hydrocarbons like tar at the bottom. "The Petrochemical Ball" is a concrete poem, with its long, narrow text split into twelve columns of different lengths and heights, representing the relative positions of heavier and lighter hydrocarbons inside the Fractionater.[52] Reminiscent of Guillaume Apollinaire's World War I poem "Du coton dans les oreilles," "The Petrochemical Ball" at first seems merely silly and fun, but, as with Apollinaire's representations of trench warfare, while reading Battler's visually loud poem the reader encounters the link between its onomatopoeic, semi-concrete forms and its disturbing content.

The speaker narrates the poem as a tour guide, with her sometimes-robotic voice represented in regular type, punctuated by statements like "please don't / feed them."[53] She walks readers through the refinery while describing both the characteristics of various hydrocarbons and the facility – a place she refers to using words such as *rococo* and *antebellum* that are out of place in the modern edifice of an oil refinery but that link it with colonialism and slavery. The hydrocarbons interrupt in boldface eruptions of sounds like "**BA-ba-de-ba-pa / ba-ba-de-BA-pa**" and "**QUEEEE- / AWNX.**"[54] These are the "pitiful / shrieks and / squawks"[55] that are reformed inside the Fractionater. As Max Karpinski notes in his reading of the poem, the narrator casts what happens inside the Fractionator as a dance party – a ball.[56] Yet, as the tour continues and the Fractionater takes on resonances with zoos, plantations, prisons, and Canada's Indian residential schools, it dawns on the visitors, as well as the reader, that the Fractionater is a site of imprisonment, forced labour, and torture. When the narrator says that the role of the facility "is to distill / volatiles" and ultimately to

re-
shape
their
alpha
bets[,][57]

the Fractionater is exposed as a way of managing the polyvalence of carbon.[58] Carbon's "alpha / bets" can be arranged into the molecular structures of desirable hydrocarbons and waste products that an oil refinery produces; these are permissible ways for hydrocarbons to spell or speak in petroculture – as energy source, plastic, pharmaceutical chemical, etc. The refinery also "bets" on the persistence of the colonial petro-economy, and along with it the dominance of particular narratives about the relationships between hydrocarbons and humans. It is the narrator's job to stick to these narratives, despite all evidence to the contrary.

Speaking over the loud noises of the hydrocarbons, the unreliable narrator says,

do not
be naïve

these pentanes
are merely
feigning pain[.]

Her warning not to be naïve about the perceived pain of hydrocarbons is a reminder of dominant colonial and modern logic that claims it would be silly to think of hydrocarbons as anything but dumb objects. Despite this, the narrator's statement that the pentanes are "merely / feigning pain" suggests that she recognizes them as sentient beings – and that she knowingly perpetrates epistemic violence by denying that hydrocarbons feel the pain of extraction, refining, or combustion. After she offers to "translate" the speech of the pentanes, the visitors cannot tell whether it is "*Pentane 1*" or the tour guide who makes the "thank god / it's Faraday" joke that reveals the Pentanes in the Fractionater are working, not playing or dancing. "*Pentane 2*" muses (through the narrator/translator),

what poet
do i quote
before i
explode?[59]

echoing both Frantz Fanon's statement "The Negro is a toy in the white man's hands; so, in order to shatter the hellish cycle, he explodes" and Langston Hughes's "Harlem," where the speaker wonders, "What happens to a dream deferred" – "*Or does it explode*?"[60] While the tour guide tries but fails to relegate the hydrocarbons to the category of inanimate objects, the hydrocarbons fail, in turn, to speak in a way that the guests can understand, or that can cross the divide created by their representation. Many of the hydrocarbons are destined to "explode" inside a combustion engine that will contain and appropriate their speech as energy. Given this future combustion, exploding instead in an industrial accident, at a moment of their own choosing, may be a means for the hydrocarbons to speak in a way that subverts their representation and commodification.

Visitors to the Fractionater are offered a disturbing sensory experience of relating to hydrocarbons in captivity, held on the visitors' behalf for the purpose of extracting energy or work from them, and rendered dangerous through their captivity. "The Petrochemical Ball" reveals that the extraction and refining of hydrocarbons is a colonial endeavour and an expression of racial capitalism.[61] That is, it shows that hydrocarbons are endangered by the same extractive ideology that treats the bodies/lives (and the language/speech) of Indigenous, Black, and racialized people as less than fully human in order to perpetrate the dispossession, violence, and injustice that capitalist economies depend on to generate and extract profit.

Why Endangered Hydrocarbons Matter

Fugitive emissions are so prevalent that more than 50,000 barrels of oil escape into water or land every day. (That's the equivalent of 450,000 escaping human slaves.)

– Andrew Nikiforuk[62]

They just lay there. *Like all fossil fuels always and everywhere,* the coal first exploited by the British was utterly impassive, plucked from underground, removed from its eternal stillness, fuels for the machines of men and fossilized to boot: by definition, instruments for the power of (some) humans.

– Andreas Malm[63]

No geology is neutral.
– Kathryn Yusoff[64]

Editors Imre Szeman and Dominic Boyer include selected poems from *Endangered Hydrocarbons* in their 2017 anthology *Energy Humanities*, which gathers key texts for scholars of energy in the humanities and social sciences. Noting this inclusion, along with the resonance between the two *EH* titles, I draw this chapter to a close by reading *Endangered Hydrocarbons* as theory that makes a vital intervention in the energy humanities' thinking about animacy. In one key example where there is room for more expansive thinking about animacy, human ecologist Andreas Malm's important historical-materialist book *Fossil Capital* demonstrates that the rise of coal-fuelled steam power was pivotal to the industrialization of cotton mills in early-nineteenth-century England and the birth of capitalism, so that capital has always been fossil capital. In his subsequent book *The Progress of This Storm*, Malm expresses derision for new-materialist scholars' interest in the agency and mattering of "inanimate" objects such as coal, as seen in the epigraph above. With respect for Malm's impactful work, and with understanding for why an interest in animacy might seem frivolous, I believe there are indeed good reasons to be more careful about our consideration of animacy in the energy humanities. *Endangered Hydrocarbons* is animacy theory that uses serious linguistic play with supposedly inanimate objects to reveal and exacerbate the deep linkages between coloniality, racism, and the petro-economy. It shows that just energy transition must involve the decolonization of energy.

The most troubling poem in *Endangered Hydrocarbons* is "Uppity Molecules," a poem that figures *fugitive emissions* (accidental leaks of hydrocarbons) as fugitive slaves.[65] Equating inefficiencies in the infrastructures of oil and slavery in a way that parallels Nikiforuk's most egregious mixed metaphors, Battler inserts the names of hydrocarbons, refinery emissions, and oil-industry infrastructures into eighteenth-century advertisements placed in the *Virginia Gazette* by enslavers seeking the return of escaped enslaved people. Battler calls the fugitive hydrocarbons *uppity*, using a term with a history of describing African American people who supposedly refuse to stay in their rightful places, beginning in the Jim Crow era and extending to recent racist comments about Barack and Michelle Obama[66] – a term that could also be used to describe the tendency of light hydrocarbons like natural gas to rise and escape. "Uppity Molecules" recasts narratives of escaped enslaved people from Virginia as narratives of fugitive emissions in Alberta, in places like Caroline (site of a sour gas field and the Caroline Gas Complex, formerly owned by Shell) and Cold Lake (site of Imperial Oil's Cold Lake in-situ heavy oil operation). Through this relocation, the poem partially materializes what historian Afua Cooper has called the "bulldozed and ploughed over" history of slavery in Canada.[67] It creates a parallel (while mocking a purported equivalence) between two areas of willful ignorance – about Canada's history as an enslaving country and as an extractive country that endangers hydrocarbons and humans.

Playful but not funny, "Uppity Molecules" leans into the mixed imagery of the energy slave; it risks straying into what might be considered intolerable content to query whether or how such mixing can be expedient, amusing, or acceptable. The absurd narrative of the escaped, bearded, fiddling, and married hydrocarbon METHYL might be comical if it were not overlaid on both a reprehensible claim on the life of an escaped enslaved human and a leak of toxic natural gas.[68] Through distorted but still-legible references to torture and the enslaver's offer of a pistol as a reward for the return of METHYL, Battler exposes the layers of violence and appropriation at work in the poem – perpetrated by the enslaver, by the *Virginia Gazette*, by her source that reprints the advertisements,[69] by Battler herself, and by other users of the energy-slave metaphor. Through its absurd substitutions, "Uppity Molecules" also condemns the audacious corporations and Albertan and Canadian petrostates that continue extracting, refining, and leaking hydrocarbons, even in the face of catastrophic climate change and Indigenous and non-Indigenous opposition and protests. "Uppity Molecules" enacts but does not really explain its animacy theory, leaving significant room for interpretation and offense in its linking of the energy systems of slavery and fossil capital. Nonetheless, I read the poem, ultimately, as calling for the decolonization of energy.

Recent interventions by Black and antiracist energy-humanities scholars have shown that fossil capitalism is, and has always been, racial-fossil capitalism. Environmental anthropologist and former energy-democracy activist Myles Lennon's article "Decolonizing Energy: Black Lives Matter and Technoscientific Expertise Amid Solar Transitions" shows that the modern energy system is modelled after the energy regimes of slavery and settler colonialism. These regimes cast African and Indigenous peoples as "less-than-human" while also denigrating and claiming ownership over non-humans, so that energy became an abstract concept, "a lifeless thing in the debased realm of matter."[70] Similarly, in her study of Black feminist theories of the inhuman in relation to "White Geology" including the proposed geological epoch of the Anthropocene,[71] Yusoff argues that anti-Blackness is foundational to and entwined with fossil capital. She notes that not only coal but also slave-produced cotton were necessary for the birth of capitalism.[72] Linked distinctions between "the *inhuman as matter* and the *inhuman as race*" create an "inhuman proximity" between Black and Indigenous subjects and hydrocarbons that exposes them to violence and harm.[73] In his book chapter "Dead Labor: On Racial Capital and Fossil Capital," anthropologist Ryan Cecil Jobson interprets W.E.B. Du Bois's 1935 book *Black Reconstruction in America, 1860–1880* as a theorization of racial-fossil capital, based on a note in Du Bois's personal papers that suggests reading the book as "[a] story of the economic development of inanimate things – land, coal, steel, etc., in which men are things."[74] Jobson contends that the concepts of both dead labour and the stockpiling of energy originate in the energy system of slavery, and must be abolished. Each of these scholars argues for radical antiracist and decolonial energy-justice work – which is also animacy work – that can bring on what Yusoff calls "*the end of this world* and the possibility of others."[75]

As these examples from recent energy-humanities theory show, the decolonization of energy is what is at stake in the naming and creative exploration of an animacy theory that links endangered humans and hydrocarbons. Written before the publication of these texts, and using innovative poetics as animacy theory, Battler's "Uppity Molecules" makes an uneasy and fraught intervention that highlights the racism of our energy system.

Conclusion

Endangered Hydrocarbons reveals that Canadians' relationships with hydrocarbons are colonial and racist; its playful and troubling poetics stimulates movement toward a decolonized conception of energy and of relationship with fossil fuels. Stó:lō poet and orator Lee Maracle has described respectful relationship with water as kin, in a way that I propose to adapt for imagining respectful relationship with oil: "*We do not own the water, the water owns itself. We are responsible for ensuring that we do not damage the water. We do not have an absolute right to use and abuse the water; we must take care of the water and ensure that we have a good relationship with it. This relationship is based on mutual respect.*"[76] The idea that oil, like water, is sovereign and owns itself undermines the many political uses to which it has been turned and demands a new ethics for relating to lively hydrocarbons, other humans, and the land, which must be part of a just energy system to come.

Safety Reminder

Lindsay Bird

Donnie's last sound was a boot
slip, sucked fifty feet down

into the tailings pond with the rest of him,
boiled in a banished concoction of chemistry.

Even the geese change their migration,
giving up instincts their parents

put into them as eggs, mapping strange
miles to avoid the air cannons.

Nothing remains of Donnie except
a murmured lunchroom tale:

the tailings ponds will eat you whole
and in a thousand years whoever's left

to wander this wasted muskeg
won't find a single human bone.

"Safety Reminder" by Linsday Bird, reprinted with permission of the author and publisher from *Boom Time* (Kentville, NS: Gaspereau, 2019), 23.

CHAPTER 7

Boom Time, Giant Time, and Other Elsewhens of Lindsay Bird's *Boom Time*

Lindsay Bird is an unmarked/white poet and CBC journalist who grew up in Toronto and who now lives in Corner Brook, Newfoundland. Her first poetry collection, *Boom Time*, was published by Gaspereau Press in 2019. *Boom Time* is a sequence of semi-autobiographical lyric poems based on the two years Bird spent living at work camps and working at Athabasca oil sands mining and construction sites near Fort McMurray, Alberta, between 2006 and 2008. Bird's post-undergraduate stint working in the tar sands coincided with the height of an oil boom that turned to bust with the financial crisis and recession of 2008.[1] The book is set during the boom, but it was written during the succession of recuperations, declines, and busts that came after, including the tragic 2016 Fort McMurray wildfire known as "The Beast" and austerity measures including the increased automation of oil-sands jobs.[2] *Boom Time* therefore layers a tone of disidentificatory irony over the mostly present-tense narration by a reticent, impersonal, mostly first-person narrator who lives in the moment, her words offering imaginative and playful imagery for her experiences and surroundings while glancing off the emotions and traumas involved in being one of the few women in a tar-sands work camp.

This chapter offers a close reading of Bird's *Boom Time* that is focused on time. Drawing on Kate Beaton's Founding Fathers comics, it situates Bird's poetry in the temporal-spatial setting of what geographer Stephanie Wakefield has called the "Anthropocene back loop" – a phase of potential dissolution or recuperation of the project of colonial modernity in which its violence, costs, and other negative impacts are laid bare.[3] From this perspective, I interpret Bird's *Boom Time* as the irreverent and questioning poetics of a daughter talking back to and reframing the narratives of industrialization as progress put forward by oil-sands founders (such as S.C. Ells, whose work is discussed in chapter 1) and other Anthropocene giants. One way of reading Bird's *Boom Time* is as a series of playful attempts to parse and perhaps balance out the scales of time and place that are jumbled in the Anthropocene and in the tar sands.[4]

Like many of the oil-worker poets I study, Bird is reluctant to criticize the oil-sands industry that employs so many hard-working people and that helped her pay off her student loans.[5] Her poetry also makes almost no reference to the Indigenous Peoples on Treaty 8 territory – Cree, Dene, and Métis peoples whose homes, territories, cultures, and well-being are intertwined with and profoundly impacted by the tar-sands industry. As Clinton N. Westman, Tara L. Joly, and Lena Gross argue in *Extracting Home in the Oil Sands*, although the Athabasca oil sands region is often constructed in the dominant settler-colonial imaginary as an "extractive zone" or a hinterland, "for many Indigenous Peoples in northern Alberta, the landscape is a homeland, full of knowing, intentional beings with whom humans are responsible for entering into just relationships."[6] Keeping these absences and elisions in mind, my reading *of* and *between* the lines of *Boom Time* takes liberties in its attention to what is implicit, unspoken, or repressed in this text.

Looping Back on Founding Fathers

Bird worked in the tar sands with her friend Kate Beaton, a now-famous comic artist who was also paying off student loans, drawing comics at night while living and working in the same work camp as Bird. Beaton's graphic memoir *Ducks: Two Years in the Oil Sands* was published to critical acclaim in 2022; it features Bird as one of the characters and tells some of the same stories that are told in *Boom Time.* Elsewhere, I have drawn on Beaton's comic series about American founding fathers to frame my work on Ells as "giving Ells the Founding Fathers treatment."[7] This chapter draws inspiration from Beaton's comics as well as Bird's poem "The Peter Pond Mall," in which notorious fur-trade founder Peter Pond

presides over
hard bargains
and one hell
of a parking
lot.[8]

Like Bird's reframing of the mall and parking lot as appropriate monuments to Pond's extractive legacy, this chapter loops back to tar-sands founding fathers, including Ells, revisiting their modernizing visions from a blighted back-loop perspective.

Beaton's comics series Founding Fathers (in a Mall) and Founding Fathers (Stuck in an Amusement Park) imagine famous American historical figures in ubiquitous twenty-first-century settings. In the first panel of one two-panel comic drawn in Beaton's rough, cartoonish style and titled "Infinity," a man in eighteenth-century garb points to a roller coaster and expresses to another his hope that the "chain of carriages" will bring them "home" – presumably back to their own time and place (see figure 7.1). In the second panel, the second founding father, who has seen the trajectory of the roller coaster, dashes the other's hopes, saying, in one speech balloon, "It is merely a circle of violence," and, in a second balloon, "and then you retch." "Infinity" can be read as metacommentary on what Daniel Marrone calls Beaton's anachronistic production of "a history that is constantly folding over on itself":[9]

Figure 7.1
"Infinity" from the series Founding Fathers (Stuck in an Amusement Park) by Kate Beaton.

the Founding Fathers comics' seemingly infinite loops of jokes and juxtapositions represent the Fathers as variously appalled and enthralled by the dystopian, late-capitalist ends to which their principles and visions have been applied. At another level, the minutes-long roller-coaster loop serves as an allegory for the violent project of homemaking on someone else's land – a "slow disturbance" that links its founders to ongoing dispossession, genocide, and harm through what architecture and media scholar Rafico Ruiz describes as infrastructural "chains of settler colonial materiality and accountability."[10] The point in the roller-coaster loop where "you retch" is a temporal marker where past promises, as seen from the back loop, are emptied out and revealed to have been part of the "circle of violence" all along. In the back loop, contemporary concerns about time are animated not only through the proposed naming of the geological epoch of the Anthropocene but also through the politics of decolonization, anticolonialism, antiracism, and reparations; the threats of catastrophic climate change, extinction, and apocalypse; and emergent visions for energy transition.

Beaton's roller-coaster scene anticipates urban geographer Stephanie Wakefield's application of resilience ecology theory to the proposed geological age of the Anthropocene in *Anthropocene Back Loop*. Like other natural-cultural systems, the Anthropocene is subject to patterns of growth, stability, fragmentation, dissolution, and adaptation that can be imagined as a figure eight, with opportunities for experimentation, resistance, and change arising especially in the back loop, where the logics and structures of the entire system are in question. Wakefield considers the twentieth-century era of megaprojects such as dams and oil-sands mines as exemplifying the front-loop sense of "being a part of an order that was going somewhere better"[11] – like a roller coaster chugging upward on its tracks. The back loop, in contrast, is "our present, the moment of the naming of the Anthropocene (as a failure), in which the past (front loop) has not disappeared, like points trailing behind on a line, but is erupting in unpredictable ways in the present."[12] What is revealed in the eruptions of climate change, precarity, fragmentation, and confusion is that the modernist-colonialist-capitalist system has always been a "circle of violence." With "the founding fathers" and giants recurring as ominous and also punning presences of so-called great men in *Boom Time*, I read this book for its back-loop perspective on the roller coaster of the tar sands.

Boom Time

The multilayered and onomatopoeic title of Bird's poetry collection is emphasized on its dust jacket, made of beige construction-paper stock, with a pen-and-ink drawing of an oil-sands refinery under construction printed and debossed along the bottom, extending from the back to the front cover in a darker-beige colour like faded newsprint or an aging photo (see figure 7.2). Near the top of the front cover, stamped into the paper like the treads of a tire or a shoe, are the staggered words *BOOM TIME*, spelled in all caps in oversized font the colour of dried blood. The word *TIME* is offset in a way that suggests motion – as if it were about to pounce on the poet's name, which is printed in a smaller, mixed-case font near the open maw of the letter *E*. The effect – of noise, violence, power, and dissonant scale-jumping – is reinforced with the page turn past the bitumen-black cover pages to an inside cover with the same heavy-set title, this time in bright-blood red, hovering like the underside of a boot above a sepia-toned drawing of a tar-sands work camp, shrinking the camp dwellers standing outside their ATCO-trailer residences to ant size (see figure 7.3). Next comes the page turn past the dedication[13] to the opening poem, "First Day in Fort Mac," where the speaker and other newcomers "stumble off the bus / in our new boots to see / what eats grass and what eats us."[14] The speaker scrambles to position herself not only in a harsh climate but also in an extractive zone and an industry food chain that treat virtually everything – fossilized prehistoric life, lakes, forests, muskeg, nearby communities, and human and non-human lives – as available to be turned into money or fuel. The work camp she has arrived at is a residential camp for migrant workers, also known as a "man camp," a toxic and dangerous location notorious for harmful effects on nearby communities and especially on Indigenous women, girls, and two-spirit people.[15] Boom time in the vicinity of the town sometimes referred to as "Fort McMoney" offers the narrator a chance to make quick cash, as long as she can handle the violence – that is, the deprivation, endangerment, and culpability – involved in oil-sands work.

Boom Time is, as the title suggests, about time – specifically, about the strange, short temporality of "boom time" as experienced by an educated-yet-unskilled worker temporarily employed as part of a transient workforce, unmoored in relation to both place and time. The title poem begins,

Figure 7.2
Boom Time front cover with illustration by Adam Smith, design by Andrew Steeves.

We swing fat and hammocked
between bust and bust,
feet up on the leather ottoman that signifies
the good life.[16]

The text of the poem zigzags or swerves, unhinged from the left-justified form of most of the other poems in the book. Turned sideways, as shown in figure 7.4, I can read this as a concrete poem: it resembles the graphs of resource prices that chart the boom-and-bust cycles to which it refers. It also resembles the tracks of a roller coaster. The imagery of Bird's first stanza in "Boom Time" uses complex and perhaps mixed metaphors. It conflates the graph, with its roller-coaster-like ups and downs, with the experiences and the lives of an indeterminate "we." This "we" may refer to industry workers; it may refer to all Canadians who ostensibly benefit from trickle-down petro-

Figure 7.3
Boom Time inside front cover with illustration by Adam Smith, design by Andrew Steeves.

economics in a petrostate; or it may refer to Anthropocene humans careening toward catastrophic climate change. In any of these cases, it privileges (or perhaps parodies) an elite subset of these groups, while marginalizing (or perhaps siding with) those who experience boom time differently. The poem constructs an image of this "we" swinging in a hammock "between bust and bust." The image is tethered, unexpectedly, to bust time, as if the bust (and not the boom) were inevitable.

I asked my child – a better artist than me – to help me draw the imagery: what does it look like? We printed out a graph produced by the independent environmental journalism website *The Narwhal*, which charts the price per barrel of Western Canadian Select crude oil from January 2006 to March 2020, using data from the Alberta government.[17] We first drew in the hammock under the plot, dangling and seemingly detached below, but it was not until we inverted the graph, making the busts the highest data points

BOOM TIME

We swing fat and hammocked
between bust and bust,
feet up on the leather ottoman that signifies
the good life.

We've made it, for a limited
time only. So we are told,
by someone on the radio
who sounds bespectacled.

Figure 7.4
Lindsay Bird's poem "Boom Time" as a boom-and-bust graph.

and letting the hammock swing into the depths of the boom, that we felt we had gotten it right (see figure 7.5). This imagery makes busts rather than booms the thing a worker relies on, comforting tethering points that ground "boom time" in a sense of self, and of home, that exists elsewhere or *elsewhen*. The hammock drawing makes me wonder: How can a person, or a culture, be so comfortable amid such precarity, like sleeping on a roller coaster? It also makes me notice how the curve of the hammock, like the very notion of a settler-colonial "good life" premised on extraction, can smooth over some of the ups and downs. This image speaks to the lulling effect of petropoetics – what Dymphny Dronyk depicts as being *rocked* (to sleep or to a kind of apathy) by business as usual, so that even fracking and the fluctuations of the boom-and-bust economy come to be seen as natural, and even comforting.[18]

Following Denise Ferreira da Silva's work on "unpayable debt" as "negative accumulation" accrued by Black and Indigenous subjects in a colonial-racial-capitalist system,[19] I note that decoding this image creates a shadow graph that registers boom as deficit and loss – a medium to chart the negative,

Figure 7.5
"Bust Hammock" by Sheldon Unrau.

undesirable, and often unnoticed objects that accumulate during "boom time." An inverted chart of boom time is a diagram of extraction as negative accumulation: the boom is an open-pit mine that deepens as it grows, accumulating dispossession, exhaustion, violence, toxicity, and pollution. This inverse relationship between accumulation/dispossession and boom/bust matches the assertion by Indigenous scholars such as Potawatomi environmental philosopher Kyle Powys Whyte that Indigenous peoples already live in "post-apocalyptic situations"[20] (in the terms of Bird's poem, a *bust*), as well as assertions by antiracist scholars such as inhuman geographer Kathryn Yusoff that the Anthropocene must be understood in terms of the "billion Black Anthropocenes" that make up its "shadow geology."[21] In a more colloquial example, an opinion piece for the *Park Rapids Enterprise* titled "The Time Thieves," Anishinaabe economist and water protector Winona LaDuke points to the absurdity of criminal charges of theft for "stealing time from Enbridge" being laid on water protectors who protested the construction of the Line 3 pipeline through Indigenous territory. From the water protectors' perspective, the pipeline company is the time thief, "taking time and natural resources from our future generations" and committing ecocide.[22] In her book *To Be a Water Protector: The Rise of the Wiindigoo Slayers*, LaDuke attributes the flawed and harmful logics of extractive industry and complicit governments to "Wiindigoo economics" – "a system based on colonization, wastefulness and ravenous greed, a system that destroys the very source of its own wealth and well-being, Mother Earth."[23] From the Anthropocene back loop, the megaprojects of the tar sands, Canadian settler colonialism, and modernity itself register as always having been negative accumulation and Wiindigoo economics.

The hammock image demonstrates how the resource economy creates and exacerbates the scalar mismatches that characterize our energy system and the dominant colonial land relations that subtend it. The human who lounges in this image is an Anthropocene or colonizing human – a giant with an oversized carbon footprint (which we might think of also as a time footprint) who, by overconsuming finite resources and emitting pollution, creates the conditions of scarcity expressed in the proclamation in the poem's second stanza that "We've made it, for a limited / time only."[24] In contrast to Indigenous notions of "the good life" (for example, the Anishinaabeg concept of minobimaatisiiwin),[25] as well as Indigenous and anticolonial notions of good land relations as involving reciprocity, relationship, and taking up one's responsibilities to the land that sustains us,[26] the hammock, the ottoman, the price index, and the "limited / time only" language of TV advertising represent tragic misrecognitions of *the good life.* Bird's narrator knows this, as demonstrated in the paltry accoutrements she mocks as symbols of a so-called good life. In a workshop I attended, "Indigenous Knowledges & Two-Eyed Seeing," Mi'kmaw Elder Albert Marshall described the inherent responsibilities that humans bear to "every living thing." Indigenous knowledge is special and sacred knowledge about those responsibilities, but, as he emphasizes, there is another sense in which all humans already know the basics of what our inherent responsibilities are.[27] Bird's italics for *the good life* signify an off-balance, extractive version of good living. The slanted letters reveal the worker's innate knowledge, fostered by moving between the separate material and ideological locations of home and mine, that "the good life" should be better than this.

If we think of the boom-and-bust cycle as a roller coaster that "we" all ride in a petro-economy, the hammock between busts represents boom time as a time when workers and other beneficiaries are buffered from the minor ups and downs. Of course, the wealth and comfort of oil sands workers who can afford, for instance, a leather ottoman or a fancy truck, is exaggerated and stereotyped in a culture where they often become the scapegoats of consumerist excess. Workers are easily condemned in individualist, neoliberal culture as perpetrators of ecocide and squanderers of resources, yet they are also treated as dispensable human resources by the corporations, executives, and billionaires they work for. Rather than lounging in hammocks or putting their feet up, they are working long hours, doing difficult and dangerous labour, and often living far away from their homes, families, and furniture. Migrant workers in the tar sands do the work of accumulation on behalf of oil companies, while treating the land where they work as an extractive zone they can take from without practising reciprocity, and while playing a role in accruing dispossession and harm for the human and non-human beings for whom the oil-sands region is a homeland. The claim to have "made it," or to be living the good life, is a disavowal of the ways in which they are also accumulating risk and harm themselves. Like that giant boot tread on the front cover, and like the "fog" of pollution that workers knowingly breathe in and sneeze out every day,[28] there are spectres that haunt the consciousness of the worker who considers themself lucky to work in the tar sands.

The title of the "Boom Time" poem may seem to privilege the chart-and-hammock metaphor for what boom time is like. But, like the "someone on the radio" who declares that "We've made it" – a supposed authority whose only qualification is that they "[sound] bespectacled" – the narrator of the poetry collection is unreliable, merely speculating, passing on rumours she hears in the work camp, and grasping for language and imagery.[29] The other poems in the book provide a range of other metaphors: boom time is watching concrete dry (48–9), or shovelling "dirt from one pile to another" (35). It is tailings ponds that resemble "[d]roopy drawers, period underwear" but with a "shimmer" that "you" can't help but be drawn toward (13). Boom time is buying a pet lizard, then deciding to take a trip, and leaving the lizard at the bus terminal to freeze in the snow (72). Boom time is having an affair, and making love while listening to the downstairs neighbour being beaten by her spouse (56). It is a grisly death on the shoulder of Highway 63, also known as the "Highway of Death," perpetrated by an unknown monster that "slunk / out of the muskeg" (44–5). It is attending a "Rager at Gregoire Lake" through a Northern summer night when "dusk touches / dawn" and the sun barely sets (14), and it is working through a winter day "as the sun barely lifts / a bored eyebrow to the horizon" (60). In the temporality structured by shift work, turnarounds, and trips home, boom time is often about "[f]illing time" (52) and killing time (27) – with parties, TV, and old-fashioned binge-watching with DVD box sets; with knitting, DIY tattoos, and outrageous bets;

with homesick rituals like a Newfoundland Screech-In where workers kiss a flown-in cod (52); and with gossip, harassment, humiliation, and threats; with the disidentifications of blending in, keeping your head down, and going along with things that make you uncomfortable, from groping superintendents to pollution and ecocide. Bird's empathetic narrative poems portray precarious and toxic working and living conditions with measures of kindness, sorrow, solidarity, and oblivion.

Elsewhen

Scattered throughout Bird's *Boom Time* is a sequence of numbered "Elsewhere" poems with titles such as "Elsewhere No. 1: Eatons, Etc" (20). Each poem is a flashback to the narrator's childhood or young-adult life before going to work in Fort McMurray – to shopping at the Eaton's department store, to a camping disaster on a family road trip, and to other scenes from a time that the narrator places "before the decline of the empire" (20). The narrator is nostalgic not only for the "elsewhere" of her memories but also for her own naïveté in unrecoverable and unredeemable *elsewhens*. The "Elsewhere" poems conjure a settler-colonial-capitalist optimism that journalist Chris Turner describes in his history of the oil sands as "the High Modern ideal of progress that defined the twentieth century, that trust in bigger machines and better technology to fuel the good life."[30] Turner argues, simplistically, that the first tar-sands megaprojects were built and the industry was born during the dominance of such a High Modernist ideal, and that the industry is now caught, unfairly, in a clash between that old ideal and a twenty-first-century ecological one. In Wakefield's terms, this condition of being caught is far from unfair; instead, the Anthropocene back loop is where the optimism and bluster of the front loop catches up with the reality that the oil-sands project has been predicated on time theft and ecocide all along. Bird's "Elsewhere" poems may express a wish to work in the industry at a time when she would not have to feel so bad about it. Living in twenty-first-century boom time involves knowing that the results of modernist projects such as the tar sands, Canadian colonialism, and the global energy system are depletion, pollution, dispossession, and extinction.

The poem "Safety Reminder" recites a camp legend, "a murmured lunchroom tale" about Donnie, a worker who slipped and was sucked into a tailings pond. It ends with another elsewhen, or perhaps an *or-elsewhen*:

the tailings ponds will eat you whole
and in a thousand years whoever's left

to wander this wasted muskeg
won't find a single human bone.[31]

This elsewhen is a terminus of settler-colonial imagination. The only end of extraction it can imagine is one in which the humans have taken everything and either died off or abandoned the now-uninhabitable land. Echoing the use of the noun *waste*, following John Locke, as a settler-colonial term that deems Indigenous land underutilized and justifies its appropriation,[32] *wasted* is, as petrocultural scholar Jennifer Wenzel has observed, an adjective used to describe colonized land treated as overburden and laid waste by extraction.[33] In the context of an industry that treats Indigenous homelands as a sacrifice zone, we might speculate that the barely imagined survivor in the Athabasca region in a thousand years is an Indigenous person. As Whyte has argued about "Indigenous Climate Studies," Indigenous peoples have deep histories that extend beyond "the brief, but highly disruptive colonial, capitalist, and industrial periods";[34] they can conceive of being the "whoever's left" that Bird's narrator struggles to imagine. "Safety Reminder" gestures, bleakly and perhaps unconsciously, beyond "boom time" to the existence of knowledges and practices for survival even in a post-extraction wasteland.

Giant Time

In a different imagined sequence of elsewhens, the unreliable narrator of *Boom Time* imagines "giant time" as both preceding and following boom time. Early in the collection, in the poem titled "Orientation," the narrator speculates,

This is where
the last giants lived
when the world decided to
        shrink to reasonable size,
and you only find
that out after the waivers,
        left to gawk at the ankles
                of everything.[35]

This speculative thread is picked up again in the final poem of the collection, titled "Giant Time," which imagines the post-apocalyptic return of the giants, who have "only been just over / the hill this whole time" (73). In the wasted landscape of the oil sands, the giants make themselves at home again:

> They snuggle rumps around
> in mine pits, a muddy lingerie.
> Snap smokestacks into cigars,
> lean back, puff and sigh.
>
> Finally put that vast sky
> into perspective. (74)

This is a playful, time-based explanation for the astonishing scale of tar-sands mines that could hold "a good / sized town down there, / with one of everything" (33), and of heavy-hauler trucks the size of two-storey houses. It resonates with the front cover images and calls to mind aerial photographs of the oil sands by Edward Burtynsky, Warren Cariou, and Louis Helbig – particularly some of Helbig's images in *Beautiful Destruction*, which evoke the sense that the trucks, pipes, and ATCO trailers they depict might be children's building blocks and other toys. The giants of "Giant Time" seem harmless enough, occupying a middle ground among Anglocentric giant tales between the blood-thirsty giant of Jack and the Beanstalk and the Friendly Giant of the long-running Canadian television series.

Bird's imagined giants may seem fantastical, and perhaps they are merely a fantasy, a fairy-tale diversion from accounting for the avarice and greed it takes for Anthropocene humans (especially the ruling classes who run corporations and petrostates) to lounge, smoke, and frolic amid the suffering of others. Yet, the cover images imply that the giants are also threatening, and the posthuman time they inhabit serves as a warning, an *or-elsewhen* of boom time that I wish to consider, briefly, as the return of the Wiindigoo or Wheetago. LaDuke writes, "In our Anishinaabe stories, the Wiindigoo is a giant murderous monster that used to rampage through the north woods, fueled by an insatiable greed and a relentless desire for human flesh. Fossil fuel era capitalism is like the Wiindigoo: a predator economics, the economics of a cannibal."[36] A similar once-human, giant monster exists in many Indigenous traditions, including the Cree Weetigo stories told in the tar-sands region. Anishinaabe scholar Basil Johnston describes the fearsome Weendigo as a warning against greed and selfishness and an exhortation to practise moderation.[37] He describes "corporations, conglomerates, and multinationals" as "Modern Weendigoes."[38] By drawing on these Indigenous traditions, I am suggesting that grasping for giant metaphors when trying to account for the distorted scales of time and space in the oil sands is an impulse driven by an "energy unconscious" of the tar sands industry;[39] it reaches, unknowingly or clumsily, for a monster who is said to have stalked the territory now known as the oil sands since long before the industry was born.

In Tłı̨chǫ Dene author Richard Van Camp's short story "On the Wings of this Prayer," a person from the future sends a message back to the present day about a zombie apocalypse to come, a world where tar-sands extraction has brought back the Wheetago.[40] They say, "You must stop the Tar Sands. Do not bring cancer to our Mother. Do not unleash them."[41] Together, Van Camp's story and LaDuke's Wiindigoo economics recast as Wiindigoo the venerated "founding fathers" of the oil sands and the corporate giants who now operate and profit from the industry, who are, like Peter Pond and the shoppers in Bird's poem "The Peter Pond Mall,"

> in search
> of a buck,
> a beaver pelt,
> bitumen,
> whatever's in demand
> with the white
> man.[42]

Workers are at risk of being infected by the cannibalistic spirit of extractive industry. So, too, are those of us who are farther removed but who have our feet up as beneficiaries of an ecocidal industry. We all bear responsibility to the land and to one another, but the most frightening monsters and giants stalking and haunting *Boom Time* are those who profit most and who have their hammocks hitched the highest, who move around resources – workers, Indigenous communities, ATCO trailers, land, and water – as if they were toys. This is the unspeakable shadow story of Lindsay Bird's *Boom Time* – the cannibalism that links boom time with giant time, glimpsed in "Safety Reminder," where the real story is that humans eat Mother Earth and other humans in the tailings ponds.

A shadow reading of *Boom Time* suggests a politics that LaDuke describes as being water protectors and Wiindigoo slayers. This does not mean killing people; instead, it means killing extractive projects such as the Trans Mountain pipeline being built by the Canadian government, despite Indigenous protests, in the midst of a climate emergency; the Coastal GasLink pipeline being built on Wet'suwet'en territory, with the Royal Canadian Mounted Police protecting the interests of TC Energy over the rights of Indigenous Peoples; and any new fossil-fuel projects at all, which the International Energy Agency has indicated are not in line with a pathway to net zero carbon emissions by 2050.[43] I like to read the lines of Bird's poem "Orientation," which are intended to refer to a past time "when the world decided to / shrink to reasonable size"[44] and when the giants went away once before as also an invitation to imagine a future world, an elsewhen shaped by a decision taken now to shrink the dominant modes of human living "to reasonable size." It is through practices of moderation, generosity, reciprocity, and care that we can slay the Wiindigoo and implement anticolonial lifeways for a just energy transition.

Birds Migrate at Night, Mostly Unseen

Kelly Shepherd

> *though they said, We will build*
> *silver paradise with a bulldozer*
> – Margaret Atwood

Earth that may once have been dug for the dead
but never deep enough to hide pipelines,
dries in the sun. Gleaming blue clay,

dark as Prairie winter night,
flakes and turns to dust
in the treads of machinery.

There's too many of us here –
we can't be seen just standing around!

The foreman pointed with his cigarette,
You four – go and hide in that trench!

Shepherd's hand on the damp trench wall,
fingers on a vein of clay,
he found a fossilized mollusc,
freshwater clamstone powdery white,
long-buried memory of pelican water
that once covered this place.

"This map is ideal for planning applications
because it shows a larger area at a smaller scale."

He hid in the trench all afternoon, being paid to hide,
one hand on cool clay, the other holding that shell.
Stillness of that bright cold lake louder in his mind.

"Birds Migrate at Night, Mostly Unseen" by Kelly Shepherd, reprinted with permission of the author and publisher from *Insomnia Bird* (Saskatoon: Thistledown, 2018), 95.

CONCLUSION

Feeling Rough: Oil-Worker Poetry, Energy Justice, and the Cultural Politics of Emotion

Kelly Shepherd is a white-settler poet, poetry editor, writing instructor, and former construction worker who was born in British Columbia and now lives in Edmonton, Alberta. His poetry about oil work includes the 2014 chapbook *Fort McMurray Tricksters* (Alfred Gustav, 2014) and individual poems collected in his poetry collections *Shift* (Thistledown, 2016) and *Insomnia Bird* (Thistledown, 2018). Influenced by the traditions of work poetry, eco-poetry, and prairie poetry, Shepherd composes his poetry first by hand in small notebooks that he carries with him everywhere – even to worksites – and in which he also records snippets of found text and conversation.[1] "Birds Migrate at Night, Mostly Unseen" is a lyric and found-text poem about pipeline-construction work from *Insomnia Bird.*[2]

The poem begins with an epigraph from Margaret Atwood's poem "A Bus along St. Clair: December," which closes her book *The Journals of Susanna Moodie.* The poem is spoken in the voice of the wilderness – a voice in tension, as in S.C. Ells's poetry, with colonial modernity, and with those who try, foolishly, to "build / silver paradise with a bulldozer." Atwood's poem concludes,

> Turn, look down:
> there is no city;

this is the center of a forest

your place is empty[.][3]

It is not surprising that Atwood's lines would occur to a Canadian poet writing about being surrounded not only by "machinery" and shining metal but also a great deal of disturbed land. Atwood's text is canonical; its settler-colonial take on wilderness as an object of repressed fascination and fear is emblematic of a dominant literary tradition that ecopoets like Shepherd seek to trouble and shift. Shepherd's poem is narrated in a third-person voice that seems at first to be distant but that turns out to be focalized through the perspective of "Shepherd," a persona of the author, describing a scene that he also participates in. Shepherd's name evokes the pastoral poetic tradition in a petropastoral scene reminiscent of Mathew Henderson's description of an oil worker's job being to "[t]end the rusted steel like a shepherd,"[4] with a palpable tension between the impulses to aestheticize even the churned-up land that resembles a "Prairie winter night" (with a capital P to draw attention to the impulse and its tradition) and to cast the land as a blighted dystopia. Shepherd's critique of extraction depends upon that tension, as seen in the mention of graves that the workers' terraforming may disturb, which reminds readers that the land has long been inhabited and cared for by Indigenous peoples for whom it remains a homeland.

Two lines of found text, "This map is ideal for planning applications / because it shows a larger area at a smaller scale," represent an "extractive view," as theorized by Macarena Gómez-Barris – a vertical, distant way of seeing that makes land appear both empty and extractible.[5] On the ground, and in a kind of middle ground of extraction, the foreman's voice is shown in italics that also equate his petropoetic voice with Atwood's. This is abrupt, imperative "rig talk"[6] that is aware of its own absurdity, yet also performing and enforcing logics of extraction that cast workers, like the resources they extract (or transport), as objects – as replaceable and interchangeable parts, "tanned gears" or "expendable machine[s]."[7] Being selected to hide in a trench for hours dehumanizes a worker who, although he is "being paid to hide," is also being shown to be a tool that can be stored away until it is needed. The narrator experiences the inhuman proximity that extractive logics create between inhuman resources such as fossils, workers as "human resources," and racialized/marginalized humans.[8]

The foreman's command for the worker to hide in the trench is an insult and an inversion that becomes a chance to see the land from a "submerged perspective"[9] – a close-up, grainy view of wet, cold clay and a fossil, embedded in the trench wall, which Shepherd clings to all afternoon. Holding on to this nonliving being that once lived in an ancient lake on the same place where he is standing, Shepherd assumes a submerged perspective where, to rephrase Atwood's line, *this is the center of a glacial lake.* Instead of feeling removed from the action above, he finds himself submerged in the land that was once water, feeling kinship with pelicans, molluscs, fossils, and human ancestors. This scene of colonial-capitalist extraction (violence to the land and its inhabitants) and exploitation (violence to the worker), is also a scene of care or love, in which an extraction worker and a fossil extend care to one another. Despite the noise of the worksite above, Shepherd is submerged in the "Stillness of that bright cold lake louder in his mind." His disidentification with oil work and identification with the land represents the potential to shift colonial geontologies (conceptions of the relationship between the living and nonliving)[10] and to imagine a different kind of petropoetics. I open this conclusion with Shepherd's image of complicity and care as a way in to thinking about what I learned by writing this book and what it offers to the energy humanities and movements for energy justice.

■ ■ ■

We don't need to identify with one another, but we need to converge at the site of our disidentification.
– Judith Butler[11]

I feel a lot of things.
– Kate Beaton[12]

The Rough Poets is a chronologically organized reading of seven poetry collections that links these works as examples of petrocultural disidentification and that claims they constitute a little-known tradition in Canadian literature. The seven chapters draw on cultural theory by non-oil workers to examine specific examples of disidentificatory performances, politics, and theories in oil-worker poetry. Yet, the academic language of disidentification would be unfamiliar and perhaps off-putting to many of the oil-worker poets I study in this book. They have their own names for ambivalent cooperation with extraction: *rig talk*, *contrary infatuation*, *shepherding*, being in *relationship with truth*, or engaging in the relations of *the lease*, *endangered hydrocarbons*, *moving to climate change hours*, or *boom time*. I have argued throughout *The Rough Poets* that oil-worker poets are theorists of petropoetics and disidentification who do not need theory to explain their work and their worlds to them. Stepping back from outsider theories of disidentification, this concluding chapter considers what oil-worker poetry has to say about mixed and ambivalent feeling as a structure of feeling of oil work. It asks how, in a climate emergency, a familiar, disidentificatory sense of feeling a lot of things at once might constitute common ground for an energy-justice movement that includes oil workers.

Disidentification combines resistance with going along with and even loving something that is problematic. Whereas other theorists are interested in the specifics of disidentification, including how to distinguish it from identification and counteridentification, I like what Judith Butler does when they note that every identification is also a disidentification, and when they suggest that it is possible to use a common-yet-undefined sense of disidentification as ground for solidarity.[13] Imagine, for example, a group of people who agree with the pro-industry slogan "I ❤ Canadian Oil & Gas." Each will have their own reasons for loving oil and gas (maybe they work in the industry, or their loved ones do, or a job in the oil patch got them through college, or they fear the Canadian economy or their local economy would collapse without oil and gas, or they think oil from Canada is more ethical than oil from other parts of the world, or they cannot imagine how Canadians would heat their homes and get around without fossil fuels). Even though they choose this identification, they may also have reasons not to love oil and gas (they are affected by environmental or health impacts, or they lost their land or way of life because of the industry, or they had a work injury, or their loved one has asthma, or they worry about climate change, or they think the industry makes them or their community look bad). Butler's proposal to "converge at the site of our disidentification" suggests that the same people who love oil and gas could also come together around not loving oil and gas. Just like everyone has their own reasons for identifying, it is possible to disidentify together for different reasons.

Whereas purity politics is about taking sides and sticking to them, a relationship with truth teaches us that to address big problems in which we are also implicated (like climate change, systemic racism, income inequality, or houselessness), we need to do better than either-or thinking and feeling. We need a politics that is adequate to the "both-and" scenarios of contrary infatuation that we find ourselves in when we feel both love and concern, fear and desire, comfort and despair. We need a politics adequate to the situation of the young-woman protagonist of an early webcomic version of Kate Beaton's *Ducks* who responds to a purist question about having lived and worked in oil-sands work camps near Fort McMurray ("Do you ever feel, like, bad about working in a place like that?") by looking down, pausing, and saying, "I feel a lot of things."[14] *The Rough Poets* shows that oil-worker poets feel solidarity with other workers and that many of them feel loyal and indebted to the companies and the industry they work(ed) for. These are the more expected and acceptable feelings for oil workers to express, but these feelings neither preclude nor cancel out other feelings that oil workers also feel. As I turn to the task of summarizing and making conclusions about *The Rough Poets*, I want to focus, following Beaton, on the dynamics and the potential of feeling a lot of things about oil work, climate change, and just transition.[15]

Confusion/Stuplimity

Beaton's protagonist's response to the presumed yes/no question "Do you ever feel, like, bad about working in a place like that?" may seem evasive or weak, but it is more accurately described as *stuplime.*[16] Mirroring the martini-drinking questioner's hesitation over the hypocrisy of her own assumptions about who should and should not be held responsible for extraction – glimpsed in the inclusion of the verbal tic or stumble with the word *like* – the protagonist holds the conversation in the muddy space of neither/nor, both/and, "a lot." In chapter 4, I draw on Sianne Ngai's concept of the "ugly feeling" of stuplimity to equate the way the production-tester narrator of Henderson's *The Lease* pretends to understand, but does not understand, things like "what a lease is," "what hands do," and "what you do"[17] with similar moments of extractive stupor in Peter Christensen's *Rig Talk* and Dymphny Dronyk's *Contrary Infatuations.* Oil-worker poetry commonly contains a sense of confusion, thickness, or slowness that might be interpreted as a doubling down on stereotypes of oil workers as simple or as having dirty hands. Like Beaton's use of thick language and feelings to point out that oil workers are not the only ones who are confused and overwhelmed by petroculture, or like Naden Parkin's adoption of a mud-man persona in *A Relationship with Truth* that accommodates both his oil work and his affection for the land, oil-worker poetry heaps up language and emotions, exposing the petromodern condition as a muddy state of feeling a lot.

Christensen was right to associate literary reviewers' questioning of whether *Rig Talk* should count as poetry at all with class snobbery and the purism of those who believe their hands are clean.[18] When he observes, in "Elegy for a Rig Worker," that few people "ever stop to think" when they enjoy the ease and the pleasures of modern life (when they "buy groceries / go to a movie" and so on) that

it's because *somebody*
stood and froze their ass off
in the steel[19]

he is being intentionally thick, crass, and slow – stopping to think about something obvious but distasteful that others tend to gloss over. Dronyk's poetry digs and lingers, similarly, in the language and the materiality of extraction, finding comfort in things like drilling fluid, being rocked by underground explosions, and drawing literal, tedious language out into long, narrow poems that might seem to say very little yet that also say a lot. Parkin's poetry plays with stupidity – "you'll never know whether I'm clever or slow"[20] – and in doing so inches toward the limits of the extractive logics he often uncritically embodies. Lesley Battler's play with thick, dense, and nonsensical language in *Endangered Hydrocarbons* enacts a different kind of muddiness, as in the obfuscations of "The Petrochemical Ball," in which the tour the reader joins may occur at a party or in a penitentiary, as well as in poems like "Tender Carbon," which echoes Gertrude Stein's *Tender Buttons* and uses arrow-shaped stanzas to depict extractive language and ideology as absurd yet having a relentless forward momentum:

petrochemists, lobbyists
guessing again and golfing again
and the best men, the very best men, decent
do-gooder democracies subsidizing subsidized enterprises
the world's third-largest watershed, six barrels water one barrel oil
four tonnes water one barrel oil. four tonnes earth
one barrel oil make a little white
no and not with pit
pit on in within[.][21]

In "Tender Carbon," the language and capital the industry accumulates (figured here as an arrow) are linked to, and inseparable from, the material violence both Henderson and Parkin describe as *punching holes*. Battler's reminder that extraction's bluster and booms are also pits matches Lindsay Bird's understated depiction of the yawning monstrosity of boom time.

Oil work brings workers into proximity with hydrocarbons, the land, experiences of exploitation, alienation, and dispossession, and hard truths about the impacts of extraction. Oil workers know, for instance, that the land from which resources are extracted is not empty but rather a homeland to Indigenous peoples, local communities, and non-humans, all of whom are harmed by extraction; that the land is not dead and inert but rather lively, dangerous, and resistant; that seemingly plentiful and cheap resources are finite and costly; that fossil fuels are not only liberating but also dangerous and threatening to petromodern subjects; that the domination of the land is linked to the domination of humans; that ownership of resources and the land is not absolute but rather contested and unstable; and that the laws of nature (including climate change) do not bend to the will of humans. Everyone knows these truths, yet they resist articulation. The feelings that come from being in relationship with these truths are "a lot," and it is easier for some people to avoid or deny them than others. The situated knowledge and affect theory of oil workers are muddy-yet-vital forms of intelligence that contradict accepted neoliberal, petromodern, and settler-colonial logics. They hold open space for puzzling over, questioning, delaying, and perhaps dismantling business as usual.

Fear

Christensen uses fear as a synonym for an oil-worker's job in *Rig Talk*, in which "keeping fear away" by laughing at it or by inflicting it on others is constitutive of oil work and of life in a petrostate.[22] The workers in Henderson's *The Lease* are likewise accustomed to and shaped by fears of accidents that threaten and are visceral in their cringing bodies.[23] Referred to as "hands,"[24] they hold on to the simultaneous fears of losing their hands or other body parts, losing their humanity by becoming mere tools, and losing their livelihoods in an energy transition to come. Fear registers in all of the oil-worker poetry I study – for example, in Dronyk's speaker's fears of and for her husband, her children, and herself in the petrocultural battlegrounds of the Gulf Wars, the Peace Country, reproductive labour, and hetero-patriarchal domestic life; in a mud man's fears about his job prospects and way of life in a post-oil future he can barely imagine in Parkin's *A Relationship with Truth*; and in the constant sense of threat and fear as a young woman in a tar-sands work camp that creeps in despite the ironic tone of Bird's *Boom Time*. Although fear may belong on the list of "What We Don't Say" in the oil patch,[25] *The Rough Poets* shows that oil workers know that fear pervades oil work and petroculture.

Of course, oil workers are not the only fearful petrocultural subjects. The global "Fridays for Future" student strike movement started by Swedish teenager Greta Thunberg is a response to the climate anxiety felt by young people watching the fossil economy and the inaction of world leaders threaten their futures. In a 2019 statement at the World Economic Forum in Davos, Thunberg calls for fear as a spark for decisive action: "I want you to panic. I want you to feel the fear I feel every day. And then I want you to act. I want you to act as you would in a crisis. I want you to act as if the house was on fire, because it is."[26] Meanwhile, in a situation in which, as UN Secretary-General António Guterres remarked at COP27, "We are on a highway to climate hell with our foot still on the accelerator,"[27] the most powerful nations, corporations, and individuals in the world have their own reasons to be afraid. As we saw at the COP28 gathering led by oil-executive Sultan al Jaber in Dubai, fossil capital is desperately trying, but has so far been unable to figure out how, to hold on to its power in a post-oil future.[28] In a global crisis, fear triggers individual and collective fight-flight-freeze responses that can look like climate anxiety, guilt, denialism, delay, geoengineering, distraction, prepping (from canned goods to bunkers and space travel), and all kinds of activism, from Indigenous land-and-water defenders and environmentalists to union organizing to the 2022 Freedom Convoy, the parental-rights movement, and pro-oil citizens' groups.

The "fight" response to crisis demands that we pick a side and start throwing literal or figurative punches, and here in Canada, fossil capital has been successful at drawing ideological battle lines in its own favour: for instance, as workers vs. environmentalists rather than extractive industry vs. planetary life. The extractive populism that enlists workers as boosters and defenders of oil and gas offers workers a sense of belonging and security within an "oil family"[29] that promises, falsely, to protect their jobs and way of life, even as the industry continues to focus on extracting profit by any means, leaving workers vulnerable to cycles of boom and bust, automation, and layoffs. For instance, Suncor CEO Rich Kruger made headlines and was called before the

House of Commons natural resources committee in 2023 for stating perhaps too baldly his commitment to shift focus back from energy transition to generating profit – a commitment Suncor is pursuing through increasing automation of oil-sands extraction and laying off 20 per cent of its workers.[30] Extractive populism mobilizes fear to create a backlash response that does nothing to address the problem at hand. It gives people a sense that they are doing something (fighting) in a crisis, but it has the effect of a "freeze" response, providing a distraction that allows the extractive economy that caused and is exacerbating the crisis to continue with business as usual.

In a blog post for the climate-justice group 350.org, Albertan journeyman machinist Stephen Buhler riffs on The Clash's song "Clampdown" to discuss how oil workers have been pitted against environmentalists and migrants, called on "to go to bat for the industry":

> For years, working people have been told to ignore warnings of an oncoming climate crisis. We've been told that these claims are drummed up by people whose interests are against ours. We are told to oppose climate activists who have come to take away our jobs and to hate the people seeking refuge from the rising seas, extreme heat, dying crops and harder lives that our high carbon economy has brought to bear.
>
> This isn't true. The "clampdown" is not coming from the environmental movement, or from people seeking refuge from the effects of climate change. It's coming from the top-down, where the wealthiest 1% control a rigged system that benefits them, and leaves the rest of us fighting over the scraps.
>
> All across Alberta, especially in the oil and gas sector, our jobs are being automated out of existence. The gap between the rich and the rest of us is growing while regressive style governments … are cutting public services, demolishing public ownership and giving handouts to wealthy corporations.
>
> **They want to divide us. Using race, gender, and religion to pit us against each other, when we all fundamentally share the same desires – a stable job, a safe community for our families, and the hope for a livable future.**[31]

As Buhler demonstrates, rather than a divisive politics, the twin crises of global warming and energy transition call for an intersectional politics – one that addresses interrelated oppressions including classism, racism, colonialism, and sexism.[32] He suggests a class basis for unity and solidarity among the 99 per cent: those who are vulnerable to climate change and economic instability, dependent on an economy that is not of our choosing and is rigged against us, and who have a shared "hope for a livable future" built on justice and care rather than extraction and exploitation.[33] Fear is a healthy response to danger or a threat. Faced with the real, imminent threat of global warming (which is linked to other threats like austerity, discrimination, and ongoing racial violence and colonial dispossession) the task, now, is to become clear about where the threat is coming from and what we are going to do about it.

Shame

When Parkin thinks about the role he plays in extractive industry and writes, "There's shame in my veins for remaining a layman,"[34] he exposes an ugly feeling about oil work that other oil-worker poets hold closer to their chests.[35] Despite this, shame is palpable in other oil-worker poetry collections, beginning with the way Ells's *Northland Trails* avoids the material conditions and the implications of his foundational work on the tar sands. Henderson's second-person narrator both admits shame and deflects it onto readers when he wonders "if you are still Catholic enough to keep a sin" and when he worries, in the closing poem, that the confessional poems themselves amount to so much whining or "howling" by a class traitor.[36] Battler's speaker manages and tries to ignore the voice of her inner critic, a judgy, idealistic "*Past Self*" who thinks she is a sellout.[37] She jokes and worries about her responsibility for the "ins / titu / tio / nal / ize / d / rac / is / m / an / d / en / de / mi / c / vio / len / ce" of the industry,[38] which disproportionately endangers Indigenous, racialized, and working-class communities while shaming and blaming them for having made bad choices like living near a refinery or doing the work of extraction. Dronyk's speaker fantasizes about shaming landowners who resist oil and gas drilling or pipelines on their land by pointing out the hypocrisies of petromodern life; her conclusion that such accusations are unspeakable testifies to the potency of shame as a structure of feeling of oil work, petropoetics, and climate change.

As I argue in chapter 3, Dronyk's speaker becomes stuck in her awareness of complicity, of what a person cannot do or say because of the "*big truck / in the yard*" or "*the purr of your furnace / switching on.*"[39] Through fantasized energy-lifeworld takedowns based on the idea that a person can't both *use* and *oppose* oil,[40] she engages in purity politics rooted in her own fear of being shamed as a hypocrite. Although such purity politics are a tactic used by industry and the oil lobby to discourage dissent, Matthew Huber shows in *Climate Change as Class War* that purity politics have also infected and undermined the climate-justice movement. He argues that because the movement has embraced both climate guilt and the idea that we must all learn to live with less, it has failed to appeal to working-class people who need visions of climate or energy justice that offer them more. Oil workers need a promise of a good life, a better life, and a "sweetness of life"[41] that is more than the "leather ottoman" that Bird mocks as a marker of having "made it,"[42] and that is also more than a band-aid fix for climate change that does not address the inequities that have caused it.

(Bad) Love

Chapter 3 reads Dronyk's *Contrary Infatuations* as petrocultural affect theory that depicts life with fossil fuels and the oil industry as an abusive relationship or bad love. A sense of being abused, exploited, and betrayed by the extractive industry to which the workers also feel loyal and indebted runs through the poetry collections I study in *The Rough Poets.* With Ells, it is the poet himself who professes to love the land and people he seeks to turn into an extractive zone. Parkin writes, "propane pays him,"[43] leaving it to readers to unpack the sense of attachment a worker feels to the industry that supports their family, allows them to keep the farm, or pays their way through university, even though the worker knows that the industry is also responsible for social and environmental harms. Yet, as Dronyk's "Love by Cell Phone" and Henderson's explorations of the land and labour relations of the lease demonstrate, despite workers' attempts to contain what they give or sell to the corporation or the industry they work for, oil work often claims extra, biting off, chewing up, and spitting out workers' hands, limbs, land, relationships, and lives. A sense of being turned into a machine, a tool, an ant, a "girl," or somebody else's "dessert" or punching bag is pervasive in oil-worker poetry.[44] In Bird's poem "Tool Crib," which begins with a listing of tools stored in the tool crib ("socket wrenches, pipe wrenches, eye bolts") but also includes workers like "Howie always boring the baloney / right out of you with those long-winded safety lectures," the entire work camp turns out to be a tool crib, storing workers in their individual boxes (rooms) for safekeeping and lumping them in with the resources being extracted in the oil sands.[45] As is evident throughout *The*

Rough Poets – from the way the safety sign looms over Ross Belot's "First Day" to the command to hide in a trench in Shepherd's "Birds Migrate at Night, Mostly Unseen" – oil-worker poetics registers workers' knowledge that the oil industry is only concerned about their safety and well-being insofar as they impact profit, is always ready to betray them, and does not love them back. Speaking from within the oil patch, the theory of contrary infatuation as bad love suggests both that the feeling of attachment is real and that the breakup with fossil fuels, although painful, is necessary for the flourishing not only of human and planetary life but also of (former) oil workers.

If a theory of contrary infatuation frames energy transition as a long-deferred breakup, it might also be considered an expression and encouragement of other forms of love. In the face of a climate crisis that world leaders and industry profiteers have failed to avert because it is a direct outcome of the profit motives, individualism, injustices, and austerity measures of the racial-fossil capitalist system that gives them their power, movements for a truly just transition must be built on decolonial, anticolonial, and anticapitalist principles of care and love.[46] They must become a gathering point for diverse groups of disidentificatory petrocultural subjects to join in solidarity *against* racial-fossil capital and *for* energy justice.

A key form of love glimpsed in *The Rough Poets* is the solidarity with other workers that each of the oil-worker poets I study (except Ells) embodies and expresses in their poetics. They do this – haltingly, tentatively, imperfectly, and sometimes unknowingly – by working out how to be in solidarity with other workers while disidentifying with extractive industry. That it is possible to do this is a key learning from oil-worker poetry in *The Rough Poets*. Henderson's narrator worries in the closing poem of *The Lease* that he – or you, the reader – will adopt a politics that betrays his coworkers,[47] but it is important to be clear about what would and would not constitute such a betrayal. Solidarity among workers is a form of disidentificatory love that must be delinked from love for commodities, industries, corporations, and extractive governments. It must also be expanded to include more people, and oil-worker poetry suggests this can be done by relinking solidarity with love and kinship with other humans and the land.

Each of the poetry collections emphasizes love for the land – as home, as kin, as mother/source of life, and as the source of knowledge for how to survive the transition from petropoetics to decolonial and postcarbon futures. Oil-worker poets' analysis of petropoetics links the exploitation of workers with ecocide and environmental harm, environmental racism, and the dispossession of Indigenous peoples. We see this in Christensen's and illustrator Jacqueline Forrie's linking of Indigenous people, rivers, nonhumans, workers, and the land at "the end of the chain" of extraction;[48] in the racist and sexist talk among workers that Henderson's poetry mimics and deconstructs; in the voyeuristic and destructive pleasure Dronyk's speaker admits to feeling as a beneficiary of past dispossessions; and even in Parkin's appropriative identifications with enslavement and indigeneity. It is perhaps most effectively conveyed in Battler's metaphor of *endangered hydrocarbons*, in the sense of kinship between humans and fossils that the animist metaphor creates, and in her linking of racial and fossil capital in playful, disturbing poems like "Eco-Terrorism in Canada," "The Petrochemical Ball," and "Uppity Molecules." Oil workers are not the only ones who have been betrayed and harmed by fossil capital. In our era of global warming, economic precarity and injustice, racial and colonial violence and solidarity movements against these (such as Black Lives Matter and Idle No More), and mounting feelings of alienation and of being embattled resulting in divisive and dangerous politics, it is time for solidarity and care among the vulnerable, betrayed, and threatened to replace fighting over the scraps of a broken system.

Muddy oil-worker poetry registers ugly and ambivalent feelings, states the obvious, and links settler colonialism, sexism, and extraction; racial capital and fossil capital; and fossil fuels and desire. In Henderson's narrator's attempt to "read the roots" of the grass on his family's property,[49] in Parkin's grasping for an unknown future that comes after both climate change and settler colonialism, and in every instance of an oil-worker poet's realization that extraction places them in a chain of violence where their job is to eat or be eaten (as we see especially in Bird's *Boom Time*), oil-worker poetry in Canada feels out and exposes racial capitalism (including settler colonialism) as the root of the climate crisis. *The Rough Poets* shows that oil workers see the negative impacts of the extractive land relations (petropoetics) that oil work enacts, that they understand that Indigenous reciprocal land relations embody better ways to relate to the land, and that, while they worry about their own livelihoods, they also hope for a transformation of land relations on territory known as Canada and the oil patch. Even as they struggle to imagine the postcarbon or decolonial futures that they anticipate or vaguely wish for (as many do at this moment of climate crisis and the early days of energy transition), they create and hold open a space for imagination and solidarity toward a just transition that repairs the injustices extraction exacerbates and exploits.

■ ■ ■

Climate change has us all feeling a lot of feelings that oil workers and oil-worker poets have been grappling with for decades. Instead of dismissing workers as backward, stupid, or unpoetic, *The Rough Poets* takes seriously the feeling-thought of oil worker poets. It posits "ugly," ambivalent, confused, and mixed feelings as potential ground for solidarity toward energy justice. My reading of oil-worker poetry agrees with Angele Alook and the other authors of *The End of This World: Climate Justice in So-Called Canada* in emphasizing Indigenous sovereignty and rights as key to a truly just transition. It also agrees with their call for a "left-wing populism" made up of "us" – "Indigenous peoples, workers, migrants and displaced people, women, LGBTQ2S+, disabled, and young people" together resisting against "them" – "a small group of mostly settler capitalists."[50] Bringing on "the end of this world" while planning to continue to live together on this land now known as Canada requires an Indigenous-led transition that involves learning how to enact good, loving land relations.

I find hope for the end of the worlds petropoetics has made, for revamped land relations, and for liveable futures in unions embracing and advocating for just transition and climate justice;[51] in workers' climate movements such as Iron and Earth, which advocates and trains workers for green energy jobs, and the Climate and Labour Campaign of the Worker Solidarity Network in BC; Indigenous and Indigenous-led resistance and land-and-water-defence movements including Indigenous Climate Action, the Keepers of the Water, the Tiny House Warriors, and the Wet'suwet'en resistance and Decolonial Solidarity movement; Indigenous renewable energy projects and the Indigenous Clean Energy Network; young people organizing for climate justice; and local grassroots, national, and global coalitions and organizations for just transition (including 350.org, the Climate Emergency Unit, the movement for a Green New Deal, and the Manitoba Energy Justice Coalition, where I find my organizing community). I also find hope in poetry, and petropoetry, as a site where we examine, work out, and reimagine our land relations toward energy justice.

Notes

TIMELINE

1 See Wendy Shearer et al., "Oil Heritage Conservation District Study," County of Lambton, 2010, 26–7, https://www.lambtononline.ca/en/county-government/resources/Documents/PlansReportsandStudies/Cultural-Services/Oil-Heritage-Study/Conservation-District-Study-Text.pdf; Stott, "Poetic Justice," 180–1.

2 Paul Horn, "The Long Tale of Exxon and Climate Change," *Inside Climate News*, 15 September, 2015, https://insideclimatenews.org/infographics/long-tale-exxon-and-climate-change.

3 Emma Graney, "Alberta Premier Jason Kenney Launches 'Energy War Room' to Take on Oil Critics," *The Globe and Mail*, 11 December 2019, www.theglobeandmail.com/canada/alberta/article-alberta-premier-kenney-launches-energy-war-room-to-take-on-oil.

4 Kieran Leavitt, "Jason Kenney's $3.5-Million Inquiry into 'Anti-Alberta' Foreign-Funded Activists Finds No Illegal Activity, Wrongdoing," *Toronto Star*, 21 October 2021, https://www.thestar.com/news/canada/jason-kenney-s-3-5-million-inquiry-into-anti-alberta-foreign-funded-activists-finds-no/article_cdef844e-6d1d-581e-8ada-89775a04ac7e.html.

INTRODUCTION

1 Although I do not devote a chapter of *The Rough Poets* to *Moving to Climate Change Hours* (because as a book only partially about oil work it falls outside the parameters of this study), I am pleased to share and discuss this poem here.

2 Neela Banerjee, Lisa Song, and David Hasemyer, "Exxon's Own Research Confirmed Fossil Fuels' Role in Global Warming Decades Ago," *Inside Climate News*, 16 September 2015, https://insideclimatenews.org/news/16092015/exxons-own-research-confirmed-fossil-fuels-role-in-global-warming; John H. Cushman Jr, "Shell Knew Fossil Fuels Created Climate Change Risks Back in 1980s, Internal Documents Show," *Inside Climate News*, 5 April 2018, https://insideclimatenews.org/news/05042018/shell-knew-scientists-climate-change-risks-fossil-fuels-global-warming-company-documents-netherlands-lawsuits; Shannon Hall, "Exxon Knew about Climate Change almost 40 Years Ago," *Scientific American*, 26 October 2015, https://www.scientificamerican.com/article/exxon-knew-about-climate-change-almost-40-years-ago.

3 Povinelli, *Geontologies*, 172.

4 Scholars have been using the term *petropoetics* or *petro-poetics* since Judith Rauscher, Ilya Kalinin, and Marina Zurkow each coined the term in 2014, in their respective fields of Canadian literature, Russian literature, and visual art. See Rauscher, "Canadian Petro-Poetics"; Balloni, "Workshop"; Kalinin, "Petropoetics"; "The Petroleum Manga: A Project by Marina Zurkow," Punctum Books 25 February 2014, https://punctumbooks.com/titles/petroleum-manga. A body of literary criticism on petropoetics is now building in Canada and elsewhere. Although I choose *petropoetics* as the term for framing and narrowing my analysis, I understand this work to be aligned with related studies of climate poetry and ecopoetics, including David Farrier's *Anthropocene Poetics*, Lynn Keller's *Recomposing Ecopoetics*, Margaret Ronda's *Remainders*, and Min Hyoung Song's *Climate Lyricism.*

5 I do this work alongside other excellent literary scholars. See, for example, Braunecker, "A Greed"; Dickinson, "Energy Humanities"; Gordon, *Unsustainable Oil*; Karpinski, "Isotopic Poetics" and "Unsettled Solutions"; Rauscher, "Canadian Petro-Poetics."

6 See Wilson, Carlson, and Szeman, *Petrocultures*; Barrett and Worden, *Oil Culture*; Bellamy and Diamanti, "Editors' Introduction"; Bellamy and Diamanti, *Materialism*; Szeman, *On Petrocultures*; Szeman and Boyer, *Energy Humanities*; Szeman, Wenzel, and Yaeger, *Fueling Culture*; Yaeger, "Editor's Column."

7 Following Sourayan Mookerjea and others, I refer to Canada as a *petrostate*, using a term commonly reserved for dictatorships and so-called "developing" countries. In "Petrocultures in Passive Revolution," Mookerjea defines a petrostate as "a polity that is subordinated and restructured according to the needs of either the Big Oil multinationals or the global political economy of oil or both"

(331). For other descriptions of Canada as a petrostate, see Cariou, "Tarhands," 17; Nikiforuk, *Energy of Slaves*, 178–203. For a discussion of the related term *resource curse*, see page 176n45.

8 I have learned about oil work through visits to oil-producing communities in Virden, MB, Fort McMurray, AB, and Leduc, AB; a visit to a refinery near Edmonton, AB; visits to oil museums in Fort McMurray, Leduc, and Aberdeen, Scotland; and conversations with oil workers I have met through my research; as well as documentary films, online research, books, and episodes of reality TV shows like *Licence to Drill* and *Black Gold*. Despite my attempts to understand oil work, I know that this book contains misunderstandings and errors, for which I take full responsibility.

9 In naming the oil industry and settler-colonial land relations in Canada as *extractive*, I employ a term coined in Latin America and most often used in reference to that region. Kristina Dietz and Bettina Engels define *extractivism* as "a national, growth-oriented development pathway based on rent-seeking activities, that is, the large-scale exploitation, production and exportation of raw materials" (*Contested Extractivism*, 2). They note the widespread effects of extractivism on social and political life, "labour, gender, class and ethnic relations," land use, and even "cultural identities" and "subjectivities" (3). While heeding petrocultures scholars Imre Szeman and Jennifer Wenzel's recent warning, in an essay titled "What Do We Talk about When We Talk about Extractivism?" about using this term with imprecision, I follow Indigenous, Black, and people of colour scholars in using this term in reference to North America/Turtle Island to link the extraction of "natural resources" with the theft of land (the ongoing dispossession of Indigenous peoples) and the theft of bodies and labour (slavery and its afterlives), along with the environmental racism that continues to expose Indigenous, Black, and Brown people disproportionally to the harmful effects of extractivism. See Ghosh, *Nutmeg's Curse*; Jobson, "Dead Labor"; Lennon, "Decolonizing Energy"; Liboiron, *Pollution Is Colonialism*; Todd, "Fossil Fuels"; Whitehead, *Making Love*. In contrast to an extractive settler-colonial approach to land relations, Glen Sean Coulthard describes Indigenous thought and practices of "*grounded normativity*," which structure Indigenous peoples' relationships with humans and non-humans, as based in an understanding of "land *as system of reciprocal relations and obligations*" (*Red Skin, White Masks*, 13). Although Western colonial frameworks and the settler-colonial nation-state have historically treated Indigenous lifeways as backward, Indigenous knowledge about how to live well on the land has persisted and constitutes demonstrated alternatives

to extractivism – alternatives that must not now be appropriated (extracted) by academics, organizations, corporations, or racial-capitalist states to address the crisis of climate change (see Whyte, "Indigenous Climate Change Studies").

10 Intergovernmental Panel on Climate Change (IPCC), *Climate Change 2021*; António Guterres, "Secretary-General Calls Latest IPCC Climate Report 'Code Red for Humanity,' Stressing 'Irrefutable' Evidence of Human Influence," United Nations, 9 August 2021, https://press.un.org/en/2021/sgsm20847.doc.htm.

11 IPCC, *Climate Change 2022*.

12 Carroll, *Regime of Obstruction*; Gunster et al., "Our Oil"; McLean, "Low Class Oil Trash."

13 See, for example, Initiative for Energy Justice, *The Energy Justice Workbook,* December 2019, https://iejusa.org/wp-content/uploads/2019/12/The-Energy-Justice-Workbook-2019-web.pdf; "About," Manitoba Energy Justice Coalition, accessed 22 December 2023, https://www.mbenergyjustice.org/about.

14 Government of Canada, *Sustainable Jobs Plan: An Interim Plan for 2023–2025 Detailing Concrete Federal Actions to Advance Economic Prosperity and Sustainable Jobs in Every Region of the Country*, 2023, https://www.canada.ca/en/services/jobs/training/initiatives/sustainable-jobs/plan.html.

15 *Oxford English Dictionary*, s.v. "poesis (*n.*), sense 2," July 2023, https://doi.org/10.1093/OED/5411289538.

16 LeMenager, *Living Oil*; Mitchell, *Carbon Democracy*; Huber, *Lifeblood*; Malm, *Fossil Capital*; Jobson, "Dead Labor"; Johnson, *Carbon Nation*; Daggett, "Petro-masculinity"; Yusoff, "Geologic Life."

17 Liboiron, *Pollution Is Colonialism*, 63.

18 Cariou, "Aboriginal," 18.

19 Todd, "Fossil Fuels," 13.

20 Povinelli, *Geontologies*, 4.

21 Gómez-Barris, *Extractive Zone.* Beginning with Cedric J. Robinson's *Black Marxism*, theories of racial capital assert that colonialism and slavery preceded and were foundational to capitalism, and therefore that any analysis of capitalism without racial capitalism is incomplete. See also Melamed, "Racial Capitalism"; Jobson, "Dead Labour"; Jenkins and Leroy, *Histories of Racial Capitalism.*

22 The colonial and racial politics of petropoetics are discussed throughout *The Rough Poets,* but see especially chapter 6.

23 Battler, *Endangered Hydrocarbons*, 15.

24 Truth and Reconciliation Commission of Canada, *A Knock*; Daschuk, *Clearing the Plains*; National Inquiry into Missing and Murdered Indigenous Women and

Girls, "Deeper Dive"; Richard Raycraft, "MPs Back Motion Calling on Government to Recognize Residential Schools Program as Genocide," CBC, October 27, 2022, https://www.cbc.ca/news/politics/house-motion-recognize-genocide-1.6632450.

25 James Yap, "Extracting Justice: The Human Rights Impact of Canadian Mining Around the World," CBC Ideas recording, 30 May 2023, https://www.cbc.ca/player/play/2214049859845.

26 In recent years, Canada went so far as to buy the Trans Mountain Pipeline from Kinder Morgan to ensure it would be built; it has persisted in using militarized police to ensure pipelines are built despite Indigenous resistance such as the Wet'suwet'en blockades against the Coastal Gaslink pipeline. See Justin Trudeau, "Prime Minister's Statement on the Trans Mountain Pipeline Project," Government of Canada, 15 April 2018, https://www.pm.gc.ca/en/news/speeches/2018/04/15/prime-ministers-statement-trans-mountain-pipeline-project; Brett Forester, "Behind the Thin Blue Line: Meet a Secretive Arm of the RCMP in B.C.," APTN News, 16 June 2022, https://www.aptnnews.ca/ourstories/cirg/.

27 McGregor, Rak, and Wunker, *Refuse*. As Emma LaRocque demonstrates in *When the Other Is Me: Native Resistance Discourse 1850–1990*, resistance and critique have existed alongside Canadian literature throughout its history. See also, for instance, Brand, *Bread out of Stone*; Chua, "Migrant Ecocriticism"; Sharpe, *Ordinary Notes*; Vernon, *Black Prairie*; Whitehead, *Making Love*; Younging, *Elements of Indigenous Style*.

28 Fee, *Literary Land Claims*, 9.

29 Frye, *Bush Garden*, 222.

30 Christensen, *Rig Talk*, 15.

31 Henderson, *The Lease*, 8.

32 See Alook et al., *End of This World*.

33 Liboiron, *Pollution Is Colonialism*, 27.

34 There is no category for non-binary or gender nonconforming workers.

35 "Employment and Labour Data," Careers in Energy, A Division of Energy Safety Canada, accessed 19 December 2023, https://careersinenergy.ca/employment-and-labour-data/.

36 "Direct and Indirect Jobs across Canada," Context: Energy Examined, Canadian Association of Petroleum Producers, last modified 11 January 2021, https://context.capp.ca/infographics/2018/infographic_jobs-across-canada. The preamble for the infographic includes these examples of ways the oil and gas industry "supports jobs and families across the country": "through the purchase of steel

from Ontario, environmental consulting from Quebec and hi-tech pipeline monitoring software from B.C."

37 Wayman, "Work and Silence," 79.

38 Atabaki, Bini, and Ehsani, *Working for Oil*, 3.

39 See also Beaton, *Ducks*.

40 Alook, Hussey, and Hill, *Indigenous Gendered Experiences*, 9.

41 Coulthard, *Red Skin, White Masks*, 13.

42 Francis, *Bush Camp*, 17.

43 Alook, Hussey, and Hill, *Indigenous Gendered Experiences*, 7.

44 Rancière, *Proletarian Nights*, x.

45 Parkin, *Relationship with Truth*, 38.

46 Henderson, "Navigating," 05:38–48.

47 Glen Sean Coulthard describes *terra nullius* as "the racist legal fiction that declared Indigenous peoples too 'primitive' to bear rights to land and sovereignty when they first encountered European powers on the continent, thus rendering their territories legally 'empty' and therefore open for colonial settlement and development" (*Red Skin, White Masks*, 175).

48 On Harold Innis's staples thesis about Canada's extractive economies and its subsequent uptake in relation to fossil fuels, see Innis, *Fur Trade in Canada*; Watkins, *Staples and Beyond* and "Rejoinder: Bitumen"; Laxer, "Alberta's Sands"; Dobson, "Canada," 65.

49 Perron, "Oil Bodies," 615.

50 Bird, *Boom Time*, 43.

51 Perron, "Oil Bodies," 606.

52 See Rauscher, "Canadian Petro-Poetics"; rob mclennan, review of *Prologue for the Age of Consequence*, by Garth Martens, rob mclennan's blog, 23 November 2014, http://robmclennan.blogspot.com/2014/11/garth-martens-prologue-for-age-of.html.

53 Rauscher, "Canadian Petro-Poetics," 104.

54 Christensen, *Rig Talk*, 67.

55 Gunster et al., "Our Oil"; McLean, "Low Class Oil Trash."

56 Gunster et al., "Our Oil," 221.

57 Eaton and Enoch, "Oil Industry Is Us," 308; 312–13.

58 Huber, *Climate Change*.

59 Eaton and Kinchy, "Quiet Voices."

60 Dronyk, *Contrary Infatuations*, 80.

61 Williams, *Marxism and Literature*, 130–1.

62 Ngũgĩ, *Globalectics*, 3–4.

63 The choice between the terms *oil sands* and *tar sands* to describe the resource that is being extracted in the Athabasca region has become polarizing. S.C. Ells preferred *bituminous sands*, a term that Jon Gordon also uses to avoid taking a position either for the industry or against it (*Unsustainable Oil*, xxxvii). Barry Ferguson uses *oil sands* and *tar sands* interchangeably (*Athabasca Oil Sands*, 5–6). I have chosen to alternate between the two terms in this book, to signal both my opposition to further tar sands development and my solidarity with oil sands workers, as well as the Indigenous and settler residents of the region.

64 Gómez-Barris, *Extractive Zone*, 12.

65 Pêcheux, *Language, Semantics and Ideology*, 67.

66 Berlant, *Cruel Optimism.*

67 Parkin, *Relationship with Truth*, 39.

68 Wakefield, *Anthropocene Back Loop*.

CHAPTER ONE

1 Readers may note inconsistencies in the spelling of Ells's name in my sources. Although Ells used *Sidney* professionally, personally, and in his print publications, it appears that his legal name was *Sydney* (as shown on the register of the Beechwood Cemetery, where he was buried ["Beechwood Cemetery Registers, 1873–1990," Ancestry.com, accessed 31 January 2018, https://www.ancestry.ca/search/collections/2168.]). I have chosen to follow his seeming preference for *Sidney.* Ells held undergraduate degrees in both arts and science from McGill University. He is often described as an engineer or a geologist, based both on his scientific background and the work that he did.

2 Gómez-Barris, *Extractive Zone.*

3 I have chosen to alternate between the terms *oil sands* and *tar sands* in reference to the deposits of bituminous sand and the industry. This imperfect gesture is meant to signal solidarity with both oil-sands industry workers and environmentalist critiques of the tar-sands industry. For more information, see page 165n63.

4 Following his retirement, Ells wrote a memoir and deposited it in his fonds at the National Archive. An unauthorized version, *Recollections of the Development of the Athabasca Oil Sands*, was published by the Department of Mines in 1962; it was reissued by Syncrude sometime in the 1970s. All citations are from the 1962 edition. Ells's many notes and revisions to the 1962 version of the memoir are available in the Sidney Clarke Ells fonds at Library and Archives Canada.

5 LaRocque, *When the Other Is Me*, 36.

6 See Westman, Joly, and Gross, "Introduction."

7 Strasbourg, *Memories of a Metis Woman*, 5.

8 Gómez-Barris, *Extractive Zone*, 12.

9 James McCook, "A Glance Down Memory Lane to $10 Billions: Ottawa Engineer First Spotted Oil Bonanza," *Ottawa Journal*, 17 October 1951, 3. See also, for example, "'Father of the Tar Sand Industry' Did 20-Year Job." *Oil in Canada*, 23 January 1950, 16–17, R4495-0-7-E, vol. 3, Sidney Clarke Ells fonds.

10 See, for instance, feminist and Womanist works on parenthood such as: hooks, "Revolutionary Parenting"; Lorde, "Man Child"; Ruddick, *Maternal Thinking*.

11 Al Wheeler, "Progress: Fort McMurray, 1928. April 1st," R4495-0-7-E, vol. 8, Sidney Clarke Ells fonds, Library and Archives Canada, Ottawa, Ontario.

12 Quoted in Ells, *Recollections*, 101.

13 See, for example, Chastko, *Developing Alberta's Oil Sands*, 7–19; Ferguson, *Athabasca Oil Sands*, 22–30; Sheppard, *Oil Sands*, 80–1; Alberta Culture and Tourism, "Sidney Ells," accessed 2 January 2024, http://www.history.alberta.ca/energy heritage/sands/unlocking-the-potential/the-federal-government/sidney-ells.

14 Although most of the content of *Northland Trails* is set in the North, there are some exceptions, including several poems and one essay about the two World Wars, an essay on the "Covered Wagon Days" in United States history (76), a short story set in ancient Egypt (133–41), and two poems imagining prehistoric human and dinosaur life (58–62; 63–7) inspired by Ells's excavation of fossil trees as part of his oil work in the Athabasca region (58A).

15 See Chasar, *Everyday Reading*.

16 The Wood Buffalo Regional Library (the public library in Fort McMurray) has a copy of Ells's *Recollections of the Development of the Athabasca Oil Sands* but no copy of *Northland Trails*. The library at Keyano College, the community college in Fort McMurray, does not hold either book, although they are available for students to borrow through the University of Alberta. I visited the Oil Sands Discovery Centre in Fort McMurray in 2017 and saw no reference to *Northland Trails*; I have since shared a copy of the book with employees at the museum. I did, however, find several copies of *Northland Trails* in the University of Manitoba libraries, including a copy once owned by Margaret Laurence.

17 Literary and visual-art examples include poetry such as Lindsay Bird's *Boom Time*, David Martin's *Tar Swan*, Garth Martens's *Prologue for the Age of Consequence*, Lesley Battler's *Endangered Hydrocarbons*, and Kelly Shepherd's *Shift* and *Insomnia Bird*, fiction such as Rudy Wiebe's "The Angel of the Tar Sands," Richard van Camp's *Godless but Loyal to Heaven*, and Warren Cariou's "An Athabasca Story"; comics and graphic novels including Kate Beaton's *Ducks: Two Years in*

the Oil Sands, Nicole Burton, Hugh Goldring, and Patrick McCurdy's *The Beast*, Joe Sacco's "Bitumen or Bust," and Cariou and Nicholas Burns's "An Athabasca Story"; and other visual texts like Cariou's petrography, Lucas Seaward's bitumen paintings, Edward Burtynsky's *Oil*, Louis Helbig's *Beautiful Destruction*, and Elizabeth LaPensée's *Thunderbird Strike.*

18 Longley, "Bitumen Exploration," 17.

19 Ibid., 22.

20 Davidson and Gismondi, "Visualizing," 39.

21 Ibid., 47; 48.

22 Gordon, *Unsustainable Oil*, 56.

23 Ibid., 57.

24 Yaeger, "Editor's Column," 306. In her essay on the periodization of literary texts according to "the energy sources that made them possible" (305) – that is, on considering energy sources as modes of production – Patricia Yaeger describes *the energy unconscious* as a version of Frederic Jameson's *political unconscious.* She writes, "since fuel sources hover in the backgrounds of texts, if they speak at all, to pursue an energy unconscious means a commitment to the repressed, the *non-dit*, and to the text as a tissue of contradictions" (310n1).

25 Ells, *Northland Trails*, 70. Unless otherwise indicated, all references are to the 1956 edition of *Northland Trails.* In the extended discussions of *Northland Trails* that follow, I use in-text, parenthetical citations of page numbers.

26 McCormack, *Fort Chipewyan*, 70.

27 Ells, *Northland Trails*, 30–2.

28 See Coulthard, *Red Skin, White Masks*, 175.

29 Unrau, "Founding Fathers," 65. The "goose's-eye view" is an adaptation of Donna Haraway's concept of the "god-trick of seeing everything from nowhere" in *Simians*, 189. See also Unrau, *The Goose.*

30 Ells uses *Athabaska*, formerly the official government spelling for the name of the Athabaska River (now *Athabasca River*), the community of Athabaska Landing (now simply *Athabasca*), and the surrounding region.

31 This chapter focuses on the poem "The Athabaska Trail," and the note that precedes it, as exemplary of the subtle and/or repressed references to Ells's oil work in *Northland Trails* (36–9). Other minor references in the 1956 edition include the note that precedes "Dawn" (58–62), a poem that imagines the age of dinosaurs in the Athabasca region, where Ells writes, "*While conducting mining operations near McMurray, Alberta, in 1930, the writer discovered excellently preserved fossil trees of Cretaceous and Jurassic age, buried in the bituminous sand .... The probability that remains of dinosaurs will also be found in the bituminous sand has*

suggested the following lines" (58A). This reference to oil work was made in prose, detached from the poem itself, and printed on a page that was accidentally left out of the 1956 edition and had to be inserted by hand – a page that was missing from the library copy I first read (see Gordon A. Burns, letter to S.C. Ells, 4 August 1961, R4495-0-7-E, vol. 8, Sidney Clarke Ells fonds.) The poem "Oilers" celebrates the role of oil and of oil tankers in World War II (213–14), mentioning neither of the two wartime oil projects in Fort McMurray – the nationalization of the Abasand tar-sands plant and the use of Fort McMurray as the staging ground for the US Army's Canol pipeline project, both of which would later be considered wasteful failures (see Comfort, *Abasand Fiasco*). "The Blazed Tree" (142–8), a short story in which the protagonist is a supervisor of prospectors in the Athabasca region, is a thinly veiled autobiographical story about Ells as a supervisor of surveyors. The veil slips when Ells accidentally names the protagonist both "Peter" and "David" (144; 148). Two other autobiographical but anonymized stories not included in the 1956 edition of *Northland Trails* are "The Message," published in a 1932 edition of the *Canadian Mining Journal*, and "Oil Shale (Being a Few Notes on Behalf of the Pioneer Women in Canada's New North)," published in the 1938 edition of *Northland Trails* (141–6). A reading of this trio of short stories would be a fascinating study but is outside the scope of this chapter.

32 O.T.G. Williamson, letter to S.C. Ells, 8 December 1962, R4495-0-7-E, vol. 1, Sidney Clarke Ells fonds.

33 Williams, *Country and the City*, 118.

34 Williams, *Ideas of Nature*, 81.

35 Ibid., 82.

36 Ibid., 81.

37 Ibid., 77.

38 Tsing, *Friction*, 50.

39 Gross, "Wastelanding the Bodies."

40 Saborimanesh, "Toward Sustainable"; Wheatley and Westman, "Reclaiming Nature," 166–74.

41 McCormack, "Conclusion," 186.

42 Wheatley and Westman, "Reclaiming Nature," 176.

43 Unsigned review of *Northland Trails*, "Amongst the New Books," *Canadian Geographical Journal*, V.

44 Ells, *Northland Trails*, 41. This route was also used for other travel – for example, by Geological Survey of Canada expeditions, by prospectors during the gold rush era, and by the 1899 Treaty 8 Commission.

45 Guy Blanchet, "The Last of the Brigades," *The Beaver*, March 1938, 12.

46 McCormack, *Fort Chipewyan*, 75–8; 134–44.
47 Ells, *Northland Trails*, 41.
48 Strasbourg, *Memories of a Metis Woman*, 8.
49 See, for instance, the historical photographs of trackers shown in "The Athabasca Brigade," *Historical Athabasca Landing, 1880–1914*, accessed 17 April 2024, http://athabascalanding.athabascau.ca/html/transportation/brigade/brigade.htm.
50 See pages 7, 13, 25, 80–2, 197, and 200 of *Northland Trails* (1956).
51 Ells, *Northland Trails*, 41.
52 Ells, *Recollections*, 10–13.
53 Ells, *Northland Trails*, 36.
54 Ibid., 36.
55 Ells, *Recollections*, 11.
56 Ibid., 11–12.
57 S.C. Ells, letter to Corporal LaNauze, 4 November 1913, R4495-0-7-E, vol. 1, Sidney Clarke Ells fonds.
58 Dyce and Opp, "Visualizing Space," 71. Some of Ells's trapper characters are Métis (Joe Pelequin is the protagonist in "The Silver Fox" [180–9] and "Big Joe" Leblanc is a minor character in "Playboy" [160]), but Indigenous men are most often represented doing other fur-trade jobs like steering, tracking, and portaging cargo along the Athabasca River (see, for example, pages 25, 36, 82, 84, 197, and 199). On the noble savage, see Berkhofer, *White Man's Indian*.
59 Ells, *Northland Trails*, 199.
60 Coulthard, *Red Skin, White Masks*, 12.
61 Cariou, "Oil Drums," 583.
62 Strasbourg, *Memories of a Metis Woman*, 71.
63 McCormack, *Fort Chipewyan*, 70.
64 Ells, "Athabaska Trail," 338.
65 Joyce e. Hunt draws a direct relationship between the development of the rail lines and the oil-sands industry in her exhaustive history *Local Push Global Pull*. In a letter to S.M. Blair dated 30 June 1928, Karl Clark describes an encounter with Ells: "I saw Ells at the Macdonald [hotel] one day and he came and spilled a line of chatter as per usual. He said he was not doing any paving this year. He could have had lots to do but would not dig sand where he had to barge it to the railway any more. Said that if the government did not extend the railway to McMurray, the tar sands were dead." (Clark, *Oil Sands*, 161). According to records of the Treaty 8 negotiations at Fort Chipewyan, however, the extension of the railway was also a demand of the Indigenous peoples of the region (Madill, *Treaty Research*, [27]).

66 Ells, *Northland Trails*, 39.

67 Lacan, "Freudian Unconscious," 25.

68 Ells, *Northland Trails*, 39.

69 Keepers of the Water, "Indigenous Water Governance in the Arctic Ocean Drainage Basin," accessed 4 January 2024, https://www.keepersofthewater.ca/indigenous-water-governance.

CHAPTER TWO

1 Roughnecks are manual labourers who work on an oil rig. They travel with the rig to different locations to drill new oil wells. Led by the driller, who operates the drill machinery, roughnecks do various jobs on the rig, including assembling and maintaining equipment; joining, disconnecting, and reattaching lengths of drill stem as the well is drilled; monitoring drilling fluids; and guiding stacks of drill stem into and out of the derrick (the tower above the rig). Although everyone who works on the rig may be called a roughneck (including workers known, for example, as floorhands, the derrickhand, or the tool push), some reserve this name for only certain workers. Watching videos is a good way to get a sense of what roughnecks do – for example, Digital Wildcatters, "What Does a Roughneck Do on a Drilling Rig?" YouTube, 11 February 2021, https://www.youtube.com/watch?v=M8s1H8gyZwc.

2 A seismic helper or jughound is a physical labourer in an entry-level position who carries and lays equipment used in seismic testing, including cables, geophones, and explosives. Seismic testing is a way to "see" below the surface of the land and determine where to drill for oil and gas. See "How Does Land Seismic Work?" *Rigzone*, accessed 13 March 2024, https://www.rigzone.com/training/insight?insight_id=301&c_id=18; "Seismic Labourer," Careers in Energy, A Division of Energy Safety Canada, accessed 13 March 2024, https://careersinenergy.ca/careers/seismic-labourer/.

3 Mark Cochrane describes the cowboy poetry of the 1980s and 1990s as performance poetry on themes of nature, work, environmentalism, and domestic life. He writes, "[t]his is a rural, anti-intellectual poetry of saddle and bedroll; rarely does it examine language as a repository of conflicting ideologies. It derives its metaphors from ranching, rodeo events, guiding, and trail riding, and from a blithe adoption of First Nations imagery; it both invokes and debunks Hollywood stereotypes of the West" (241). Cochrane, "COWBOY POETRY," 240–1. Cochrane resists the idea that most (or the best) cowboy poets are men – although there is, of course, a privileging of men in the tradition's name. Christensen's later poetry about his work as a park ranger fits more squarely

within this tradition, but the simple, vernacular, and nature-focused poetry in *Rig Talk* demonstrates Christensen's cowboy style. In its content, and in its attention to language and ideology, *Rig Talk* is related to yet also diverges from cowboy poetry.

4 Cochrane, "CHRISTENSEN, Peter," 206.

5 Christensen, *Rig Talk*, 61. Other examples of clipped sonnets include "The Oil Rush Has Come" (9), "Inside" (35), and "Heroes" (47).

6 Thistledown Press, "RIG TALK by Peter Christensen," [1981], MSS 116 (A.01–36), box 34, folder 52, Thistledown Press Ltd fonds, University of Manitoba Archives, Winnipeg, Manitoba.

7 Christensen, *Rig Talk*, 25. In the extended discussions of *Rig Talk* that follow, I use in-text, parenthetical citations of page numbers.

8 Tripping pipe is pulling the drill stem out of an oil well to replace a worn-out drill bit or to address another issue, then putting it back in. Rather than disconnecting each piece of pipe, longer lengths are pulled up and stacked in the derrick (the tower on the rig), then reattached so that the rig can continue drilling.

9 Peter Christensen, "The Plains Are Alive with the Campfires of Millionaires," 1980, MSS 116 (A.90–64), box 16, folder 2, Thistledown Press Ltd fonds.

10 Christensen, *Rig Talk*, 32.

11 Ibid., 38.

12 Ibid., 39.

13 The naming of people as Slavey (as well as the naming of the Slave River and the two Slave Lakes) comes from the colonial adoption of Cree pejoratives used to refer to the Indigenous peoples who live in the region (see Asch, "Slavey," 348).

14 See, for instance, R. Buckminster Fuller, "World Energy," *Fortune*, February 1940, 57; Nikiforuk, *Energy of Slaves*.

15 Christensen, *Rig Talk*, 42–3.

16 These are poems of the type Dennis Cooley would soon celebrate in *The Vernacular Muse* (1987).

17 Christensen, *Rig Talk*, 50.

18 Wayman, *Inside Job*.

19 Smith, "Rink Rats," 17.

20 For favourable reviews of *Rig Talk*, see: Cuelho, review of *Rig Talk*; Faiers, "Work, Love"; Frank Moher, "Poems from the Oil Patch: Tough Talk about the Human Costs of Drilling for Oil," *Alberta Report*, 9 October 1981, 44; O'Brien, "Coming Through Fire"; Alan O'Conner, "Working Poetry," review of *Rig Talk* by Peter Christensen and *Going for Coffee: Poetry on the Job* edited by Tom Wayman. *The Lexicon* [York University], December 1981, MSS 166 (A.90–64), box 34, folder 52,

Thistledown Press Ltd fonds; Pilon, review of *Rig Talk*; Patricky Tivy, "Exposing the Work of Prairie Poets," *The Calgary Herald*, 9 January 1982, E3; Tom Wayman, "Three Work Poets," rev. of *On the Line* by Jim Daniels, *The Grievance: Poems from the Shop Floor* by Martin Glaberman, and *Rig Talk* by Peter Christensen, *Industrial Worker*, December 1982, 6, *Underground Newspaper Collection 1982*, roll 389, item 5. For negative and lukewarm reviews, see: Rosemary Aubert, "New Stars in the Galaxy of Canadian Poetry," *Quill & Quire*, April 1982, 30; Lorne Daniel, "Poet Puts Oil Rig Experiences to Work in New Collection," *Lethbridge Herald*, 4 July 1981, 38; Lane, "Saskatchewan Presses," 53–4; Kenneth McGoogan, review of *Rig Talk* by Peter Christensen, *The Calgary Herald*, 29 August 1981, F4; Smith, "Rink Rats"; Wiseman, "Deep Pleasure"; Zacharin, review; Francis Zichy, "Poetry Review: A Poor Photographer / Rig Talk / Disturbances," review of *A Poor Photographer* by John Barton, *Rig Talk* by Peter Christensen, and *Disturbances* by Greg Simison, *NeWest Review*, March 1982, 10–11. For other literary criticism, see New, "Tops and Tales"; Ricou, "Poetry," 11.

21 Zichy, "Poetry Review," 11.

22 Peter Christensen, Letter to Glen Sorestad, 30 April 1982. MSS 116 (A.90–64), box 6, folder 7, Thistledown Press Ltd fonds.

23 Keller, *Recomposing Ecopoetics*, 10.

24 Bate, *Song of the Earth*, 64.

25 Jonathan Skinner, "What Is Ecopoetics?" [2011], https://jacket2.org/commentary/conceptualizing-field.

26 Christensen, *Rig Talk*, 15.

27 Keller, *Recomposing Ecopoetics.* Keller's subtitle is *North American Poetry of the Self-Conscious Anthropocene.*

28 LaDuke, *Water Protector*, 83.

29 Christensen, *Rig Talk*, 16.

30 These quotations are from "Lorna's Bones," a poem that unfairly attacks prairie poet Lorna Crozier because of a conflict Christensen had with her partner, Patrick Lane. Lane refused to edit *Rig Talk* for Thistledown. He would later opine that Christensen's book "should not have been published at all" and that "[t]he quality of the poetry is extremely marginal" (Lane, "Saskatchewan Presses," 54). It was after Lane declined to edit his book that Christensen changed the title of this poem from "Poem to Remind Me" to "Lorna's Bones" (see the original and working manuscripts for *Rig Talk*, MSS 116 [A.90–64], box 16, Thistledown Press Ltd fonds).

31 Johnson, *Carbon Nation.*

32 Ibid., xx.

33 Ibid., 145.
34 Yusoff, *Billion Black Anthropocenes*, xii.
35 Christensen, *Rig Talk*, 9.
36 Ibid., 14; 32.
37 Pêcheux, *Language, Semantics and Ideology*, 60.
38 Althusser, "Ideology and Ideological State Apparatuses."
39 Pêcheux, *Language, Semantics and Ideology*, 157.
40 Ibid., 158; 136.
41 Ibid., 195.
42 Ibid., 150.
43 Muñoz, *Disidentifications*, 147.
44 Ibid., 15.
45 Ibid., 196.
46 Butler, "Solidarity/Susceptibility," 5.
47 Muñoz, *Disidentifications*, 168.
48 Christensen, *Rig Talk*, 7.
49 Ibid., 25.
50 Merchant, *Death of Nature*.
51 Christensen, *Rig Talk*, 27.
52 Ibid., 31.
53 Armstrong, "Land Speaking," 184.
54 Christensen, *Rig Talk*, 15.
55 Armstrong, "Land Speaking," 178.
56 Christensen, *Rig Talk*, 18.
57 Ibid., 67. This poem is used with permission of the author.
58 Christensen, *Rig Talk*, 47.
59 Zichy, "Poetry Review," 11.
60 Muñoz, *Disidentifications*, 185.
61 Cariou, "Tarhands."
62 My use of the term "racial-fossil-capitalist" here refers to the work of Black and antiracist scholars including Myles Lennon, Ryan Cecil Jobson, and Kathryn Yusoff, who add to Andreas Malm's argument that capital has always been fossil capital: capital has always been racial-fossil capital. On racial capitalism, see my earlier discussion on page 162n21; see also Robinson, *Black Marxism*; Melamed, "Racial Capitalism"; Jenkins and Leroy, *Histories of Racial Capitalism*. On racial capital and fossil capital, see Lennon, "Decolonizing Energy"; Jobson, "Dead Labor"; Yusoff, *Billion Black Anthropocenes*; Malm, *Fossil Capital*. This is discussed in more detail on page 161n9 and in chapters 5 and 6.

CHAPTER THREE

1 Dronyk, *Contrary Infatuations*, 77.

2 Ibid., 13.

3 See Deshaye, "Wolf, Star, and Ash"; Rettie, "Interiors."

4 Ngai, *Ugly Feelings*, 271. See Ngai's full chapter on "Stuplimity" (248–97). About the seeming stupidity of stuplimity, and in contrast to the sublime, Ngai writes, "[w]hat stuplimity relies on is an anti-auratic, anti-cynical tedium that at times deliberately risks seeming obtuse, as opposed to making claims for spiritual transcendence or ironic distance" (278). This seems to describe Dronyk's poetics. See my extended discussions of stuplimity in chapter 4 and the conclusion.

5 Dehsaye, "Wolf, Star, and Ash," n. pag.

6 Dronyk, *Contrary Infatuations*, 13.

7 Williams, *Marxism and Literature*, 131.

8 Ibid., 132.

9 Berlant, *Cruel Optimism*, 4.

10 Berlant coined the term *cruel optimism* in a journal article in 2006 (see Berlant, "Cruel Optimism"); I am suggesting that Berlant and Dronyk developed these concepts around the same time but independently of one another.

11 Berlant, *Cruel Optimism*, 24.

12 Ibid., 249.

13 Dominic Boyer and Imre Szeman, "The Rise of the Energy Humanities," *University Affairs*, March 2014, 40, https://www.universityaffairs-digital.com/university affairs/201403/?pm=1&u1=friend&pg=42#pg42; Petrocultures Research Group, *After Oil*, 15–16.

14 Federici, *Caliban and the Witch*, 97.

15 Dronyk, *Contrary Infatuations*, 76.

16 Gordon Jaremko, "'The Only Girl at the Rig' Uses Experience to Mediate Industry and Landowner Conflicts," *Alberta Oil: The Business of Energy*, 1 April 2009, accessed 11 September 2017.

17 Dronyk, *Contrary Infatuations*, 76.

18 See, for example, Gordon Jaremko, "The Blunt Bard of Wiebo Country; Dymphny Dronyk Immortalizes Oilpatch," *Edmonton Journal*, 9 May 2008, D1. ProQuest Canadian Major Dailies.

19 Dronyk, *Contrary Infatuations*, 80.

20 Yaeger, "Editor's Column," 306.

21 Lauren Berlant, "Lauren Berlant on her book *Cruel Optimism*," ROROTOKO, 5 June 2012, https://rorotoko.com/interview/20120605_berlant_lauren_on_cruel_optimism/.

22 LeMenager, *Living Oil*, 11.

23 Dronyk, *Contrary Infatuations*, 22.

24 Ibid., 25.

25 Ibid., 24.

26 Hurst, *United States and Iraq*, 8, 106; McQuaig, *It's the Crude*, 273–6.

27 Dronyk, *Contrary Infatuations*, 28. The citations in the extended discussions of *Contrary Infatuations* that follow are made using in-text parenthetical citations.

28 Dronyk dedicates the book to "Levi – who taught me that unconditional love is not always a tired old cliché," making a troubling statement in relation to the theme of contrary infatuation. It suggests that the husband taught the wife unconditional love not by showing it but by requiring it of her.

29 Yusoff, "Geologic Life," 781; 791.

30 Ibid., 791; 780.

31 Yusoff, *Billion Black Anthropocenes*, xii.

32 Dronyk, *Contrary Infatuations*, 85.

33 See "Drilling Fluids," Work Safe BC, accessed 8 January 2024, https://www.worksafebc.com/en/health-safety/hazards-exposures/drilling-fluids; "Drilling Mud," Energy Glossary, Schlumberger, accessed 8 January 2024, https://glossary.slb.com/Terms/d/drilling_mud.aspx. Despite the toxicity and often unknown composition of drilling fluids (also known as drilling mud), these materials are often splashed on workers on oil rigs. See, for example, videos of roughnecks working: A A, "Drilling Rig Canada," YouTube, 19 January 2013, https://www.youtube.com/watch?v=UVh_Jvon1ZQ; sleazyeddy, "The Roughneck Mudcan," YouTube, 30 May 2011, https://www.youtube.com/watch?v=FKASZx-8qos.

34 Perforation of a well may increase oil or gas production on its own, or it may be a first step before water is injected into the well to further break up the rock formation in a process known as *hydraulic fracturing* or *fracking*.

35 Dronyk, *Contrary Infatuations*, 88.

36 Ibid., 87.

37 De Luca, "Blake and Burke," 102.

38 Ngai, *Ugly Feelings*, 271.

39 Dronyk, *Contrary Infatuations*, 86.

40 Quoted in Jordan G. Teicher, "Inside the Temporary Homes of North Dakota Oil Workers," *Slate*, 14 March 2016, https://slate.com/culture/2016/03/kyle-cassidy-photographs-the-homes-of-oil-workers-in-north-dakota-in-the-bakken-goes-boom.html.

41 Dronyk, *Contrary Infatuations*, 91.

42 Ibid., 21.

43 Nikiforuk, *Saboteurs*, 26–7.

44 Christie Blatchford, "Wiebo's Dynamite: He Is a Man of Unyielding Beliefs, Adept at Manipulating Public Opinion. But Who Is this Oilpatch Crusader Who Has Created Such Fear in this Alberta Farming Community? A Report from the Front," *National Post*, 8 April 2000, B1. ProQuest Canadian Major Dailies.

45 Literary scholar Jennifer Wenzel describes and critiques the notion of the "resource curse": "[t]he 'resource curse' argument holds that bad governance and violent conflict are the inevitable lot of states unlucky enough to be so well-endowed with desirable natural resources that they can base their entire economies on extraction – at least for a while, until things turn sour. This diagnosis sees the problem as the resource itself. It also assumes the absence of traditions of democratic accountability in the places, disproportionately in the Global South, seen as accursed; Norway is cited endlessly as the exception that proves the resource curse rule. Eliding the histories through which such states are drawn into global capitalism, the resource curse analysis construes an abundance of particular minerals or plants – rather than, say, Chiquita or the CIA – as a threat to democratic rule and social welfare … [I]t is appealing in First World analyses precisely because it lets consumers, their governments, and multinational corporations off the hook" (*Disposition*, 106–7). Wenzel avoids using this term in reference to the Niger Delta, but applying the term to places usually considered to be exempt from the "resource curse" may be another way to shift thinking about the impacts of oil extraction away from myth and exoticism and toward accountability. Although Rob Nixon argues that Canada is "resource rich but not resource cursed" (*Slow Violence*, 70), some scholars disagree with this assessment. In her study of a potential "resource curse" on Indigenous peoples affected by the mining of oil sands in northern Alberta, Brenda Parlee takes in such factors as unemployment, lost access to the land and traditional ways of life, and increased rates of cancer and illness. She concludes "that symptoms of the resource curse are present in northern Alberta and felt acutely by Indigenous communities" ("Avoiding the Resource Curse," 434). Sourayan Mookerjea includes both Indigenous and settler communities when he writes that "[the regional municipality of] Wood Buffalo, along with much of Alberta, has been living with what scholars of boom-and-bust resource economies call the 'resource curse' ever since the oil and gas industry displaced agriculture and forestry over the postwar decades as the primary sector of production in terms of investment and growth" ("Petrocultures in Passive Revolution," 329).

46 Andreas Malm's recent polemic *How to Blow Up a Pipeline* (2021) makes a case for sabotage of "CO_2-emitting devices" as a tactic for a radical arm of the

climate movement (67), one that might serve as leverage to demand more immediate and drastic government action and emissions reduction. The story of Wiebo Ludwig and Trickle Creek suggests that sabotage can also have the effect of alienating potential allies and entrenching support for the industry. See James Wilt's critique of Malm's argument in "How to Blow Up a Movement: Andreas Malm's New Book Dreams of Sabotage but Ignores Consequences," *Canadian Dimension*, 3 March 2021, https://canadiandimension.com/articles/view/how-to-blow-up-a-movement-malms-new-book-dreams-of-sabotage-but-ignores-consequences.

47 Gunster et al., "Our Oil," 212.

48 Dronyk, *Contrary Infatuations*, 81.

49 Shotwell, *Against Purity*, 7.

50 Blatchford, "Wiebo's Dynamite," B1.

51 Dronyk, *Contrary Infatuations*, 78–9.

52 Dronyk, *Contrary Infatuations*, 16; 17. Rather than a more neutral term like *observers* or even *beneficiaries*, Dronyk uses the term *voyeurs*, with its suggestion that they watch with pleasure. See Sontag, *Regarding the Pain of Others*, 42.

53 Dronyk, *Contrary Infatuations*, 16–17. This is an example of what Eve Tuck and K. Wayne Yang call the "settler move to innocence" of "settler harm reduction" ("Decolonization Is Not a Metaphor," 21), where the conscientization of the settler replaces "the more uncomfortable task of relinquishing stolen land" (19).

54 Dronyk, *Contrary Infatuations*, 79.

55 Liboiron, *Pollution Is Colonialism*, 6.

56 Ibid., 134.

57 Dronyk, *Contrary Infatuations*, 81.

58 Liboiron, *Pollution Is Colonialism*, 88.

59 Dronyk, *Contrary Infatuations*, 83.

60 Ibid.

CHAPTER FOUR

1 Sally Cole, "Poet of the Oil Patch," *The Guardian* [Prince Edward Island], 3 June 2013 [updated 30 September 2017], https://www.theguardian.pe.ca/living/poet-of-the-oil-patch-109128/.

2 Mathew Henderson, "Mathew Henderson on Lust and Loneliness in the Oilfields," interview with Julie Wilson, 49th Shelf, 16 October 2013, https://49thshelf.com/Blog/2013/10/16/Mathew-Henderson-on-Lust-and-Loneliness-on-the-Oilfields.

3 See Alberta Learning and Information Service, "Oil and Gas Well Tester," YouTube,

10 April 2012, https://www.youtube.com/watch?v=1S70rpXcsD4; Jeffrey Landreth, "Brief Description of Flowback Operations," YouTube, 8 February 2017, https://www.youtube.com/watch?v=F1IVAu6to5U.

4 Henderson, *The Lease*, 8.

5 Ibid., 9.

6 See Robertson, "How Pastoral"; McSweeney, *The Necropastoral.*

7 Karpinski, "Unsettled Solutions," 207.

8 In *Jackpine Sonnets*, PEI-born poet Milton Acorn describes the form as "a short poem with a dialectical play of argument" that is "not always limited to fourteen lines" (16), with line lengths of "roughly, between 7 and 13 syllables" (19), and with "irregular rhyme" (20). Henderson's Jackpines, either in one long stanza or broken up into stanzas that echo Shakespearean or Petrarchan sonnet forms, make up the greater part of *The Lease*: thirty-nine of the fifty poems fall within Acorn's capacious parameters, and many of the remaining poems also follow sonnet-like patterns.

9 Henderson, *The Lease*, 7.

10 Dwight Garner, "On the Job, and Reading Between the Gritty Lines," *The New York Times*, 26 February 2013, https://www.nytimes.com/2013/02/27/books/the-lease-poetry-by-mathew-henderson.html.

11 Matthew Tierney, "The Trillium Conversations: Matthew Tierney and Mathew Henderson," *National Post*, 17 June 2013, https://nationalpost.com/entertainment/books/the-trillium-conversations-matthew-tierney-and-mathew-henderson.

12 Clarke, review of *The Lease.*

13 Rauscher, "Canadian Petro-Poetics," 105.

14 This statement must also now be read in light of George Elliott Clarke's recent collaborations with and defence of Stephen Kummerfield (now known as Stephen Brown), a white poet who was convicted of manslaughter and who served a short sentence for the 1995 murder in Regina of Pamela George, a Saulteaux woman who was also a poet. Clarke shows here that Henderson's privileging of class over race is not neutral; critics of Clarke, including Misty Longman (Saulteaux) of the ta-tawâw Student Centre at the University of Regina, have likewise argued that academic freedom should not be privileged over respect for missing and murdered Indigenous women and girls and their families. See Bonnie Allen and Alicia Bridges, "Case of Killer's Poetry Ignites Conversation about Indigenization and Academic Freedom," CBC Saskatchewan, 4 January 2020, https://www.cbc.ca/news/canada/saskatchewan/indigenization-academic-freedom-george-elliott-clarke-steven-kummerfield-1.5414821.

15 Rauscher, "Canadian Petro-Poetics," 104.
16 Henderson, "Navigating," 05:38–48.
17 Henderson, *The Lease*, 64.
18 Christensen, *Rig Talk*, 67.
19 Henderson, "Navigating."
20 Henderson, "Lust and Loneliness."
21 Henderson, *The Lease*, 48.
22 Ibid., 52. In a smart intertextual reference by Henderson, Dave unknowingly echoes Philip Levine's poem "What Work Is" and its exploration of disidentification through what Michel Pêcheux calls an "epistemological break" (*Language, Semantics and Ideology*, 139).
23 Henderson, *The Lease*, 30; 67. The subtle politicization of the narrator's confessional rig talk is signalled in Henderson's glancing reference to Allen Ginsberg's *Howl* in the closing line of the book, "As if you've ever stopped your howling" (67).
24 Henderson, *The Lease*, 10.
25 Ibid., 14.
26 Ibid., 67.
27 Wenzel, *Disposition of Nature*, 167.
28 Ibid., 18.
29 Henderson, "Navigating," 05:38–48.
30 Pêcheux, *Language, Semantics and Ideology*, 139.
31 Ibid., 137.
32 Henderson, *The Lease*, 38.
33 Christensen, *Rig Talk*, 15; Dronyk, *Contrary Infatuations*, 88.
34 Ngai, *Ugly Feelings*, 271.
35 Yusoff, "Geologic Life."
36 Henderson, *The Lease*, 10.
37 Ibid., 35.
38 Ibid., 14.
39 Perron, "Oil Bodies," 616.
40 Ibid., 612.
41 Oil extraction, as what Andreas Malm has called "*primitive accumulation of fossil capital*" (*Fossil Capital*, 291), is predicated on the prior and ongoing accumulations of settler colonialism, racism, and patriarchy. See Coulthard, *Red Skin, White Masks*, 12–13; Jobson, "Dead Labour," 221; Liboiron, *Pollution Is Colonialism*, 13; Yusoff, *Billion Black Anthropocenes*; Federici, *Caliban and the Witch*.
42 Tailfeathers, *Bloodland*.

43 Henderson, *The Lease*, 17. In the extended discussion of content from *The Lease* that follows, I use parenthetical, in-text citations.

44 Merchant, *Death of Nature*, 190.

45 Henderson, *The Lease*, 50.

46 Ibid.

47 Muñoz, *Disidentifications*, 31.

48 Henderson, *The Lease*, 49; see also 31.

49 Ibid., 49.

50 Butler, "Solidarity/Susceptibility," 5.

CHAPTER FIVE

1 Parkin, *Relationship with Truth*, 23.

2 Ibid., 28.

3 Cultural studies is interested in popular culture as a potential site of resistance and social change, yet also as continually co-opted and contained by the dominant culture (see Hall, "Notes").

4 For instance, the portrayal of a coworker as "slow" in Mathew Henderson's poem "Todd" (*The Lease*, 38), discussed in chapter 4.

5 Williams, *Country and the City*, 144.

6 Parkin, *Relationship with Truth*, 1.

7 Williams, *Marxism and Literature*, 131.

8 Parkin has some college education but no degree. He trained as a drilling fluids specialist in Houston, Texas. Subsequent to the publication of *A Relationship with Truth*, and after working as a "mud man" for twelve years, Parkin moved to British Columbia for a job in the mining industry. He is now a salesperson marketing wholesale building supplies and agricultural feed.

9 Dronyk, *Contrary Infatuations*. See my discussion of Dymphny Dronyk's poetic theorization of "contrary infatuation" as a structure of feeling of petromodernity in chapter 3.

10 *A Relationship with Truth* was published in April 2014, two months before the oil bust that saw the price of oil decline from around US$110 per barrel between 2011 and June 2014 to a low point of US$29 per barrel in January 2016. See Reinhard Ellwanger, Benjamin Sawatzky, and Konrad Zmitrowicz, "Factors Behind the 2014 Oil Price Decline," *Bank of Canada Review*, Autumn 2017, https://www.bankofcanada.ca/wp-content/uploads/2017/11/boc-review-autumn2017-ellwanger.pdf. The decline led oil companies to tighten their belts through automation, corporate restructuring, mergers and acquisitions, and the elimination of oil and gas jobs, many of which would not be reinstated. See "Workforce In-

sights: Impacts of the Oil and Gas Downturn on the Future and Attitudes of Workers," PetroLMI, Energy Safety Canada, 2017, 3, https://careersinenergy.ca/wp-content/uploads/2021/08/LabourSupplyReport_FINAL1.pdf; "2019 Oil and Gas Labour Market Update," PetroLMI, Energy Safety Canada, 2019, 5, https://careersinenergy.ca/wp-content/uploads/2021/08/2019_Labour_Market_Update_FINAL-1.pdf.

11 Yaeger, "Editor's Column," 306.

12 Parkin, *Relationship with Truth*, 37.

13 Because I am a scholar of poetry, and for simplicity's sake, I refer to the individual verses/poems as poems for the remainder of this chapter.

14 Bradley, *Book of Rhymes*, xv.

15 In both its form and its content that negotiates the tension between "modernity and wilderness" (Gordon, *Unsustainable Oil*, 56), Parkin's poetics bears comparison with S.C. Ells's popular, rhyming poetry, which is discussed in chapter 1.

16 According to some of the top *Urban Dictionary* definitions of *fronting*, it means "Acting like you are more, or you have more than what really exists" (Stacy, 14 November 2022); "Trying to pass yourself off as something you are not" (Nitro Survivor, 2 July 2010); and "Misrepresenting yourself, in regards to what you have or how you feel" (Oz, 25 November, 2022). See "fronting," Urban Dictionary, accessed 11 January 2024, https://www.urbandictionary.com/define.php?term=fronting. In the Fugees' "Fu-Gee-La," fronting is "A boy on the side of Babylon, trying to front like he's down with Mount Zion."

17 Parkin, *Relationship with Truth*, 24. In the extended discussions of *A Relationship with Truth* that follow, I use in-text parenthetical citations of page numbers.

18 Drawing on critiques of the exoticist term *magical realism* to describe fantastical literatures from the Global South and reading examples of petro-magic-realism about the Niger Delta, Wenzel describes *petro-magic* as a sense of promise surrounding oil that turns out to be a betrayal and form of violence. She writes, "[p]etro-magic offers the illusion of wealth without work; petro-magic-realism pierces such illusions, evoking a recognizably devastated, and recognizably fantastic, landscape." Wenzel, *Disposition of Nature*, 126. See my earlier discussion of the "resource curse" on page 176n45.

19 Parkin, *Relationship with Truth*, 53. With the author's permission, I have corrected a typographic error in this quotation.

20 Ibid., 20.

21 Notably, in another poem, titled "Surviving," Naden describes his job to "punch holes in her [nature's] frame," saying that he does it, in part, "[s]o I can afford the things / I want for my wife" (Parkin, *Relationship with Truth*, 72). See my

discussion of a similar use of "punching holes" in Mathew Henderson's *The Lease* in chapter 4, beginning on page 87.

22 Merchant, *Death of Nature*, 39.

23 Ibid., 288.

24 For two examples of Indigenous representations, see Tailfeathers, *Bloodland*; LaDuke, *Water Protector*, 192.

25 Watts, "Petro-Violence," 189.

26 Turcotte, "Contextualizing," 201.

27 Parkin, *Relationship with Truth*, 54.

28 See also Parkin, *Relationship with Truth*, 9–10; 59.

29 Karl Marx and Friedrich Engels write in *The Communist Manifesto*, "Not only are [labourers] slaves of the bourgeois class, and of the bourgeois State; they are daily and hourly enslaved by the machine, by the overlooker, and above all, by the individual bourgeois manufacturer himself" (88). See also Tracy, Lutgen-Sandvik, and Alberts, "Nightmares, Demons," in which the metaphor of slavery is considered among the "naturally occurring metaphors" of abused and bullied workers (150); and the *Oxford English Dictionary* definitions of *slave* as noun and verb that include "a person who works very hard without proper remuneration or appreciation" and "[t]o toil; to work hard," respectively. *Oxford English Dictionary*, s.v. "slave (*n.* & *adj.*)," December 2023, https://doi.org/10.1093/OED/1339272053; *Oxford English Dictionary*, s.v. "slave (*v.*2)," July 2023, https://doi.org/10.1093/OED/3907400868.

30 See Gabrielle P. Foreman, et al., "Writing about Slavery/Teaching about Slavery: This Might Help" community-sourced document, NAACP Culpeper #7058, accessed 11 January 2024, https://naacpculpeper.org/resources/writing-about-slavery-this-might-help/; da Silva, "Unpayable Debt," 101–2; Soyinka, "Slave Talk."

31 Parkin, *Relationship with Truth*, 9.

32 da Silva, "Unpayable Debt," 88.

33 See Brand, *Map*; Cooper, *Hanging of Angélique*; Hartman, *Scenes of Subjection*; Sharpe, *In the Wake*; International Labour Organization, *Global Estimates.*

34 Parkin, *Relationship with Truth*, 33.

35 Wynter, "Unsettling"; See also Garba and Sorentino, "Slavery Is a Metaphor," 778; Yusoff, *Billion Black Anthropocenes*, 63.

36 Here, Parkin uses the trope of the Noble Savage, which, as Robert Berkhofer Jr shows in *The White Man's Indian,* white people have used for centuries to critique European or settler-colonial culture while also reinforcing white supremacy.

37 Parkin, *Relationship with Truth*, 10.

38 Ibid., 9.

39 Melamed, "Racial Capitalism," 77.

40 Parkin, *Relationship with Truth*, 10.

41 Haraway, *Staying with the Trouble*, 78.

42 Parkin, *Relationship with Truth*, 37.

43 Ibid., 52.

44 Ibid., 22; 23; 39–40; 43.

45 Although both Young and Parkin use extractive metaphors, Young's description of a lifelong process of "searching for a heart of gold" in his song reveals that a heart of gold is more properly described as being made through ongoing relationship with the land, not as a property or possession that can be taken from it. An environmental, anti-war, and Indigenous-rights activist, Young visited the oil sands and the Athabasca Chipewyan First Nation (ACFN) in September 2013, then did an "Honour the Treaties" tour to benefit the legal defence fund for the ACFN in January 2014. He made explicit statements criticizing the tar sands at both times. See "Neil Young Blasts Tar Sands & Harper Government," YouTube, 12 January 2014, https://www.youtube.com/watch?v=p41EnK7hd7M; Marty Klinkenberg and Mariam Ibrahim, "Rocker Helps Bankroll Oilsands Battle; Benefit Concerts for First Nation," *Edmonton Journal*, 10 December 2013, LexisNexis Uni.

46 See Margery Fee's *Literary Land Claims* on how literary texts can make Indigenous and settler-colonial claims on land.

47 Gaudry and Andersen, "*Daniels v. Canada*," 27.

48 Parkin, *Relationship with Truth*, 17.

49 See Daschuk, *Clearing the Plains*.

50 Parkin, *Relationship with Truth*, 7; 55.

51 Shell's Groundbirch project is on Treaty 8 land and the traditional territory of the West Moberly First Nations near Dawson Creek, BC.

52 Parkin, *Relationship with Truth*, 43.

53 See, for example, Northrop Frye's discussion of the "garrison mentality" (*Bush Garden*, 227) and Margaret Atwood's characterization of Canadian literature as having an "ever-present feeling of menace," with "survival" as its central symbol (*Survival*, 25; 27).

54 Parkin, *Relationship with Truth*, 42. See also 10; 36; 55.

55 Liboiron, *Pollution Is Colonialism*, 7n19.

56 Ibid., 42–6.

57 Tuck and Yang, "Decolonization Is Not a Metaphor," 6.

58 Hern and Johal, *Global Warming*, 30.

59 Ibid., 172.

60 Young, "Heart of Gold."

CHAPTER SIX

1 Brand, *No Language Is Neutral*, 19.

2 Levant, *Ethical Oil*, 107.

3 Nikiforuk, *Energy of Slaves*, 66.

4 Sleydo' (Molly Wickham), "Dramatic Video Shows Militarized Canadian Police Raid Wet'suwet'en Land Defenders & Journalists," filmed by Michael Toledano. YouTube, uploaded by Democracy Now, 24 November 2021, https://www.youtube.com/watch?v=raO_s9W09po.

5 António Guterres, "Secretary-General Warns of Climate Emergency, Calling Intergovernmental Panel's Report 'a File of Shame,' While Saying Leaders 'Are Lying,' Fuelling Flames," United Nations, 4 April 2022, www.un.org/press/en/2022/sgsm21228.doc.htm.

6 Greta Thunberg, "'Blah Blah Blah': Greta Thunberg Dismisses World Leaders' Climate Rhetoric." YouTube, uploaded by NBC News, 28 September 2021, https://www.youtube.com/watch?v=UryIL4kUcx8.

7 Oilfield technology company Schlumberger has recently been rebranded as SLB, a "global technology company, driving energy innovation for a balanced planet." "Who We Are," SLB, accessed 12 January 2024, https://www.slb.com/about/who-we-are. Schlumberger's *Oilfield Glossary* has been renamed the *Energy Glossary*. "Energy Glossary." SLB, accessed 12 January 2024, https://glossary.slb.com. The rebranding and repositioning of extractive industry are part of the management of language and information that Battler examines in *Endangered Hydrocarbons*.

8 See Battler, *Endangered Hydrocarbons*, 77–83; 133–42. See *Oxford English Dictionary*, s.v. "sinister (*adj.*, *n.*, & *adv.*)," December 2023, https://doi.org/10.1093/OED/1718144737.

9 Chen, *Animacies*, 106.

10 Eichorn and Milne, *Prismatic Publics*, 9.

11 Zolf, "Irritating and Stimulating," 32.

12 Battler, *Endangered Hydrocarbons*, 7.

13 Ibid., 15.

14 Ibid., 77.

15 Sloane, review of *Endangered Hydrocarbons*, 2.

16 Battler, *Endangered Hydrocarbons*, 173.

17 Battler, "Quarclet: The Poetics of Big Oil," *ARC Poetry*, 2011, https://arcpoetry.ca/editorials/quarclet-lesley-battler/.

18 Levant, *Ethical Oil*, 12.

19 Ibid., 12; 14; 43; 47.

20 Battler, *Endangered Hydrocarbons*, 108.

21 Frye, *Bush Garden*, 227.

22 Battler, *Endangered Hydrocarbons*, 109.

23 Ibid., 108; 109.

24 See Barker, *Red Scare*; Proulx, "Colonizing Surveillance."

25 Battler, *Endangered Hydrocarbons*, 109.

26 Ibid., 110.

27 Barker, *Red Scare*, 5.

28 Battler, *Endangered Hydrocarbons*, 110.

29 The criminalization of dissent against extractive projects in recent years includes the Province of Alberta's passing of the Critical Infrastructure Defence Act (Bill 1) in 2020, the Province of Manitoba's attempt to pass a similar act, the Protection of Critical Infrastructure Act (Bill 57) in 2021, and the British Columbia RCMP's establishment of the Community-Industry Response Group, a militarized police body that defends corporate interests and has been called "The Pipeline Police." See Emily Chan, "Explainer: Alberta's Controversial Critical Infrastructure Defence Act," Canadian Civil Liberties Association, 14 April 2022, https://ccla.org/get-informed/talk-rights/explainer-albertas-controversial-critical-infrastructure-defence-act/; Brendan Devlin, "Critical Infrastructure Protection: Dangerous Politics in Manitoba, Alberta and Beyond," *Canadian Dimension*, 17 February 2021, https://canadiandimension.com/articles/view/critical-infrastructure-protection-dangerous-politics-in-manitoba-alberta-and-beyond; Brett Forester, "Behind the Thin Blue Line: Meet a Secretive Arm of the RCMP in B.C.," *APTN News*, 16 June 2022, https://www.aptnnews.ca/ourstories/cirg.

30 Nikiforuk, *Energy of Slaves*, xi. Slavery has never, in fact, been abolished. As Cedric J. Robinson observes in *Black Marxism: The Making of the Black Radical Tradition*, slavery cannot be conceived as a precapitalist mode of production and accumulation. Rather, "[f]or more than 300 years slave labor persisted beyond the beginnings of modern capitalism, complementing wage labor, peonage, serfdom, and other methods of labor coercion" (4). This is one of the reasons Robinson gives for conceiving of capitalism as always racial capitalism.

31 Johnson, "Energy Slave," 963. Johnson tracks the history of the terms *mechanical servant*, *electric servant*, and *energy slave*, extending to a proliferation of writing on the energy slave in the early twenty-first century (956).

32 See Girvan, *Carbon Footprints*, 193; Mouhout, "Past Connections."

33 See Jobson, "Dead Labor"; Lennon, "Decolonizing Energy"; Mirzoeff, "Not the Anthropocene."

34 Battler, *Endangered Hydrocarbons*, 36.

35 I experienced this firsthand when I heard Battler read the poem at a Forum on Poetics, Energy, and Extraction that I co-hosted at the University of Manitoba Institute for the Humanities in March 2022.

36 George Caffentzis, "The Petroleum Commons," CounterPunch, 15 December 2004, https://www.counterpunch.org/2004/12/15/the-petroleum-commons/.

37 *Oxford English Dictionary*, s.v. "animate (*adj.* & *n.*)," September 2023, https://doi.org/10.1093/OED/7146672614; *Oxford English Dictionary*, s.v. "inanimate (*adj.* & *n.*)," December 2023, https://doi.org/10.1093/OED/6254819292.

38 Chen, *Animacies*, 2.

39 Ibid., 27.

40 Ibid., 24–7.

41 Ibid., 9; 30; 11.

42 Ibid., 10.

43 Ibid., 13; 203.

44 Ibid., 13.

45 Chen, *Animacies*, 106; and see 102–6.

46 See Bezan and McKay, *Animal Remains*.

47 Chen, *Animacies*, 28.

48 Todd, "Fish, Kin, and Hope," 104.

49 Battler, *Endangered Hydrocarbons*, 56.

50 Yusoff, "Geologic Life," 789. See my discussion of the proposed geological epoch of the Anthropocene in chapter 7, beginning on page 130; see also 188n4.

51 On the silencing and marginalization of geologic life and of Indigenous/Animist peoples through "geontologies" that are foundational to modern, colonial life, see Povinelli, *Geontologies*.

52 In his argument that oil is the lifeblood of American culture, geographer Matthew Huber contends that "refineries can be seen as particular expressions of the historically specific relations between petroleum and society" (*Lifeblood*, 70). The Fractionater is central to Huber's metaphor of the privatized and entrepreneurial "*fractionated lives*" of neoliberal American subjects (64), but he also notes that oil refineries are toxic and endangering to nearby communities, disproportionately communities of colour, as in the example of "Cancer Alley" on the Gulf Coast (69). A Canadian example is the Aamjiwnaang First Nation near Sarnia, Ontario, which is surrounded by petrochemical processing plants and whose

people suffer the health effects of polluted air, water, and land (see Wiebe, *Everyday Exposure*; Murphy, "2. Some Keywords"). With refineries representing and producing environmental racism – and with hydrocarbons that escape the Fractionater through flaring or leakage serving as the agents of violence – Battler's implied parallels with slavery and genocide are, sadly, appropriate.

53 Battler, *Endangered Hydrocarbons*, 56.

54 Ibid., 57.

55 Ibid., 59.

56 Karpinski, "Isotopic Ecopoetics," 116. Karpinski reads *Endangered Hydrocarbons* as a "poetics of appropriation" that enacts a "politicized ecopoetics" (108).

57 Battler, *Endangered Hydrocarbons*, 56.

58 See Girvan, "Trickster Carbon."

59 Battler, *Endangered Hydrocarbons*, 57.

60 Fanon, *Black Skin, White Masks*, 140; Hughes, "Harlem."

61 See my earlier discussions of racial capitalism, especially on pages 100 and 162n21.

62 Nikiforuk, *Energy of Slaves*, 180.

63 Malm, *Progress of this Storm*, 99.

64 Yusoff, *Billion Black Anthropocenes*, 108.

65 Battler, *Endangered Hydrocarbons*, 103–4.

66 *Oxford English Dictionary*, s.v. "uppity (*adj.*)," July 2023, https://doi.org/10.1093/OED/8446255801; "uppity," Urban Dictionary, accessed 12 January 2024, https://www.urbandictionary.com/define.php?term=uppity; Elspeth Reeve, "Yep, 'Uppity' Is Racist," *The Atlantic*, 22 November 2011, https://www.theatlantic.com/politics/archive/2011/11/yep-uppity-racist/335160.

67 Cooper, *Hanging of Angélique*, 7. Many Canadians do not know that our colonial history up until the abolition of slavery in the British Empire in 1833 includes over 200 years during which the enslavement of Indigenous people, Africans, and their descendants was both legal and common in Canada (70).

68 Battler, *Endangered Hydrocarbons*, 103.

69 I have chosen not to reproduce or quote "Uppity Molecules" to mitigate harm. The found text for this poem comes from the book *Country: The Twisted Roots of Rock 'n' Roll*, where the author, Nick Tosches, cites the ads somewhat disinterestedly as references to "fiddling slaves" (168). Battler lists Tosches's biography of minstrel/blackface performer Emmett Miller, *Where Dead Voices Gather*, in her "Partial list of sources" (*Endangered* 174), but the ads are not quoted in that book.

70 Lennon, "Decolonizing Energy," 24; 25.

71 Yusoff, *Billion Black Anthropocenes*, xii.

72 Ibid., 16.

73 Ibid., 5; xii.

74 Quoted in Jobson, "Dead Labor," 215

75 Yusoff, *Billion Black Anthropocenes*, 101.

76 Maracle, "Water," 37.

CHAPTER SEVEN

1 See page 165n63 for an explanation of my decision to alternate between *oil sands* and *tar sands*.

2 Tim Querengesser, "Automation Vs. Humanity and the Future of Alberta's Oilsands," *The Huffington Post*, 22 November 2018, https://www.huffpost.com/archive/ca/entry/automation-vs-humanity-and-the-future-of-albertas-oil-sands_a_23563966.

3 Wakefield, *Anthropocene Back Loop*.

4 The Anthropocene is a proposed geological epoch profoundly shaped by humans. While the Anthropocene Working Group of scientists has been debating the validity of the theory and proposed start dates, parallel debates have been going on in the humanities and social sciences. Some notable contributions include Davis and Todd, "Importance of a Date"; Farrier, *Anthropocene Poetics*; Haraway's chapter on "Tentacular Thinking: Anthropocene, Capitalocene, Chthulucene" in *Staying with the Trouble*, 30–57; Mirzoeff, "Not the Anthropocene"; Moore, "Anthropocene or Capitalocene"; Povinelli, *Geontologies*; Yusoff, *Billion Black Anthropocenes*.

5 Bird discusses this in a podcast interview that is no longer available online: Lindsay Bird, "The Poetry of the Oil Sands," *Bookings: The King's Co-op Bookstore Podcast*, 27 May 2019.

6 Westman, Joly, and Gross, "Introduction," 10.

7 Unrau, "Founding Fathers," 73.

8 Bird, *Boom Time*, 37.

9 Marrone, "Hark! Anachronism," 176.

10 Ruiz, *Slow Disturbance*, 7.

11 Wakefield, *Anthropocene Back Loop*, 26.

12 Ibid., 32.

13 The dedication is to Kate Beaton's sister Becky, who also worked in the oil sands with Beaton and Bird, and who died of cancer.

14 Bird, *Boom Time*, 9.

15 As part of its final report, *Reclaiming Power and Place* (2019), the National Inquiry into Missing and Murdered Indigenous Women and Girls does what it

calls a "Deeper Dive" into "Resource Extraction Projects and Violence against Indigenous Women." The report links "man camps" to violence against Indigenous women, girls, and 2SLGBTQQIA people; it concludes by assigning responsibility not only to governments and industry but also to "all Canadians, including those workers who may contribute to the problem by participating in violence themselves, or by creating situations in which violence is ignored and normalized as part of the work environment" (593).

16 Bird, *Boom Time*, 43.

17 The Narwhal, "Western Canadian Select Prices," in "Alberta's Record-Low Oil Prices: What the Coronavirus and a Supply Glut Mean for the Province," by Sharon J. Riley, 20 March 2020, https://thenarwhal.ca/albertas-record-low-oil-prices-what-the-coronavirus-and-a-supply-glut-mean-for-the-province.

18 Dronyk, *Contrary Infatuations*, 88. See my discussion of Dymphny Dronyk's *Contrary Infatuations* in chapter 3.

19 da Silva, "Unpayable Debt," 108. da Silva argues that "global capital lives off the total value expropriated from slave labour and native lands" (88). Where value has been generated by capitalists through the "total violence" of land theft and enslavement (86), an "economic deficit" comes to be attributed to the dispossessed as if it were a "natural [racial] deficit, but which is nothing more than the effect of colonial expropriation and later juridical, symbolic, and everyday violence" (108).

20 Whyte, "Indigenous Climate Change Studies," 160.

21 Yusoff, *Billion Black Anthropocenes*, 59.

22 Winona LaDuke, "The Time Thieves," *Park Rapids Enterprise*, 14 January 2022. The piece is no longer available on the *Park Rapids Enterprise* website; it is available at https://www.winonaladuke.com/winona-blog/2022/1/14/the-time-thieves.

23 LaDuke, *Water Protector*, 83.

24 Bird, *Boom Time*, 43.

25 LaDuke, *Water Protector*, 14.

26 See, for example, Liboiron, *Pollution Is Colonialism*; Kimmerer, *Braiding Sweetgrass*; Todd, "Fossil Fuels."

27 Marshall, "Indigenous Knowledges." See also Bartlett, Marshall, and Marshall, "Two-Eyed Seeing."

28 Bird, *Boom Time*, 35.

29 Ibid., 43. The poem "Celebrity Gossip with Charlie Yahyahkeekoot" reveals the speaker likes to gossip (63). In the extended discussion of *Boom Time* that follows, I use in-text parenthetical citations of page numbers.

30 Turner, *The Patch*, xxiv.

31 Bird, *Boom Time*, 23.
32 See, for example, oil sands industry founder and civil servant S.C. Ells's early twentieth-century description of "the empty woods and white wastes of the North" (*Northland Trails*, 187).
33 Wenzel, "Improvement and Overburden."
34 Whyte, "Indigenous Climate Change Studies," 159.
35 Bird, *Boom Time*, 12.
36 LaDuke, *Water Protector*, 83.
37 Johnston, "Weendigo," 222–3.
38 Ibid., 235.
39 Yaeger, "Editor's Column," 306. This impulse is related to, but distinct from, the one that drives settler-colonial writers in Canada to represent animate land as monstrous, perhaps most famously with E.J. Pratt's giant Laurentian reptile in *Towards the Last Spike*. Pratt's modernist epic about the modernizing project of the construction of the Canadian railway is representative of the Anthropocene front loop: it uses the monstrous to repress and contain the resistance of Indigenous peoples and the land against colonization. In a poetic reversal of pathetic fallacy, the wilderness that is supposedly conquered by colonial modernism strikes back in the back loop, turning out to be real, and alive, after all. From the back loop, the modernizing project itself is recognizable as always having been violent and monstrous, along with the humans who advance ecocidal and genocidal projects, including the tar sands.
40 Van Camp, *Godless but Loyal*, 12.
41 Ibid., 16. Other examples of contemporary Wiindigoo stories include Cherie Dimaline's *The Marrow Thieves* and Waubgeshig Rice's *Moon of the Crusted Snow* and *Moon of the Turning Leaves*.
42 Bird, *Boom Time*, 36.
43 International Energy Agency, *Net Zero by 2050*, 21.
44 Bird, *Boom Time*, 12.

CONCLUSION

1 Shepherd, "Pocket Notebook Poetics."
2 An earlier version of this poem was published as "Excavators" in issue 9 (2016) of the UK-based *Dark Mountain* journal. I do not include a chapter on Kelly Shepherd's poetry because as poetry collections only partially about oil work, his books do not fit the parameters of this study, but I am glad to feature this poem and to alert readers to Shepherd's work. Shepherd is my colleague and friend; we

have collaborated on conference panels, a book review, and a planned poetry anthology.

3 Known by many as a prescient author of feminist dystopian fiction and climate fiction, Atwood has recently been embroiled and outspoken in the UBC Accountable scandal. Even as the TV adaptation of *The Handmaid's Tale* has resonated with and served to critique the recent rise of anti-abortion, anti-queer, anti-immigrant, and racist ideology, Atwood's doubling down in defense of an accused sexual predator came to be emblematic of Canadian Literature being, and always having been, a "dumpster fire" (see Elliott, "Raging Dumpster Fire"). As the editors of *Refuse: CanLit in Ruins* write, the crises sparked by UBC Accountable, other revelations of sexual harassment in creative-writing and English departments, the crass discussion among magazine and newspaper editors about creating an "Appropriation Prize," and the unfolding revelations of "Pretendian" (that is, pretending-to-be-Indigenous) creators and scholars are only the most recent manifestations of "long-standing problems in CanLit related to racism, colonialism, sexism, the literary star system, and economic privilege" (McGregor, Rak, and Wunker, *Refuse*, 10).

This citation of Atwood's poem about a bus ride in Toronto recalls a passage about a bus ride in Vancouver in Dionne Brand's *A Map to the Door of No Return*. See Brand, *Map*, 219–21. In Atwood's poem, and in a move typical of the settler-colonial tropes of fear and denial of the wilderness, the land is personified as an "old woman / sitting across from you on the bus" who shoots from her eyes "secret / hatpins" that destroy and dissolve the bus, the street, and the city. The speaker of Brand's poetic contemplation of "lost maps" is a Black diasporic woman sitting with a friend on a city bus driven by a Black diasporic man (221). A Coast Salish woman boards the bus and asks for directions ("redundantly," because she is presumably lost on her own territory). Brand concludes, about the four characters in this story, "We have perfected something – each of us something different. One drives through lost paths, one asks the way redundantly, one floats and looks, one looks and floats – all marvel at their ability to learn and forget the way of lost maps. We all feign ignorance at the rupture in mind and body, in place, in time. We all feel it" (221). Where the wilderness's dissolution of the bus and its surroundings in Atwood's poem comes off as a postmodern trick, connected to but actively repressing the colonial and racial dispossession and violence (the ruptures) it symbolically unravels, Brand's text draws attention to the ruptures created through the colonization of Africa and the Americas, the dispossession of Indigenous peoples, and the trans-Atlantic slave trade. Canadian literature, like Canadian subjectivity, is built on *feigning*, rather than *being*, ignorant of the violence that constitutes it, and, even as the subjects in Brand's story go along with the bus ride and the story they are part of, the sense that "We all feel it" prefigures modes for decolonial and anticolonial subjectivity.

4 Henderson, *The Lease*, 9.

5 Gómez-Barris, *Extractive Zone*, 6.

6 Christensen, *Rig Talk*.

7 Henderson, *The Lease*, 14; Christensen, *Rig Talk*, 32.

8 Yusoff, *Billion Black Anthropocenes*.

9 Gómez-Barris, *Extractive Zone*, 1.

10 Povinelli, *Geontologies*.

11 Butler, "Solidarity/Susceptibility," 18.

12 Kate Beaton, "Ducks," part 5, *Hark! A Vagrant*, 7 April 2014, https://beatonna.tumblr.com/post/81993262830/here-is-a-sketch-comic-i-made-called-ducks-in.

13 This is in keeping with Judith Butler's theory of gender performativity. See Butler, *Gender Trouble*.

14 Beaton, "Ducks," part 5. While I was writing this book, Cape Breton comics artist Kate Beaton published her long-anticipated graphic memoir about working in the oil sands, *Ducks*. Beaton's book depicts life as a young woman in work camps near Fort McMurray, Alberta, in the early 2000s, including the Long Lake camp that also features in Shepherd's oil-work poems (see Shepherd's poem "Long Lake Camp, Fort McMurray," in *Shift*, 51). Although Beaton's award-winning book is not oil-worker poetry, it is oil-worker poetics, and my scholarly and creative work on petropoetics has developed in conversation with *Ducks*.

15 The writing for this conclusion began in response to a call for papers on "Climate, Justice, and the Politics of Emotion." The resulting symposium was renamed "Environment, Justice, and the Politics of Emotion" and was held in April 2023. The titles for both the symposium and this conclusion refer to the foundational feminist and queer affect theory of Sara Ahmed, including *The Cultural Politics of Emotion*. My engagement with oil-worker affect theory here is also in conversation with and indebted to other affect theory including Ahmed's *The Promise of Happiness*, Lauren Berlant's *Cruel Optimism*, Mel Chen's *Animacies*, José Esteban Muñoz's *Disidentifications*, Sianne Ngai's *Ugly Feelings*, Eve Kosofsky Sedgwick's *Touching Feeling*, Nicole Seymour's *Bad Environmentalism*, and Christina Sharpe's *In the Wake*.

16 See Ngai, *Ugly Feelings*, 248–97.

17 Henderson, *The Lease*, 17; 48; 64.

18 Peter Christensen, Letter to Glen Sorestad, 30 April 1982. MSS 116 (A.90–64), box 6, folder 7, Thistledown Press Ltd fonds. This is discussed in chapter 2.

19 Christensen, *Rig Talk*, 32.

20 Parkin, *A Relationship with Truth*, 23.

21 Battler, *Endangered Hydrocarbons*, 156.

22 Christensen, *Rig Talk*, 18.

23 Henderson, *The Lease*; 54.

24 Ibid., 48.

25 Dronyk, *Contrary Infatuations*, 80.

26 Greta Thunberg, "'I want you to panic': 16-Year-Old Issues Climate Warning at Davos," *YouTube*, 25 January 2019, https://www.youtube.com/watch?v=RjsLm5PCdVQ.

27 António Guterres, "Secretary-General's Remarks to High-Level Opening of COP27," *United Nations*, 7 November 2022, https://www.un.org/sg/en/content/sg/speeches/2022-11-07/secretary-generals-remarks-high-level-opening-of-cop27.

28 As novelist Amitav Ghosh shows in *The Nutmeg's Curse: Parables for a Climate in Crisis*, fossil fuels are essential to the dominant geopolitical order established through Western colonial capitalism, and those who sit at the pinnacle of wealth and power have not yet figured out how to hold on to their power without fossil fuels. See Ghosh, *Nutmeg's Curse*, 105–20.

29 Massie and Jackson, "Standing Up," 55. On extractive populism, see Gunster et al., "Our Oil."

30 Amanda Stephenson, "Suncor Has Been Too Focused on Energy Transition, Must Get Back to Fundamentals: CEO," CBC, 15 August 2023, https://www.cbc.ca/news/canada/calgary/suncor-too-focused-on-energy-transition-rich-kruger-says-1.6937360; Mia Rabson, "Suncor CEO Says Company Committed to Decarbonization, Is Accused of Greenwashing," CBC, 17 October 2023, https://www.cbc.ca/news/canada/calgary/suncor-rich-kruger-commons-steven-guilbeault-george-chahal-1.6997365.

31 Stephen Buhler, "I Work in the Fossil Fuel Industry and I Believe in a Green New Deal," *Our Time*, 22 April 2019, https://our-time.ca/stephen. Emphasis in original. Reprinted with the permission of the author.

32 On Kimberlé Crenshaw's theory of intersectionality, see, for example, Crenshaw, "Mapping the Margins."

33 Similarly, in *Climate Change as Class War*, Matthew Huber proposes a broadened concept of the ecological working class as the basis for an effective movement for climate justice (18–23; 187–90). Alienated from the land and dependent on the

oil-centred economy, those who belong to this loosely defined class of "the masses who rely on the market to survive" (188) are dependent on fossil fuels and easily compelled to admit that they/we love oil, but Huber suggests that the ecological working class could band together to overthrow fossil capital instead of propping it up.

34 Parkin, *A Relationship with Truth*, 53.

35 See Ngai, *Ugly Feelings*.

36 Henderson, *The Lease*, 64; 67.

37 Battler, *Endangered Hydrocarbons*, 7.

38 Ibid., 102.

39 Dronyk, *Contrary Infatuations*, 82.

40 On "energy lifeworld" arguments, see Gunster et al., "Our Oil," 199; 219.

41 Hern and Johal, *Global Warming and the Sweetness of Life*.

42 Bird, *Boom Time*, 43.

43 Parkin, *A Relationship with Truth*, 53.

44 Dronyk, *Contrary Infatuations*, 75–6; Bird, *Boom Time*, 26.

45 Bird, *Boom Time*, 22.

46 See the Care Collective, *Care Manifesto*; Alook et al., *End of This World*.

47 Henderson, *The Lease*, 67.

48 Christensen, *Rig Talk*, 43; 45.

49 Henderson, *The Lease*, 17.

50 Alook et al., *End of This World*, 156.

51 See, for example, Canadian Labour Congress, "A Future that Works," accessed 14 March 2024, https://futurethatworks.ca; UNIFOR, "Environment," accessed 28 January 2024, https://www.unifor.org/node/7872; CUPE, *Working Harmoniously on the Earth: CUPE's National Environmental Policy*, 2021, https://cupe.ca/sites/cupe/files/cupe_environmental_policy_2021_eng.pdf.

Bibliography

ARCHIVAL SOURCES

Sidney Clarke Ells fonds, Library and Archives Canada, Ottawa, Canada.

Thistledown Press Ltd. fonds, University of Manitoba Archives, Winnipeg, Canada.

PRINT SOURCES

Acorn, Milton. *Jackpine Sonnets.* Toronto: Steel Rail Educational Publishing, 1977.

Ahmed, Sara. *The Cultural Politics of Emotion*. New York: Routledge, 2004.

– *The Promise of Happiness.* Durham, NC: Duke University Press, 2010.

Alook, Angele, Emily Eaton, David Gray-Donald, et.al. *The End of This World: Climate Justice in So-Called Canada*. Toronto: Between the Lines, 2023.

Alook, Angele, Ian Hussey, and Nicole Hill. *Indigenous Gendered Experiences of Work in an Oil-Dependent, Rural Alberta Community*. Parkland Institute. 21 February 2019. https://www.parklandinstitute.ca/indigenous_gendered_experiences_of_work.

Althusser, Louis. "Ideology and Ideological State Apparatuses (Notes towards an Investigation)." 1970. In *Lenin and Philosophy and Other Essays*. Translated by Ben Brewster, 61–83. New York: Monthly Review, 2001.

Apollinaire, Guillaume. "Du coton dans les oreilles." In *Calligrammes: Poèmes de la paix et de la guerre 1913–1916.*, Paris: Gallimard, 1925, 140–4.

Armstrong, Jeannette C. "Land Speaking." In *Speaking for the Generations: Native Writers on Writing*, edited by Simon J. Ortiz, 174–94. Tucson: University of Arizona Press, 1998.

Asch, Michael I. "Slavey." In *Subarctic*, edited by June Helm, 338–49. 1981. Vol. 6 of *Handbook of North American Indians*. Edited by William C. Sturtevant. Washington: Smithsonian Institution, 1978–.

Atabaki, Touraj, Elisabetta Bini, and Kaveh Ehsani, eds. *Working for Oil: Comparative Social Histories of Labor in the Global Oil Industry*. London: Palgrave Macmillan, 2018. https://doi.org/10.1007/978-3-319-56445-6.

Atwood, Margaret. "A Bus along St. Clair: December." In *The Journals of Susanna Moodie*. 1970. Illustrated by Charles Pachter. Macfarlane Walter & Ross, 1997, n.pag.

– *Survival: A Thematic Guide to Canadian Literature*. 1972. Toronto: Anansi, 2012.

Balloni, Massimo. "Workshop, 'After Censorship, Before Freedom: Mapping Contemporary Russian Literature,' Princeton University, 28–9 March 2014." *Russian Journal of Communication* 6, no. 3 (2014): 324–35. https://doi.org/10.1080/19409419.2014.957005.

Barker, Joanne. *Red Scare: The State's Indigenous Terrorist*. Berkeley: University of California Press, 2021, doi.org/10.1525/9780520972674.

Barrett, Ross, and Daniel Worden, eds. *Oil Culture*. Minneapolis: Minnesota University Press, 2014.

Bartlett, Cheryl, Murdena Marshall, and Albert Marshall. "Two-Eyed Seeing and Other Lessons Learned with a Co-Learning Journey of Bringing Together Indigenous and Mainstream Knowledges and Ways of Knowing." *Journal of Environmental Studies and Sciences* 2, no. 4 (2012): 331–40. https://doi.org/10.1007/s13412-012-0086-8.

Bassey, Nnimmo. *We Thought It Was Oil but It Was Blood*. Ibadan, NG: Kraft, 2002.

Bate, Jonathan. *The Song of the Earth*. London: Picador, 2000.

Battler, Lesley. *Endangered Hydrocarbons*. Toronto: BookThug, 2015.

Beaton, Kate. *Ducks: Two Years in the Oil Sands*. Montreal: Drawn & Quarterly, 2022.

Bellamy, Brent Ryan, and Jeff Diamanti. "Editors' Introduction: Envisioning the Energy Humanities." *Reviews in Cultural Theory* 6, no. 3 (2016): 1–4. http://reviewsinculture.com/archive/volume-6-issue-3/.

– eds. *Materialism and the Critique of Energy*. Chicago, IL: MCM, 2018. http://www.mcmprime.com/books/marxism-and-energy.

Belot, Ross. *Moving to Climate Change Hours*. Hamilton, ON: James Street North Books, 2020.

Berkhofer, Robert F. Jr. *The White Man's Indian: Images of the American Indian from Columbus to the Present*. 1978. New York: Vintage, 1979.

Berlant, Lauren. "Cruel Optimism." *Differences: A Journal of Feminist Cultural Studies* 17, no. 3 (2006): 20–36. https://doi.org/10.1215/10407391-2006-009.

– *Cruel Optimism*. Durham, NC: Duke University Press, 2011.

Bezan, Sarah, and Robert McKay, eds. *Animal Remains*. New York: Routledge, 2021. https://doi.org/10.4324/9781003129806.

Bird, Lindsay. *Boom Time*. Kentville, NS: Gaspereau, 2019.

Bradley, Adam. *Book of Rhymes: The Poetics of Hip Hop*. New York: Basic, 2009. EBSCOhost Academic eBook Collection.

Brand, Dionne. *Bread out of Stone: Recollections Sex Recognitions Race Dreaming Politics*. Toronto: Coach House, 1994.

– *A Map to the Door of No Return: Notes to Belonging*. Toronto: Vintage Canada, 2002.

– *No Language Is Neutral*. 1990. Toronto: McClelland & Stewart, 1998.

Braunecker, Melanie. "A Greed to Which We Agreed? Representations of the Oil Industry in Canadian Petro-Literature." PhD diss., University of Graz, 2020.

Brown, Howard. *So You Want to Be a Roughneck: Tales from the Alberta Oil Rigs in the 1960s*. Self-published, 2009.

Brydges, David C. *Crude Truths*. Self-published: Brydge Builder Press, 2013.

Butler, Judith. *Gender Trouble*. 1990. New York: Routledge, 1999.

– "Solidarity/Susceptibility." *Social Text* 36, no. 4 (2018): 1–20.

The Care Collective [Andreas Chatzidakis, Jamie Hakim, Jo Littler, Catherine Rottenberg, and Lynne Segal]. *The Care Manifesto: The Politics of Interdependence*. London: Verso, 2020.

Cariou, Warren. "Aboriginal." In *Fueling Culture: 101 Words for Energy and Environment*, edited by Imre Szeman, Jennifer Wenzel, and Patricia Yaeger, 17–20. New York: Fordham University Press, 2017.

– "Oil Drums: Indigenous Labour and Visions of Compensation in the Tar Sands Zone." In *Materialism and the Critique of Energy*, edited by Brent Ryan Bellamy and Jeff Diamanti, 581–602. Chicago, IL: MCM, 2018. http://www.mcmprime.com/books/marxism-and-energy.

– "Tarhands: A Messy Manifesto." *Imaginations* 3, no. 2 (2012): 17–34. http://dx.doi.org/10.17742/IMAGE.sightoil.3-2.3.

Carroll, William K, ed. *Regime of Obstruction: How Corporate Power Blocks Energy Democracy*. Athabasca, AB: Athabasca University Press, 2021. https://doi.org/10.15215/aupress/9781771992893.01.

Chasar, Mike. *Everyday Reading: Poetry and Popular Culture in Modern America*. New York: Columbia University Press, 2012. Proquest Ebook Central Academic Complete.

Chastko, Paul. *Developing Alberta's Oil Sands: From Karl Clark to Kyoto*. Calgary, AB: University of Calgary Press, 2004.

Chen, Mel Y. *Animacies: Biopolitics, Racial Mattering, and Queer Affect*. Durham, NC: Duke University Press, 2012.

Christensen, Peter. *Rig Talk*. Saskatoon: Thistledown, 1981.

Chua, Rina Garcia. "Migrant Ecocriticism: Unbinding Movements and Spaces in Anthologies of Ecopoetry." PhD diss., University of British Columbia Okanagan, 2022.

Clark, Karl A. *Oil Sands Scientist: The Letters of Karl A. Clark, 1920–1949*, edited by Mary Clark Sheppard. Edmonton: University of Alberta Press/Alberta Culture and Multiculturalism, 1989.

Clarke, George Elliott. Review of *The Lease* by Mathew Henderson, and *Here for the Music* by Laurie Brinklow. *Maple Tree Literary Supplement* no. 15 (2013). https://www.mtls.ca/issue15/writings/reviews/george-elliott-clarke/2/.

Cochrane, Mark. "CHRISTENSEN, Peter." *Encyclopedia of Literature in Canada*, edited by William H. New, 206. Toronto: University of Toronto Press, 2002.

– "COWBOY POETRY." *Encyclopedia of Literature in Canada*, edited by William H. New, 240-1. Toronto: University of Toronto Press, 2002.

Comfort, Darlene J. *The Abasand Fiasco: The Rise and Fall of a Brave Pioneer Oil Sands Extraction Plant.* Self-published, 1980.

Cooley, Dennis. *The Vernacular Muse: The Eye and Ear in Contemporary Literature.* Winnipeg: Turnstone Press, 1987.

Cooper, Afua. *The Hanging of Angélique: The Untold Story of Canadian Slavery and the Burning of Old Montreal.* Toronto: HarperCollins, 2006.

Coulthard, Glen Sean. *Red Skin, White Masks: Rejecting the Colonial Politics of Recognition.* Minneapolis: University of Minnesota Press, 2014.

Crenshaw, Kimblerlé. "Mapping the Margins: Intersectionality, Identity Politics, and Violence against Women of Color." *Stanford Law Review* 43, no. 6 (1991): 1241–99. https://www.jstor.org/stable/1229039.

Cuelho, Art. Review of *Rig Talk* by Peter Christensen. *Hard Row to Hoe: Reviews from Rural America* 1, no. 7 (1984): 2–3.

Daggett, Cara. "Petro-masculinity: Fossil Fuels and Authoritarian Desire." *Millennium: Journal of International Studies* 47, no. 1 (2018): 25–44. https://doi.org/10.1177/0305829818775817.

Daschuk, James. *Clearing the Plains: Disease, Politics of Starvation, and the Loss of Aboriginal Life.* Regina: University of Regina Press, 2013.

Davidson, Debra J., and Mike Gismondi. "Visualizing the Tar Sands Through Time." In *Challenging Legitimacy at the Precipice of Energy Calamity*. New York: Springer, 2011, 39–68. https://doi.org/10.1007/978-1-4614-0287-9.

Davis, Heather, and Zoe Todd. "On the Importance of a Date, or, Decolonizing the Anthropocene." ACME: *An International Journal for Critical Geographers* 16, no. 4, (2017): 761–80. https://acme-journal.org/index.php/acme/article/view/1539.

De Luca, V.A. "Blake and Burke in Astonishment!" *Blake: An Illustrated Quarterly* 23, no. 2 (1989): 100–4. https://bq.blakearchive.org/23.2.deluca.

Deshaye, Joel. "Wolf, Star, and Ash." *Canadian Literature* no. 205 (2010): 140–1. ProQuest One Literature.

Dickinson, Adam. "Energy Humanities and Metabolic Poetics." *Reviews in Cultural Theory* 6, no. 3 (2016): 17–21. http://reviewsinculture.com/2016/03/09/energy-humanities-and-metabolic-poetics.

Dietz, Kristina, and Bettina Engels, eds. *Contested Extractivism, Society and the State: Struggles over Mining and Land*. London: Palgrave Macmillan, 2017. https://link.springer.com/book/10.1057/978-1-137-58811-1.

Dimaline, Cherie. *The Marrow Thieves*. Toronto: Cormorant, 2017.

Dobson, Kit. "Canada." In *Fueling Culture: 101 Words for Energy and Environment*, edited by Imre Szeman, Jennifer Wenzel, and Patricia Yaeger, 65–7. New York: Fordham University Press, 2017.

Dronyk, Dymphny. *Contrary Infatuations*. Calgary, AB: Frontenac House, 2007.

Dyce, Matt, and James Opp. "Visualizing Space, Race, and History in the North: Photographic Narratives of the Athabasca-Mackenzie River Basin." In *The West and Beyond: New Perspectives on an Imagined Region*, edited by Alvin Finkel, Sarah Carter, and Peter Fortna, 65–93. Athabasca, AB: Athabasca University Press, 2010.

Eaton, Emily, and Simon Enoch. "The Oil Industry Is Us: Hegemonic Community Economic Identity in Saskatchewan's Oil Patch." In *Regime of Obstruction: How Corporate Power Blocks Energy Democracy*, edited by William K. Carroll, 307–30. Athabasca, AB: Athabasca University Press, 2021. https://doi.org/10.15215/aupress/9781771992893.01.

Eaton, Emily, and Abby Kinchy. "Quiet Voices in the Fracking Debate: Ambivalence, Nonmobilization, and Individual Action in Two Extractive Communities (Saskatchewan and Pennsylvania)." *Energy Research & Social Science* 20 (2016): 22–30. https://doi.org/10.1016/j.erss.2016.05.005.

Eichorn, Kate, and Heather Milne. *Prismatic Publics: Innovative Canadian Women's Poetry and Poetics*. Toronto: Coach House, 2009.

Elliott, Alicia. "CanLit Is a Raging Dumpster Fire." In *Refuse: CanLit in Ruins*, edited by Hannah McGregor, Julie Rak, and Erin Wunker, 93–8. Toronto: Book*hug, 2018.

Ells, S.C. "Athabaska Trail." *Canadian Geographical Journal* 18, no. 6 (1939): 328–39.

– "The Message." *Canadian Mining Journal* December 1932, 537–40.

– *Northland Trails*. Toronto: Garden City Press, 1938.

– *Northland Trails*. New and enlarged edition. Toronto: Burns & MacEachern, 1956.

– *Recollections of the Development of the Athabasca Oil Sands*. Ottawa: Canada Department of Mines and Technical Surveys, 1962.

Faiers, Chris. "Work, Love and Small Towns." Review of *Rig Talk* by Peter Christensen, *Disturbances* by Greg Simison, and *The Life of Ryley* by Monty Reid. *Cross-Canada Writers Quarterly* 4, no. 2–3 (1982): 44–5.

Fanon, Frantz. *Black Skin, White Masks*. Translated by Charles Lam Markmann. New York: Grove, 1967.

Farrier, David. *Anthropocene Poetics: Deep Time, Sacrifice Zones, and Extinction*. Minneapolis: University of Minnesota Press, 2019.

Federici, Silvia. *Caliban and the Witch: Women, the Body, and Primitive Accumulation*. Brooklyn, NY: Autonomedia, 2004.

Fee, Margery. *Literary Land Claims: The "Indian Land Question" from Pontiac's War to Attawapiskat*. Waterloo, ON: Wilfrid Laurier University Press, 2015.

Ferguson, Barry Glen. *Athabasca Oil Sands: Northern Research Exploration 1875–1951*. Edmonton: Alberta Culture/Canadian Plains Research Center, 1985.

Fisher, Kathy. *Prairie Wheel: A Vision of Turnaround*. Self-published, 2014.

Francis, Marvin. *Bush Camp*. Winnipeg: Turnstone, 2008.

Frye, Northrop. *The Bush Garden: Essays on the Canadian Imagination*. 1971. Concord, ON: Anansi, 1995.

The Fugees. "Fu-Gee-La." *The Score*. Sony/ATV, 1995.

Fuller, R. Buckminster. "World Energy." *Fortune*, February 1940, 57.

Gale, Ron. *The Oil Patch (Cowboy Poems Four)*. Self-published: Bergen Ranch Products, [2017].

Garba, Tapji, and Sara-Maria Sorentino. "Slavery Is a Metaphor: A Critical Commentary on Eve Tuck and K. Wayne Yang's 'Decolonization Is Not a Metaphor.'" *Antipode* 52, no. 3 (2020): 764–82. https://doi.org/10.1111/anti.12615.

Gaudry, Adam, and Chris Andersen. "*Daniels v. Canada*: Racialized Legacies, Settler Self-Indigenization, and the Denial of Indigenous Peoplehood." TOPIA 36 (2016): 19–30. https://topia.journals.yorku.ca/index.php/topia/article/view/40396.

Ghosh, Amitav. *The Nutmeg's Curse: Parables for a Planet in Crisis*. Chicago, IL: University of Chicago Press, 2021.

Girvan, Anita. *Carbon Footprints as Cultural-Ecological Metaphors*. Milton Park, GB: Routledge, 2018.

– "Trickster Carbon: Stories, Science, and Postcolonial Interventions for Climate Justice." *Journal of Political Ecology* 24 (2017): 1038–54.

Gómez-Barris, Macarena. *The Extractive Zone: Social Ecologies and Decolonial Perspectives*. Durham, NC: Duke University Press, 2017.

Gordon, Jon. *Unsustainable Oil: Facts, Counterfacts, and Fictions*. Edmonton: University of Alberta Press, 2015.

Gross, Lena. "Wastelanding the Bodies, Wastelanding the Land: Accidents as Evidence in the Albertan Oil Sands." In *Extracting Home in the Oil Sands: Settler Colonialism and Environmental Change in Subarctic Canada*, edited by Clinton Westman, Tara L. Joly, and Lena Gross, 82–100. London: Routledge, 2020.

Gunster, Shane, Robert Neubauer, John Bermingham, and Alicia Massie. "'Our Oil': Extractive Populism in Canadian Social Media." In *Regime of Obstruction: How Corporate Power Blocks Energy Democracy*, edited by William K Carroll, 197–224. Athabasca, AB: Athabasca University Press, 2021

Hall, Stuart. "Notes on Deconstructing 'the Popular.'" 1981. In *Cultural Theory and Popular Culture: A Reader*, edited by John Storey. 4th ed., 508–18. Harlow, GB: Pearson Education, 2009.

Haraway, Donna J. *Simians, Cyborgs, and Women: The Reinvention of Nature*. London: Free Association, 1991.

– *Staying with the Trouble: Making Kin in the Chthulucene*. Durham, NC: Duke University Press, 2016.

Hartman, Saidiya. *Scenes of Subjection: Terror, Slavery, and Self-Making in Nineteenth-Century America*. New York: Oxford University Press, 1997.

Helbig, Louis. *Beautiful Destruction*. [Victoria, BC]: Rocky Mountain Books, [2014].

Henderson, Mathew. *The Lease*. Toronto: Coach House, 2012.

– "Navigating Class and Ethics in *The Lease*." Panel D: Writing Oil. Cultures of Energy 5 Spring Symposium, Rice University, Houston, 23 April 2016. YouTube, https://www.youtube.com/watch?v=oT3IdoIkjTA.

Hern, Matt, and Am Johal, with Joe Sacco. *Global Warming and the Sweetness of Life: A Tar Sands Tale*. Cambridge, MA: MIT Press, 2018.

hooks, bell. "Revolutionary Parenting." 1984. In *Maternal Theory: Essential Readings*, edited by Andrea O'Reilly, 145–56. Toronto: Demeter, 2007.

Huber, Matthew. *Climate Change as Class War: Building Socialism on a Warming Planet*. London: Verso, 2022.

– *Lifeblood: Oil, Freedom, and the Forces of Capital*. Minneapolis: University of Minnesota Press, 2013.

Hughes, Langston. "Harlem [2]." In *Montage of a Dream Deferred*. 1951. *The Collected Poems of Langston Hughes*, edited by David Roessel, 426. New York: Alfred A. Knopf, 1996.

Hunt, Joyce e. *Local Push Global Pull: The Untold History of the Athabaska Oil Sands, 1900–1930*. Self-published: PushPull, 2011.

Hurst, Steven. *The United States and Iraq Since 1979: Hegemony, Oil and War*. Edinburgh, GB: Edinburgh University Press, 2009.

Innis, Harold A. *The Fur Trade in Canada*. 1930. Rev. ed. Toronto: University of Toronto Press, 1999.

Intergovernmental Panel on Climate Change (IPCC). *Climate Change 2021 – The Physical Science Basis: Working Group I Contribution to the Sixth Assessment Report of the Intergovernmental Panel on Climate Change.* Cambridge: Cambridge University Press, 2023. https://doi.org/10.1017/9781009157896.

– *Climate Change 2022: Mitigation of Climate Change. Contribution of Working Group III to the Sixth Assessment Report of the Intergovernmental Panel on Climate Change.* Cambridge: Cambridge University Press, 2022. https://doi.org/10.1017/9781009157926.

International Energy Agency. *Net Zero by 2050: A Roadmap for the Global Energy Sector.* July 2021. https://www.iea.org/reports/net-zero-by-2050.

International Labour Organization. *Global Estimates of Modern Slavery: Forced Labour and Forced Marriage.* Geneva, SE: International Labour Organization, Walk Free, and International Organization for Migration, 2022. https://www.ilo.org/global/topics/forced-labour/publications/WCMS_854733/lang—en/index.htm.

Jenkins, Destin, and Justin Leroy, eds. *Histories of Racial Capitalism.* New York: Columbia University Press, 2021. EBSCO eBook Collection.

Jobson, Ryan Cecil. "Dead Labor: On Racial Capital and Fossil Capital." In *Histories of Racial Capitalism*, edited by Destin Jenkins and Justin Leroy, 215–30. New York: Columbia University Press, 2021. EBSCO eBook Collection.

Johnson, Bob. *Carbon Nation: Fossil Fuels in the Making of American Culture.* Lawrence, KS: University Press of Kansas, 2014.

– "Energy Slave: Carbon Technologies, Climate Change, and the Stratified History of the Fossil Economy." *American Quarterly* 68, no. 4 (2016): 955–79. https://doi.org/10.1353/aq.2016.0074.

Johnston, Basil. "Weendigo." In *The Manitous: The Spiritual World of the Ojibway*, 221–37. New York: Harper Collins, 1995.

Kalinin, Ilya. "Petropoetics." In *Russian Literature Since 1991*, edited by Evgeny Dobrenko, 120–44. Cambridge: Cambridge University Press, 2015.

Karpinski, Max. "Isotopic Poetics: The Petrocultural Appropriations of Lesley Battler's *Endangered Hydrocarbons.*" *Imaginations: Journal of Cross-Cultural Image Studies* 13, no. 1 (2022): 107–28. https://doi.org/10.17742/IMAGE.PM.13.1.7.

– "Unsettled Solutions: Petropastoral Poetics in Rita Wong's *undercurrent.*" *Studies in Canadian Literature / Études en littérature canadienne* 45, no. 2 (2020): 205–28. https://doi.org/10.7202/1080280ar.

Keller, Lynn. *Recomposing Ecopoetics: North American Poetry of the Self-Conscious Anthropocene.* Charlottesville: University of Virginia Press, 2017.

Kimmerer, Robin Wall. *Braiding Sweetgrass: Indigenous Wisdom, Scientific Knowledge, and the Teachings of Plants.* Minneapolis: Milkweed Editions, 2013.

Lacan, Jacques. "The Freudian Unconscious and Ours." In *The Four Fundamental*

Concepts of Psycho-Analysis, edited by Jacques-Alain Miller, translated by Alan Sheridan, 7–28. London: Routledge, 2004. EBSCOhost.

LaDuke, Winona. *To Be a Water Protector: The Rise of the Wiindigoo Slayers.* Halifax: Fernwood/Spotted Horse, 2020.

Lane, Patrick. "The Saskatchewan Presses." *Grain* 9, no. 4 (1981): 52–7.

LaRocque, Emma. *When the Other Is Me: Native Resistance Discourse, 1850–1990.* Winnipeg: University of Manitoba Press, 2010.

Laxer, Gordon. "Alberta's Sands, Staples, and Traps." In *The Staple Theory @ 50: Reflections on the Lasting Significance of Mel Watkins's "A Staple Theory of Economic Growth,"* edited by Jim Stanford, 53–7. Canadian Centre for Policy Alternatives, April 2014. https://policyalternatives.ca/publications/reports/staple-theory-50.

LeMenager, Stephanie. *Living Oil: Petroleum Culture in the American Century.* Oxford: Oxford University Press, 2014.

Lennon, Myles. "Decolonizing Energy: Black Lives Matter and Technoscientific Expertise amid Solar Transitions." *Energy Research & Social Science* 30 (2017): 18–27. https://doi.org/10.1016/j.erss.2017.06.002.

Levant, Ezra. *Ethical Oil: The Case for Canada's Oil Sands.* Toronto: McClelland & Stewart, 2010.

Levine, Philip. "What Work Is." In *What Work Is.* New York: Alfred A. Knopf, 1991, 18–19.

Liboiron, Max. *Pollution Is Colonialism.* Durham, NC: Duke University Press, 2021.

Longley, Hereward. "Bitumen Exploration and the Southern Re-Inscription of Northeastern Alberta: 1875–1967." *RCC Perspectives,* no. 4 (2016): 17–24. www.jstor.org/stable/10.2307/26241385.

Lorde, Audre. "Man Child: A Black Lesbian Feminist's Response." 1979. In *Sister Outsider: Essays & Speeches.* Freedom, CA: The Crossing Press, 1984, 72–80.

Madill, Dennis F.K. *Treaty Research Report: Treaty Eight (1899)*, Treaties and Historical Research Centre, Indian and Northern Affairs Canada, 1986. https://www.aadnc-aandc.gc.ca/eng/1100100028809/1100100028811.

Malm, Andreas. *How to Blow Up a Pipeline: Learning to Fight in a World on Fire.* London: Verso, 2021.

– *Fossil Capital: The Rise of Steam Power and the Roots of Global Warming.* London: Verso, 2016.

– *The Progress of this Storm: Nature and Society in a Warming World.* London: Verso, 2018.

Maracle, Lee. "Water." In *Downstream: Reimagining Water*, edited by Rita Wong and Dorothy Christian, 44–9. Waterloo, ON: Wilfrid Laurier University Press, 2017. Scholars Portal Books.

Marrone, Daniel. "Hark! Anachronism: Kate Beaton's Metafiction." In *The Canadian Alternative: Cartoonists, Comics, and Graphic Novels*, edited by Dominick Grace and Eric Hoffman, 176–88. Jackson: University Press of Mississippi, 2017. https://doi.org/10.14325/mississippi/9781496815118.003.0012.

Marshall, Albert. "Indigenous Knowledges & Two-Eyed Seeing." Lecture at Prairie Climate Centre, University of Winnipeg, Winnipeg, MB, 10 November 2021.

Martens, Garth. *Prologue for the Age of Consequence*. Toronto: Anansi, 2014.

Martin, David. *Tar Swan*. Edmonton: NeWest, 2018.

Marx, Karl, and Friedrich Engels. *The Communist Manifesto.* Translated by Samuel Moore. 1888. Harmondsworth, GB: Penguin, 1967.

Massie, Alicia, and Emma Jackson. "'Standing Up for Canadian Oil & Gas Families': Tracing Gender, Family, and Work in the Alberta Petro-Economy." *Media Tropes* 7, no. 2 (2020): 40–66. https://doi.org/10.33137/mt.v7i2.33669.

McBride, Robert. *Poems Satirical & Sentimental, On Many Subjects Connected with Canada, Including a Complete Exposure of Our County Court, and Division Court System, in Several Theatrical Acts & Dialogues, Showing How the People Have Been, and Are Now Victimized. All Tending to Prove on the Part of Those Indicated, A Complete Conspiracy Set Up by Them for the Purpose of Enslaving the People of this Country. Also a Dissertation on the Doings of the Canada Company's Land, Jobbing, and Other Matters.* London, ON: Dawson & Brother, Book & Job Printers, 1869.

McCormack, Patricia A. "Conclusion: Studying the Social and Cultural Impacts of 'Extreme Extraction' in Northern Alberta." In *Extracting Home in the Oil Sands: Settler Colonialism and Environmental Change in Subarctic Canada*, edited by Clinton Westman, Tara L. Joly, and Lena Gross, 180–98. London: Routledge, 2020.

– *Fort Chipewyan and the Shaping of Canadian History, 1788–1920s: "We like to be free in this country."* Vancouver: UBC Press, 2010.

McGregor, Hannah, Julie Rak, and Erin Wunker. eds. *Refuse: CanLit in Ruins*. Toronto: Book*hug, 2018.

McLean, Jacob. "Low Class Oil Trash and the Politico-Aesthetics of the Fossilized Proletariat." *Canadian Literature* no. 251 (2022): 97–118.

McQuaig, Linda. *It's the Crude, Dude: War, Big Oil and the Fight for the Planet.* Toronto: Doubleday Canada, 2004.

McSweeney, Joyelle. *The Necropastoral: Poetry, Media, Occults.* Ann Arbor: University of Michigan Press, 2015. https://doi.org/10.3998/mpub.7573327.

Melamed, Jodi. "Racial Capitalism." *Critical Ethnic Studies* 1, no. 1 (2015): 76–85. https://doi.org/10.5749/jcritethnstud.1.1.0076.

Merchant, Carolyn. *The Death of Nature: Women, Ecology and the Scientific Revolution.* 1980. New York: HarperCollins, 1990.

Mirzoeff, Nicholas. "It's Not the Anthropocene, It's the White Supremacy Scene; or, The Geological Color Line." In *After Extinction*, edited by Richard Grusin, 123–49. Minneapolis: University of Minnesota Press, 2018.

Mitchell, Timothy. *Carbon Democracy: Political Power in the Age of Oil.* 2nd ed. London: Verso, 2013.

Mookerjea, Sourayan. "Petrocultures in Passive Revolution: The Autonomous Domain of Treaty Poetics." In *Petrocultures: Oil, Politics, Culture*, edited by Sheena Wilson, Adam Carlson, and Imre Szeman, 325–54. Montreal: McGill-Queen's University Press, 2017.

Moore, Jason W. "Anthropocene or Capitalocene? On the Nature and Origins of Our Ecological Crisis." In *Capitalism in the Web of Life: Ecology and the Accumulation of Capital*. London: Verso, 2015, 169–92.

Mouhout, Jean-François. "Past Connections and Present Similarities in Slave Ownership and Fossil Fuel Usage." *Climactic Change* 105, no. 1–2 (2011): 329–55. https://doi.org/10.1007/s10584-010-9982-7.

Muñoz, José Esteban. *Disidentifications: Queers of Color and the Performance of Politics.* Minneapolis: University of Minnesota Press, 1999.

Murphy, Michelle. "2. Some Keywords toward Decolonial Methods: Studying Settler-Colonial Histories and Environmental Violence from Tkaronto." *History and Theory: Studies in the Philosophy of History* 59, no. 3 (2020): 376–84. https://doi.org/10.1111/hith.12165.

National Inquiry into Missing and Murdered Indigenous Women and Girls. "Deeper Dive: Resource Extraction Projects and Violence against Indigenous Women." In *Reclaiming Power and Place: The Final Report of the National Inquiry into Missing and Murdered Indigenous Women and Girls*, vol. 1a (2019): 584–94. https://www.mmiwg-ffada.ca/final-report.

New, W.H. "Tops and Tales: Mountain Anecdote and Mountain Metaphor." *Canadian Poetry* 55 (2004), 111–31. http://www.canadianpoetry.ca/cpjrn/vol55/new.htm.

Ngai, Sianne. *Ugly Feelings.* Cambridge, MA: Harvard University Press, 2005.

Ngũgĩ wa Thiong'o. *Globalectics: Theory and the Politics of Knowing.* New York: Columbia University Press, 2012.

Nicholson, Owain. *Digsite.* Gibsons, BC: Nightwood, 2016.

Nikiforuk, Andrew. *The Energy of Slaves: Oil and the New Servitude.* Vancouver: Greystone, 2012.

– *Saboteurs: Wiebo Ludwig's War against Big Oil.* 2002. 2nd ed. Vancouver: Greystone, 2014.

Nixon, Rob. *Slow Violence and the Environmentalism of the Poor.* Cambridge, MA: Harvard University Press, 2011.

O'Brien, T. Peter. "Coming Through Fire." Review of *The Whisky Vigil* by Erin Mouré and *Rig Talk* by Peter Christensen. *McGill Literary Journal* 3, no. 2 (1982): 86–8.

Parkin, Naden. *A Relationship with Truth: Poem and Verse Born in the Canadian Oil Patch.* Self-published, 2014.

Parlee, Brenda L. "Avoiding the Resource Curse: Indigenous Communities and Canada's Oil Sands." *World Development* 74 (2015): 425–36. https://doi.org/10.1016/j.worlddev.2015.03.004.

Pêcheux, Michel. *Language, Semantics and Ideology*. 1975. Translated by Harbans Nagpal. London: Macmillan Press, 1982.

Perron, Dominique. "The Oil Bodies: Workers of Fort McMurray." Translated by Wafa Gaiech. In *Materialism and the Critique of Energy*, edited by Brent Ryan Bellamy and Jeff Diamanti, 605–25. Chicago, IL: MCM, 2018. http://www.mcmprime.com/books/marxism-and-energy.

Petrocultures Research Group, *After Oil*. Edmonton: Petrocultures Research Group, 2016.

Pilon, Ellen. Review of *Rig Talk* by Peter Christensen. *Canadian Book Review Annual 1981*, edited by Dean Tudor and Ann Tudor, 153–4. Toronto: Simon & Pierre, 1983.

Povinelli, Elizabeth A. *Geontologies: A Requiem to Late Liberalism.* Durham, NC: Duke University Press, 2016.

Pratt, E.J. *Towards the Last Spike.* Toronto: Macmillan, 1952.

Proulx, Craig. "Colonizing Surveillance: Canada Constructs an Indigenous Terror Threat." *Anthropologica* 56, no. 1 (2014): 83–100. www.jstor.org/stable/24469643.

Rancière, Jacques. *Proletarian Nights: The Workers' Dream in Nineteenth-Century France.* 1981. Translated by John Drury. London: Verso, 2012.

Rauscher, Judith. "Canadian Petro-Poetics: Masculinity, Labor, and Environment in Mathew Henderson's *The Lease*." In *Energy in Literature: Essays on Energy and Its Social and Environmental Implications in Twentieth and Twenty-First Century Literary Texts*, edited by Paula Anca Farca, 99–111. Oxford: TrueHeart Academic, 2014.

Rettie, Alex. "Interiors: Quartet 2007 Gets Personal." *Alberta Views* 10, no. 8 (2007): 59. EBSCOhost Canadian Reference Centre.

Rice, Waubgeshig. *Moon of the Crusted Snow*. Toronto: ECW, 2018.

– *Moon of the Turning Leaves*. Toronto: Random House, 2023.

Ricou, Laurie. "Poetry." In *Literary History of Canada: Canadian Literature in English.* 2nd ed. Vol. 4. Edited by W.H. New, 3–45. Toronto: University of Toronto Press, 1990.

Robertson, Lisa. "How Pastoral: A Manifesto." In *Telling It Slant: Avant-Garde Poetics of the 1990s*, edited by Mark Wallace and Steven Marks, 21–6. Tuscaloosa: University of Alabama Press, 2002.

Robinson, Cedric J. *Black Marxism: The Making of the Black Radical Tradition*. 3rd ed. Chapel Hill: University of North Carolina Press, 2020.

Ronda, Margaret. *Remainders: American Poetry at Nature's End*. Stanford, CA: Stanford University Press, 2018.

Ruddick, Sara. *Maternal Thinking: Toward a Politics of Peace*. 1989. Boston: Beacon Press, 1995.

Ruiz, Rafico. *Slow Disturbance: Infrastructural Mediation on the Settler Colonial Resource Frontier*. Durham, NC: Duke University Press, 2021.

Saborimanesh, Nayereh. "Toward Sustainable Remediation of Oil Sands Fine Tailings – A Review." *Journal of Environmental Management* 288 (2021): 1–10. https://doi.org/10.1016/j.jenvman.2021.112418.

Sedgwick, Eve Kosofsky. *Touching Feeling: Affect, Pedagogy, Performativity*. Durham, NC: Duke University Press, 2003.

Seymour, Nicole. *Bad Environmentalism: Irony and Irreverence in the Ecological Age*. Minneapolis: University of Minnesota Press, 2018.

Sharpe, Ada, and Sarah-Jean Krahn. *Alberta Holed 'Em: Playin for Girls, Gold and Oil*. Self-published, 2009.

Sharpe, Christina. *In the Wake: On Blackness and Being*. Durham, NC: Duke University Press, 2016.

– *Ordinary Notes*. Toronto: Alfred A. Knopf, 2023.

Shepherd, Kelly. *Fort McMurray Tricksters*. North Vancouver: Alfred Gustav, 2014.

– *Insomnia Bird*. Saskatoon: Thistledown, 2018.

– "Pocket Notebook Poetics." *Canadian Literature* no. 251 (2022): 157–60.

– *Shift*. Saskatoon: Thistledown, 2016.

Sheppard, Mary Clark. "The Post War Years and a New Pilot Plant." In *Oil Sands Scientist: The Letters of Karl A. Clark, 1920–1949*, edited by Mary Clark Sheppard, 80–6. Edmonton: University of Alberta Press/Alberta Culture and Multiculturalism, 1989.

Shotwell, Alexis. *Against Purity: Living Ethically in Compromised Times*. Minneapolis: University of Minnesota Press, 2016.

Siebert, Melanie. *Deepwater Vee*. Toronto: McClelland & Stewart, 2010.

da Silva, Denise Ferreira. "Unpayable Debt: Reading Scenes of Value against the Arrow of Time." In *The documenta 14 Reader*, edited by Quinn Latimer and Adam Szymczyk, 81–113. Munich: Prestel, 2017.

Sloane, Michael D. Review of *Endangered Hydrocarbons* by Lesley Battler. *The Goose* 14, no. 2 (2016). https://scholars.wlu.ca/thegoose/vol14/iss2/1/.

Smith, Douglas. "Rink Rats and Ravens." *Books in Canada* 11, no. 3 (1982): 16–17.

Song, Min Hyoung. *Climate Lyricism*. Durham, NC: Duke University Press, 2022.

Sontag, Susan. *Regarding the Pain of Others.* New York: Picador, 2003.

Soyinka, Wole. "Slave Talk: Between Metaphor and Reality." Henry Louis Gates Jr Lecture, Yale University, 9 April 2014. YouTube, www.youtube.com/watch?v=nVSwUtB6pyA.

Spivak, Gayatri Chakravorty. "Can the Subaltern Speak?" 1988. In *Colonial Discourse and Post-Colonial Theory: A Reader*, edited by Patrick Williams and Laura Chrisman, 66–111. New York: Columbia University Press, 1994.

Stott, Gregory. "Poetic Justice: Corruption in Lambton County, Canada West, 1854–1858." *Ontario History* 105, no. 3 (2013): 160–82. https://doi.org/10.7202/1050732ar.

Strasbourg, Alvena. *Memories of a Metis Woman: Fort McMurray Yesterday & Today.* Self-published: [1998].

Szeman, Imre. *On Petrocultures: Globalization, Culture, and Energy*. Morgantown: West Virginia University Press, 2019.

Szeman, Imre, and Dominic Boyer. *Energy Humanities: An Anthology.* Baltimore, MD: Johns Hopkins University Press, 2017.

Szeman, Imre, and Jennifer Wenzel. "What Do We Talk about When We Talk about Extractivism?" *Textual Practice* 35, no. 3 (2021): 505–23. https://doi.org/10.1080/0950236X.2021.1889829.

Szeman, Imre, Jennifer Wenzel, and Patricia Yaeger, eds. *Fueling Culture: 101 Words for Energy and Environment.* New York: Fordham University Press, 2017.

Tailfeathers, Elle-Máijá. *Bloodland*, 2011. YouTube, https://www.youtube.com/watch?v=LSfBWMSl1rw.

Todd, Zoe. "Fish, Kin, and Hope: Tending to Water Violations in *amiskwaciwâskahikan* and Treaty Six Territory." *Afterall* 43 (2017): 102–7, https://doi.org/10.1086/692559.

– "Fossil Fuels and Fossil Kin: An Environmental Kin Study of Weaponised Fossil Kin and Alberta's So-Called 'Energy Resources Heritage.'" *Antipode* 8 November 2022, https://doi.org/10.1111/anti.12897.

Tosches, Nick. *Country: The Twisted Roots of Rock 'N' Roll.* New York: Da Capo, 1996.

Tracy, Sarah J., Pamela Lutgen-Sandvik, and Jess K. Alberts. "Nightmares, Demons, and Slaves: Exploring the Painful Metaphors of Workplace Bullying." *Management Communication Quarterly* 20, no. 2 (2006): 148–85. https://doi.org/10.1177/0893318906291980.

Truth and Reconciliation Commission of Canada. *A Knock on the Door: The Essential History of Residential Schools from the Truth and Reconciliation Commission of Canada.* Winnipeg: University of Manitoba Press/National Centre for Truth and Reconciliation, 2016.

Tsing, Anna Lowenhaupt. *Friction: An Ethnography of Global Connection*. Princeton, NJ: Princeton University Press, 2005.

Tuck, Eve, and K. Wayne Yang. "Decolonization Is Not a Metaphor." *Decolonization* 1, no. 1 (2012): 1–40. https://jps.library.utoronto.ca/index.php/des/article/view/18630.

Turcotte, Heather. "Contextualizing Petro-Sexual Politics." *Alternatives: Global, Local, Political* 36, no. 3 (2011): 200–20. https://doi.org/10.1177/0304375411418597.

Turner, Chris. *The Patch: The People, Pipelines, and Politics of the Oil Sands.* Toronto: Simon & Schuster, 2017.

Unrau, Melanie Dennis. "Founding Fathers (in a Tailings Pond)." *Imaginations: Journal of Cross-Cultural Image Studies* 13, no. 1 (2022): 55–79. https://doi.org/10.17742/IMAGE.PM.13.1.5.

– *The Goose.* Ottawa: above/ground, 2022.

Van Camp, Richard. *Godless but Loyal to Heaven: Stories.* Winnipeg: Enfield & Wizenty, 2012.

Vandersteen, Max. *Work of Words: Poems.* Self-published: Beret Days, 2020.

Vernon, Karina. *The Black Prairie Archives: An Anthology*. Waterloo, ON: Wilfrid Laurier University Press, 2020.

Wakefield, Stephanie. *Anthropocene Back Loop*. London: Open Humanities Press, 2020. http://www.openhumanitiespress.org/books/titles/anthropocene-backloop.

Watkins, Mel. *Staples and Beyond: Selected Writings of Mel Watkins*, edited by Hugh Grant and David Wolfe. Montreal: McGill-Queen's University Press, 2006.

– "Rejoinder: Bitumen as Staple." In *The Staple Theory @ 50: Reflections on the Lasting Significance of Mel Watkins's "A Staple Theory of Economic Growth,"* edited by Jim Stanford, 127–33. Canadian Centre for Policy Alternatives, April 2014. https://policyalternatives.ca/publications/reports/staple-theory-50.

Watts, Michael. "Petro-Violence: Community, Extraction, and Political Ecology of a Mythic Commodity." *Violent Environments*, edited by Nancy Lee Peluso and Michael Watts, 189–212. Ithaca, NY: Cornell University Press, 2001.

Wayman, Tom, ed. *Going for Coffee: Poetry on the Job.* Madeira Park, BC: Harbour, 1981.

– *Inside Job: Essays on the New Work Writing.* Madeira Park, BC: Harbour, 1983.

– "Work and Silence." In *The Order in Which We Do Things: The Poetry of Tom Wayman*, edited by Owen Percy, 79–85. Waterloo, ON: Wilfrid Laurier University Press, 2014.

– ed. *Paperwork: Contemporary Poems from the Job.* Madeira Park, BC: Harbour, 1991.

Wenzel, Jennifer. *The Disposition of Nature: Environmental Crisis and World Literature.* New York: Fordham University Press, 2020.

– "Improvement and Overburden." *Postmodern Culture* 26, no. 2 (2016): n.pag. https://doi.org/10.1353/pmc.2016.0003.

Westman, Clinton, Tara L. Joly, and Lena Gross. "Introduction: At Home in the Oil Sands." In *Extracting Home in the Oil Sands: Settler Colonialism and Environmental Change in Subarctic Canada*, edited by Clinton Westman, Tara L. Joly, and Lena Gross, 1–22. London: Routledge, 2020.

Wheatley, Katherine, and Clinton N. Westman. "Reclaiming Nature? Watery Transformations and Mitigation Landscapes in the Oil Sands Region." In *Extracting Home in the Oil Sands: Settler Colonialism and Environmental Change in Subarctic Canada*, edited by Clinton Westman, Tara L. Joly, and Lena Gross, 160–79. London: Routledge, 2020.

Whitehead, Joshua. *Making Love with the Land*. Toronto: Alfred A. Knopf Canada, 2022.

Whyte, Kyle Powys. "Indigenous Climate Change Studies: Indigenizing Futures, Decolonizing the Anthropocene." *English Language Notes* 55, no. 1–2 (2017): 153–62.

Wiebe, Sarah Marie. *Everyday Exposure: Indigenous Mobilization and Environmental Justice in Canada's Chemical Valley*. Vancouver: UBC Press, 2016.

Williams, Raymond. *The Country and the City*. 1973. London: Vintage, 2016.

– *Marxism and Literature*. Oxford: Oxford University Press, 1977.

– "Ideas of Nature." *Problems in Materialism and Culture*, 67–85. London: Verso, 1980.

Wilson, Sheena, Adam Carlson, and Imre Szeman. *Petrocultures: Oil, Politics, Culture*. Montreal: McGill-Queen's University Press, 2017.

Wiseman, Christopher. "Deep Pleasure." Review of *Disturbances* by Greg Simison, *Alternate Endings* by Jill Rogers, *Rig Talk* by Peter Christensen, *Land of the Peace* by Leona M. Gom, and *Winter Your Sleep* by John V. Hicks. *Canadian Literature* 93 (1982): 140–2. https://canlit.ca/full-issue/?issue=93.

Wynter, Sylvia. "Unsettling the Coloniality of Being/Power/Truth/Freedom: Towards the Human, After Man, Its Overrepresentation – An Argument." *CR: The New Centennial Review* 3, no. 3 (2003): 257–337. www.jstor.org/stable/41949874.

Yaeger, Patricia. "Editor's Column: Literature in the Age of Wood, Tallow, Coal, Whale-Oil, Gasoline, Atomic Power and Other Energy Sources." *PMLA* 126, no. 2 (2011): 305–10. www.jstor.org/stable/41414106.

Young, Neil. "Heart of Gold." *Harvest*. Reprise, 1972.

Younging, Gregory. *Elements of Indigenous Style: A Guide for Writing By and About Indigenous Peoples*. Edmonton: Brush Education, 2018.

Yusoff, Kathryn. *A Billion Black Anthropocenes or None*. Minneapolis: University of Minnesota Press, 2018.

– "Geologic Life: Prehistory, Climate, Futures in the Anthropocene." *Environment and Planning D: Society and Space* 31 (2013): 779–95. https://doi.org/10.1068/d11512.

Zacharin, Noah. Review of *Disturbances* by Greg Simison and *Rig Talk* by Peter Christensen. *Quarry* 31, no. 1 (1982): 86–90.

Zolf, Syd. "*Irritating and Stimulating.*" *Beyond Stasis: Poetics and Feminism Today*. Special issue of *Open Letter* 13, no. 9 (2009): 28–33.

Index